T0250552

Lecture Notes in Computer Science 777

Edited by G. Goos and J. Hartmanis

Advisory Board: W. Brauer   D. Gries   J. Stoer

Kai von Luck · Heinz Marburger (Eds.)

Management and Processing of Complex Data Structures

Third Workshop on Information Systems
and Artificial Intelligence
Hamburg, Germany, February 28 - March 2, 1994
Proceedings

Springer-Verlag
Berlin Heidelberg New York
London Paris Tokyo
Hong Kong Barcelona
Budapest

Kai von Luck   Heinz Marburger (Eds.)

Management and Processing of Complex Data Structures

Third Workshop on Information Systems
and Artificial Intelligence
Hamburg, Germany, February 28 - March 2, 1994
Proceedings

Springer-Verlag

Berlin Heidelberg New York
London Paris Tokyo
Hong Kong Barcelona
Budapest

Series Editors

Gerhard Goos
Universität Karlsruhe
Postfach 69 80
Vincenz-Priessnitz-Straße 1
D-76131 Karlsruhe, Germany

Juris Hartmanis
Cornell University
Department of Computer Science
4130 Upson Hall
Ithaca, NY 14853, USA

Volume Editors

Kai von Luck
Fachhochschule Hamburg
Berliner Tor 3, D-20099 Hamburg, Germany

Heinz Marburger
MAZ GmbH
Karnapp 20, D-21079 Hamburg, Germany

CR Subject Classification (1991): H.1-2, I.2.3-4, E.1

ISBN 3-540-57802-1 Springer-Verlag Berlin Heidelberg New York
ISBN 0-387-57802-1 Springer-Verlag New York Berlin Heidelberg

CIP data applied for

This work is subject to copyright. All rights are reserved, whether the whole or part
of the material is concerned, specifically the rights of translation, reprinting, re-use
of illustrations, recitation, broadcasting, reproduction on microfilms or in any other
way, and storage in data banks. Duplication of this publication or parts thereof is
permitted only under the provisions of the German Copyright Law of September 9,
1965, in its current version, and permission for use must always be obtained from
Springer-Verlag. Violations are liable for prosecution under the German Copyright
Law.

© Springer-Verlag Berlin Heidelberg 1994
Printed in Germany

Typesetting: Camera-ready by author
SPIN: 10131968   45/3140-543210 - Printed on acid-free paper

Preface

The third workshop on "Information Systems and Artificial Intelligence" took place at the FH Hamburg, February 28 - March 2, 1994. The contributors were invited by the organizing committee on the basis of their previous work concerning management and processing of complex data structures, which is the topic of this workshop.

After 'integration aspects', which was the topic of the first IS/KI workshop[1], and 'modelling', which was the topic of the second IS/KI workshop[2], the actual topic was chosen as one of the most interesting common research and development areas in the fields of databases, information systems, and artificial intelligence.

The broad scope of the papers in these proceedings shows the wide range of common interests. Most papers stress the demands for new or extended formalisms and their deductive capabilities, including an analysis of their – formal – properties for managing complex structures. Looking at the contributions it is hard to see the borderlines between the work in the research areas of databases, information systems, and artificial intelligence. With these proceedings we hope to contribute to the discussions in all of these areas showing common research interests.

The IS/KI-94 was jointly organized by the special interest groups 1.1.4 (Knowledge Representation), 2.5.1 (Databases), and 2.5.2 (Methods for Developing Information Systems and Their Application) of the GI e.V. (German Computer Science Society). We would like to thank those of our colleagues who helped to set up this workshop, and in particular the members of the organizing committee, D. Karagiannis (Vienna), G. Lausen (Mannheim), C.-R. Rollinger (Osnabrück), H. Schweppe (Berlin), R. Studer (Karlsruhe), and H. Thoma (Basel). Thanks go also to the people who helped in the local organization at the FH Hamburg and the MAZ GmbH Hamburg. Last but not least we owe an inestimable debt to all contributors and participants at IS/KI-94 for their good will and manifold assistance.

Hamburg, January 1994   Kai von Luck
                                                       Heinz Marburger

---

[1] D. Karagianis (ed.): *Informations Systems and Artificial Intelligence: Integration Aspects.* Lecture Notes in Computer Science Vol. 474, Springer, 1991.

[2] R. Studer (ed.): *Informationssysteme und Künstliche Intelligenz: Modellierung.* Informatik Fachberichte Band 303, Springer, 1992.

Contents

Complex Structures in (Deductive) Database Systems:
Variables and Open Property Sets

B. Walter and S. Benzschawel

Universität Trier

Abstract. It is widely agreed on that (deductive) database systems for knowledge based applications should support complex data structures. From a database point of view this usually means to provide a collection of constructors that allow to build complex objects out of simpler objects, perhaps combined with some inheritance mechanisms. This way of thinking is determined by such applications as CAD or Multi Media. However, knowledge engineers like to enrich objects with more eccentric items like variables, active values, or open property sets. Taking the pragmatic view point of a database implementer, we will discuss the problems associated with supporting variables and open property sets.

1 Introduction

When constructing a database system for the support of knowledge based systems some of the features asked for most frequently by knowledge engineers are the following:

- Support of complex objects. Complex objects are built from simpler ones by applying constructors. The simplest objects are constants of such atomic types as integer or symbol, popular constructors include tuples, lists, and sets. The structure of complex objects relates to the structure of terms in first order predicate logic with the constructors being interpreted functors.
- Support of inheritance hierarchies. A type denotes a set of admissible objects. Types usually model concepts of the real world. Since such concepts form natural hierarchies of super- and subconcepts (e.g. animal, dog, beagle) the database system should support a similar structured system of super- and subtypes. If the type system forms a lattice, it can be related to the order sorted variant of first order predicate logic.
- Support of variables. If first order logic is used as a knowledge representation method, all formulas may include variables. Thus supporting variables seems to be a natural extension to database systems.
- Support of open sets of properties (sometimes also called feature tuples). In the traditional database world, the philosophy is that any object can be uniquely described by a fixed and well known set of properties. Hence, objects of the same type are described by the same set of properties. However, in natural language systems, objects, that due to semantical reasons belong to

the same type, may nevertheless be described by differing sets of properties. Two real world speakers describing the same object, will usually not name the same characteristics. Also it is not known in advance which properties a speaker will actually use.

If one considers the current state of the art in the database field, one can see, that the problem of supporting complex objects has been one of the most popular topics of database research for quite a while. They are supported in already commercially available object oriented database systems (e.g. O2 [4] or Orion/Ithaska [12]), in prototypes of term-oriented deductive databases [6, 9], and in extended relational database systems [2]. Complex objects will even find their way into the next version of the SQL-standard [5].

Most of the systems supporting complex objects also support some kind of inheritance hierarchy. However, additional research is needed especially concerning efficient implementation technics.

Since research on complex objects and inheritance hierarchies was initiated from the fields of computer aided design and object oriented databases and not from the field of knowledge representation, the question of how to support variables was not a prominently featured problem during the last few years. However, several work was done on such related problems as 'incomplete information' or 'null values' Since most of this work is strongly theoretical, in the most cases only rudimentary implementation techniques are discussed in the literature.

The problem of openness of property sets has been investigated in some detail in the area of computer linguistics. As a result several representation methods have been suggested including so-called feature logics. Based on these formalisms a few proposals have been developed in the areas of logic programming [3] and deductive databases [7].

In the following discussions we will first focus on the problem of supporting variables. Although the research was done in the context of deductive database systems (LILOG-DB [6] and more recently T^2D^2 (Trier Term oriented Deductive Database system)) supporting complex objects, we will, for the sake of simplicity, restrict ourselves to the case of relational databases. The concepts to be presented here are widely sufficient for more complex data structures as well. However, the use of the well known relational data model helps us to keep the focus on the special problems induced by the introduction of variables.

We will then extend our proposal in order to be able to handle open property sets as well.

Our presentation will be given from a strictly pragmatical point of view. We will primarily try to show what can be implemented and what are the common pitfalls. A more formal treatment and a thorough analysis of performance issues is the subject of a long version of this paper.

Since our database system is intended to have only inference machines as users we will not discuss the representation of results to end users.

The remainder of the paper is organized as follows. First, we shortly discuss the characteristics of the facts (section 2) that must be stored in the database if predicate logic is used as the underlying knowledge representation mechanism.

We then introduce our concept of naming (section 3) and suggest various levels of certainty to be associated with stored and computed data items (section 4). After discussing the problems of constraints (section 5) and redundant representations (section 6) we show how the traditional operators of the relational algebra can be changed in order to handle variables (section 7). Finally, it is shown that open property sets can easily be integrated into our concept of variables (section 8).

2 From well formed formulas to tuples and relations

Since we are discussing database techniques for the support of knowledge based systems, we have to state first on which kind of knowledge representation method we like to base our investigation. Since relational and deductive databases are essentially logic based and since logic based knowledge representation methods are the most accepted and the best documented, we will assume, that all relevant knowledge of our universe of discourse is formulated using first order predicate logic. All true statements that are of interest in our application area are formulated by means of WFFs (well formed formulas).

Typically, values will be used for describing properties of objects, functors are either used as data constructors (e.g. for grouping related values or related objects) or as value computing functions (e.g. for computing time dependent values at query time). At this stage of the modelling process there is a real world interpretation for any functor used. Additionally, variables may be used either as short notations ('for all' to indicate that any value is suitable) or to describe certain kinds of incomplete knowledge ('it exists' to indicate that at least one value does exist, but that the real values are not (yet) known).

As already stated above, for the sake of keeping things simple, we will not discuss complex objects, hence we will omit functors in the design stage.

In order to enable more efficient processing strategies, all WFFs are transformed into clausal form. This includes the step of skolemization where new functors may be introduced. The general form of a clause is

$$Q_1 \vee \ldots \vee Q_n \leftarrow P_1 \wedge \ldots \wedge P_m$$

with Q_i and P_j being atomic formulas, i.e. predicates.

For the moment we will assume, that all clauses are in fact Horn clauses ($n = 1$). In order to reach essentially the power of such languages as Prolog or Datalog, negated subgoals may be supported in the usual way (stratified negation with perfect model semantics) that not perfectly follows classical logic.

A clause is called a fact if $m = 0$, otherwise it is called a rule. Facts that do not contain variables or skolem functions are called ground facts. Facts are stored in the database, whereas rules can be interpreted as definitions of views or as preformulated programs and thus are stored separately.

In a relational database facts are represented by tuples, and all facts with the same predicate name and the same arity are represented by tuples of the same relation.

Now that we have roughly outlined our intentions, we will investigate in more detail the meaning of variables occurring in facts.

Besides constants, facts include variables which are universally quantified (in the following called ∀-variables) and skolem functions (skolem constants if the arity of the functions is 0). Skolem functions stand for constants with unknown values. Skolemization, i.e. the introduction of skolem functions as a replacement for existentially quantified variables (∃-variables) is not an equivalence transformation. Whereas an ∃-variable denotes 'at least one' a skolem-function denotes 'exactly one'. However, in both cases the valid instantiations are unknown. Consequently, we will regard skolem functions as being ∃-variables. Additionally we will adopt the 'at least one'–semantics of such variables. To make it clear, if skolemization is applied to the formula

$$\forall X \; \exists Y \; (P(X, Y))$$

then we get

$$\forall X \; (P(X, G(X))$$

meaning 'exactly one'. If however, we adopt the meaning 'at least one' we use this skolemized formula as a short notation for the formula

$$\exists G \; \forall X \; (P(X, G(X))$$

which of course is a second order formula. So what we do in this case, is to use first order syntax with keeping second order semantics in mind.

Thus unlike in traditional relational databases, tuples in our context do not only include constants but also ∀- and ∃-variables.

Views or programs (both written as Datalog programs) are translated to a relational algebra, which (in the case of datalog with negation and recursion) should include the equivalent of the algebraic operations selection, projection, cross product, union, and difference as well as a fix point operator. The usually implemented join can be expressed by cross product, selection and projection. Renaming is not necessary if every column can be identified by its column number.

3 Naming

In order to be able to design a clean concept for naming variables in a database, we will now discuss in more detail the meaning and information content of the occurring ∀- and ∃-variables.

∀-variables allow short notations. If X is a ∀-variable, then

$$(X, a)$$

stands for a whole set of ground tuples. In fact this set could have an infinite number of members. Hence, the use of ∀-variables enables us to represent knowledge, which in traditional relational databases is not representable at all.

A ∀-variable may have multiple occurrences within the same tuple. If X is a ∀-variable then the tuple

$$(X, b, X)$$

stands for all ground tuples that have the same value in the first and in the third position as well as an 'b' in the second position. However, since

$$\forall X \ (P(X) \wedge Q(X)) = \forall X \ (P(X)) \wedge \forall Y \ (Q(Y))$$

it makes no sense that the same $\forall$-variable has multiple occurrences in different tuples (of the same or of different relations).

So for $\forall$-variables it seems to be a good idea to have a naming concept with globally unique names. However, assume that we want to compute the cross product of the above tuple with itself. Then the result is (X, b, X, X, b, X), i.e. we now have equality over positions 1, 3, 4 and 6. Since (X, b, X) stands for a set of ground tuples, the correct result should instead be a set where any single ground tuple is combined with every ground tuple in the set. Hence, the correct result should have been something like (X, b, X, Y, b, Y) with equality between positions 1 and 3 and between 4 and 6.

We therefore suggest to replace all $\forall$-variables with an anonymous variable, written as $\forall$, and to express equality via constraints. The above tuples are now written as

$(\forall, b, \forall)$ with ($\$1 = \$3$)

$(\forall, b, \forall, \forall, b, \forall)$ with ($\$1 = \$3$) $\wedge$ ($\$4 = \$6$)

with $\$i$ identifying position i.

An $\exists$-variable is also something like a short notation, however, we do not know, which tuples are really included in the such described set, we do not even know, how many tuples are exactly included. In fact, a tuple that includes at least one $\exists$-variable, represents knowledge about possible worlds. At least one ground tuple represents a true fact in all possible worlds, all other instances represent facts that are true in at least one world.

The parameter list of a skolem function identifies dependencies. It should be clear that even in the same world the facts

$$P(X, Y, F)$$
$$P(X, Y, F(X))$$
$$P(X, Y, F(Y))$$
$$P(X, Y, F(X, Y))$$
$$P(X, Y, F(X, Y, Z))$$

all may stand for different sets of ground facts, i.e. they denote different knowledge. Although it might be possible, that in some world all these facts do have the same ground instances, they still represent different dependencies, being valid in all possible worlds. In the general case, the described sets of ground facts are not comparable.

In a first approach assume that we adopt the names as introduced during skolemization. Then the WFF

$$\forall X \ \exists Y \ (P(X, Y) \wedge Q(Y))$$

can be transformed to

$$P(X, F(X))$$

and

$$Q(F(X)).$$

Obviously, the occurrence of F(X) in both facts defines an equality between the second position of P and the only position of Q. If we arbitrarily select one out of the possible worlds, then the values that make Q true are the same that may occur in the second position of P in order to make P true.

Additionally, for the set of ground facts described by P(X,F(X)) F(X) denotes a dependency relation. If we adopt the 'exactly one'–semantics, this is a functional dependency, if we adopt the 'at least one'–semantics, then F(X) denotes something like a 'multiple functional' dependency (because our second order semantics F(X) stands for a set of functions). This means, that in any possible world the knowledge of the X-value would us enable to determine the F(X)-value(s). However, since we cannot determine the possible world in which we actually are, we cannot determine the valid interpretation of F. Nevertheless, we have the knowledge that such dependencies exists.

If we now store the tuples representing these two facts in the database and perform a cross product, then the result would be

$$(X, F(X), F(X))$$

Now, F(X) on position 2 would denote a dependency whereas F(X) on position 3 would not. Additionally, we may deduce, that the values admissible at position 2 are the same which are admissible at position 3. But we may not deduce, that all ground tuples carry the same values at positions 2 and 3.

The concept of using anonymous variables as in the case of $\forall$-variables is not applicable here, since in a given possible world $\exists$-variables with different names also may stand for different sets of admissible values.

So what we suggest is a compromise between anonymous variables and the direct import of the names generated by skolemization. Two skolem functors with different names denote usually differing sets of admissible values in any possible world we might select.

Hence, it is a suitable approach to apply a one-to-one mapping of functor names to names for $\exists$-variables. For the sake of readability in database tuples we will now write $\exists$- variables as $\exists F$, $\exists G$, ...

Besides associating for each possible world an individual but unknown set of admissible values, we do not adopt any further meanings with these variables. If we write

$$(b, \exists F, \exists F)$$

this just means, that in any selected world all values that occur in position 2 of some ground tuple will also occur in position 3 of some (other) ground tuple.

If we want to express the equality of the values occurring in the ground tuples, we again have to use constraints and then for instance can write

$$(b, \exists F, \exists F) \text{ with } (\$2 = \$3)$$

If we additionally want to keep the knowledge about dependencies we have to notate this separately, e.g. by writing

$$(b, \forall, \exists G) \text{ with\_d } (\$3(\$2))$$

in order to state that for the described set of ground tuples the value at position 3 depends on the value on position 2.

It should be clear, that if we have the two facts

$$P(X) \text{ and } Q(Y, G(X,Y))$$

then there is no dependency to keep track of.

The dependencies are only guarantied to hold as long as no further constraints are added. For instance assume a relation R that includes the tuple

$$(\forall, \exists F) \text{ with\_d } (\$2(\$1))$$

Assume further, that because of some database operations we are forced to add a further constraint, say ($2 \neq 3$), then the dependency is no longer guarantied to hold and we may only notate

$$(\forall, \exists F) \text{ with } (\$2 \neq 3)$$

Remembering our second order interpretation of skolem functions, we can say, that at least one of the functions represented by F is no longer defined for some value in position 1. In the remainder of this paper we will not discuss such dependencies any further.

As a result of this section we may note, that we use anonymous ∀-variables and individually named ∃-variables. If two ∃-variables have different names then the associated sets of values are generally incomparable. Equalities are expressed by means of constraints.

4   Status of Certainty

In traditional relational database systems all tuples included in the database or in computed results represent true facts, i.e. the represented knowledge is always guarantied to be true. As will be seen, the introduction of ∃-variables implies the existence of facts which we can neither proof to be true nor proof to be false. For this purpose we attach to each tuple its associated status of certainty (or status for short). We introduce three possible status values: 'true', 'mixed', and 'maybe', with 'true' being the highest and 'maybe' being the lowest attachable value (tuples with status 'false' are not stored in the database).

A tuple is allowed to carry any status value up to 'true' if it only includes constants or ∀-variables, e.g. we may notate

$$(a, \forall, 5, \forall).true$$

Such tuples exactly describe a set of facts. For any fact it is clearly known whether it is included or not. During query processing a tuple that initially is 'true' may be manipulated in a way that its status may change to 'mixed' or 'maybe'.

Whenever required by the application, the knowledge engineer may directly use 'maybe' when inserting such tuples into the database.

Tuples including ∃-variables may only carry a status value that does not exceed 'mixed', e.g. we may write

$$(\exists F, b, \exists G, 7).\text{mixed}$$

As stated above, tuples like this actually describe sets of possible worlds. At least one combination of values for $\exists F$ and $\exists G$ leads to a ground fact that is true in all possible worlds. Additionally there are further combinations of values for $\exists F$ and $\exists G$ that lead to ground facts that are individually 'true' in some of the possible worlds and 'false' in others. It should be clear, that whenever in the course of computation the set of facts represented by such a tuple is restricted by adding a constraint, then the existence of facts that are 'true' in any possible world can no longer be guarantied.

So, if the original range of an $\exists$- variable has been restricted, i.e. a constraint has been added, then we require that the corresponding tuple may only be annotated with status value 'maybe', e.g. we may notate

$$(\exists F, b, \exists G, 7).\text{maybe with } (\$1 \neq 2)$$

In this case any combination of values for $\exists F$ and $\exists G$ leads to ground facts that individually may be 'true' in some of the possible worlds and 'false' in all others.

Whenever required by the application, the knowledge engineer may insert tuples with status 'mixed' into the database that include $\exists$-variables as well as constraints already restricting the range of these $\exists$-variables. However, as soon as the original range (as at insertion time) is further restricted in the course of query processing, the status will of course be reduced to 'maybe'.

At a first sight it seems, that during query processing a status may only change from higher to lower values. However, there are cases where a change occurs from a lower to a higher value. Examples will be given in the section on algebraic operations (in the case of a projection) and in the section on constraints.

5 Constraints

Constraints are always applied to tuples. In fact we could use a mixed solution where some constraints are notated at the relational level. However, for the sake of simplifying our presentation we will attach all constraints directly to the corresponding tuples.

As already could be seen above, we use the following notation for simple constraints:

$$\$i \; \theta \; a$$
$$\$i \; \theta \; \$j$$

with '$\$i$', '$\$j$' representing the columns i and j, 'a' being a value and 'θ' being an arithmetical comparison operator (one out of $\{=, \neq, >, \geq, <, \leq\}$).

In the same way as a tuple with variables stands for a non-empty set of ground tuples, also a constraint over variables denotes a non-empty set of constraints over instances. For instance, the meaning of

$$(\exists F, b, \exists G, \exists G).\text{maybe with } (\$1 > \$3)$$

is that in any ground tuple the value in the first column (coming from the domain of F) must be greater than the value in the third column (coming from the domain of G). Clearly in at least some of the possible worlds some values of F and G will not qualify for inclusion in tuples satisfying the attached constraint.

Whether this concept of identifying columns by their position is always sufficient depends on further design decisions.

For this purpose consider the following tuple
$$(a, \forall, \exists F, \exists F).\text{mixed}$$
If we now perform some computations on this tuple, we might first add a constraint and get
$$(a, \forall, \exists F, \exists F).\text{maybe with } (\$2 < \$3)$$
In the further course of the computation we might loose our interest in the third column and thus get something we are not yet able to write down.

In fact, at this point we do have two design choices:

a) Delete all constraints concerning variables that have been excluded from the corresponding tuple. Additionally, if one of the deleted constraints also was a restriction for a $\forall$-variable, then this $\forall$-variable is reduced to an anonymous $\exists$-variable. In our example this would lead to
$$(a, \exists, \exists F).\text{maybe}$$
Of course, any appearance of an anonymous $\exists$-variable denotes a different set of ground values.

b) Collect all constraints in order to enable the later reconstruction of the original range of a variable. So in the case that a column holding an $\exists$- variable is deleted, we must support further references to this variable. For this purpose we must introduce fresh variables, which are $\forall$-variables with unique names. Fresh variables are needed to avoid confusion that could be caused by the fact that an $\exists$-variable or an anonymous $\forall$-variable might have multiple occurrences within the same tuple. In our example we may then write
$$(a, \forall, \exists F).\text{maybe with } (\$2 < \forall X) \wedge (\forall X = \exists F)$$
where we have introduced the fresh $\forall$-variable X which then is restricted to the domain of F and used to replace all occurrences of the old identifier $3. $\forall X$ and $\exists F$ could be seen as denoting something like virtual columns.

As the next example demonstrates, we could really make use of all the constraints we now would be carrying along. If for instance in the further course of processing our result relation includes the tuples

$$(a, \forall, \exists F).\text{maybe with } (\$2 < \forall X) \wedge (\forall X = \exists F)$$
$$(a, \forall, \exists F).\text{maybe with } (\$2 \geq \forall Y) \wedge (\forall Y = \exists F)$$

these can be recombined to
$$(a, \forall, \exists F).\text{mixed}$$
i.e. later on we could even extract
$$(a).\text{true}$$
However, it must be guarantied, that the status of the original tuple really was higher than 'maybe'. This can for instance be achieved by explicitly remembering the original status.

The first alternative follows the philosophy that whenever a tuple has reached the status 'maybe' we do not know whether it really exists. Consequently, it can no longer be used to construct a tuple that is guarantied to be 'true'.

The philosophy of the second alternative is, that status 'maybe' just means, that currently not enough information is available to support a stronger statement. If, however, at a later point of time more information is available, then a stronger statement and hence a higher status might be possible.

Although we have a slight preference for the first strategy we will discuss both alternatives when necessary.

6   Redundant Representation

Assume the following two tuples

$$(a, \forall).true$$
$$(\forall, b).true$$

both standing for a set of ground tuples. Obviously, the intersection of these sets includes

$$(a, b).true$$

Naively, we could try to solve this problem by using constraints, i.e. by explicitly excluding this fact from one of the two sets. This would lead to

$$(a, \forall).true \text{ with } (\$2 \neq b)$$
$$(\forall, b).true$$

or

$$(a, \forall).true$$
$$(\forall, b).true \text{ with } (\$1 \neq a)$$

However, assume that there are thousands of facts structured in the same way as $(a, \forall).true$ and thousands of facts structured in the same way as $(\forall, b).true$, then the use of constraints becomes practically infeasible.

So it is certainly better to accept, that the database may include a redundant representation of facts.

From a traditional database point of view, redundancy leads to problems in the handling of duplicates. If we perform a projection, we will not easily be able to decide whether a duplicate is was caused by redundant representation or if it is a real duplicate. In the case of $\exists$-variables we sometimes even do not know whether duplicates do exist or not, i.e. there may be duplicates that exist in only some of the possible worlds. For instance, the intersection of the sets of ground facts represented by the following tuples could be nonempty in some of the possible worlds

$$(\forall, \exists F, a).mixed$$
$$(b, c, \exists G).mixed$$

In fact, this problem only occurs since at this point database technology deviates from the underlying theory, which is set oriented and hence does not know about duplicates. So in a logic database, i.e. a database system supporting knowledge based systems and especially inference machines this might be no problem at all.

Before we are able to discuss some possibilities of how to reduce redundancy we must define, what equality and subsumption of tuples means in our context.

Two tuples t1 and t2 are equal, if they represent the same set of ground facts. In order to represent the same set of tuples ∃-variables at corresponding positions must have the same names and the same set of associated restrictions.

Tuple t1 subsumes tuple t2, if t1 represents a superset of the ground facts represented by t2.

Disregarding all restrictions expressed by constraints, the following procedure tests whether a given tuple t1 with arity n subsumes another tuple t2 with the same arity:

```
FUNCTION SUBSUMPTION (t1, t2, n)
i := 1;
subs := 'true';
WHILE (i < n) ∧ (subs = 'true') DO
    IF (t1(i) ≠ ∀) ∧ (t1(i) ≠ t2(i))
        THEN RETURN 'false';
    i:=i+1;
ENDWHILE
RETURN 'true'
```

If there are constraints, we additionally have to check these as well. To give an example, assume the tuple
$$(\exists F, \exists G, a).\text{maybe with } (\$1 = \$2)$$
then this would now be subsumed by
$$(\exists G, \forall, a).\text{mixed}$$
i.e. the above algorithm becomes more complex.

Now we can say, that redundancy can sometimes be slightly reduced, for instance if a tuple is totally subsumed by some other tuple, e.g. $(\exists F, 5, a)$.mixed is subsumed by $(\exists F, \forall, a)$.mixed and can thus be ignored.

7 Algebraic Operations

In this section we will consider what happens when we apply the usual database operations to tuples that include variables. Since we consider relational databases, we will limit our discussion to those operations that may occur when we use database languages like SQL or Datalog. Both languages can be implemented via the well known relational algebra.

In order to implemented Datalog without negation we need at least the algebra operators projection, selection, cross product, and union (we omit renaming and thus choose to identify each column by its position number). If additionally a fixpoint operator is supplied, we are able to implement recursive Datalog. If instead of a fixpoint operator difference is supported we can have SQL or nonrecursive Datalog with negation. If both is supported we get recursive Datalog with negation, which in the current state of the art is the most powerful language that can still be implemented efficiently, at least in the context of databases without variables.

If we follow the philosophy of never being able to construct a 'true'-tuple out of 'maybe'-tuples, we also loose some of the well known characteristics of relational algebra. However, a precise description of the characteristics of the enhanced operators are a subject of the long version of this paper.

7.1 Projection

If we are only interested in a subset of the columns of a relation we have to apply a projection to this subset. In traditional relational databases this operation can usually be performed in two ways, either with or without duplicate elimination. As pointed out above, in our case it does not make sense to further distinguish between these two cases. However, for the sake of small intermediate results, one should in any case try to reduce redundant representations as far as possible, e.g. by deleting tuples that are subsumed by others.

The projection operation gives us further arguments supporting the above introduction of a status for every tuple. Consider for instance the following tuple without annotation, which might be part of an intermediate result
$$(\exists F, d) \text{ with } (\$1 > 5)$$
representing a set of ground facts that may be empty in some possible world and hence would have status 'maybe'. Because of the $\exists$-variable this status is clear even without annotation.

If we now apply a projection onto the second column, we get the result
$$(d)$$
which would now denote a true fact for all possible worlds, which certainly is not what we originally should have intended. If instead we use annotation, we can easily keep track of the real status, which of course is 'maybe'.

In the case of a projection we can also see that a status might change from a lower to a higher value. If for instance the tuple
$$(\exists F, d).\text{mixed}$$
is projected onto column 2, then we get
$$(d).\text{true}$$
i.e. we have performed a projection onto that part the tuple that represents a part of at least one fact that is guaranted to be true in any possible world.

After applying a projection we must be very careful with updating the associated constraints, especially if, for the sake of later reconstructions, we follow the philosophy of keeping track of all constraints that are associated directly or indirectly with $\exists$-variables that have been projected out of the tuple.

We must also be able to guarantee that before applying a projection no tuple does stand for an empty set of ground facts. If for instance
$$(\forall, 5).\text{true with } ((\$1 < 3) \wedge (\$1 = \$2))$$

is projected onto column 2, we get the result (5).true although the starting point was already an empty set.

7.2 Selection

Whereas projection is used to select columns, selection is used to select rows (tuples). It is well known that any selection expression can be transformed to a conjunction of simple conditions. A simple condition is either a comparison column-to-value or column-to-column. A column is either identified by its names (provided that they are unique) or by its position number which we will prefer in order to omit renaming. Let '$i', '$j' represent the columns i and j, let 'a' be a value and 'θ' be an arithmetical comparison operator (one out of $\{=, \neq, >, \geq, <, \leq\}$), then

$$\$i \ \theta \ a$$
$$\$i \ \theta \ \$j$$

are simple conditions, noted in the same way as constraints. Note that we do not need the logical 'or' since instead we can use the union operator discussed below.

Up to now some readers might still be in doubt that constraints are really necessary and that a different naming concept might have avoided constraints. So it is time to demonstrate, that we will not be able to go along without constraints. For this purpose assume the relation

$$(\forall, a).true$$
$$(7, b).true$$
$$(3, c).true$$
$$(\exists F, d).mixed$$

and the selection condition $\$1 > 5$

Obviously, without constraints we are not able to write down the tuples in the result. Since the range of $\forall$-variables is usually infinite, we are not able to expand the given tuple to a set of ground tuples. As a consequence, selections must be regarded as a main source for the addition of further constraints.

The selection operation can be described in more detail by the following tables.

a) Selection with simple condition '$i = a$' as an example for '$i \ \theta \ a$'

value in column i	condition evaluates to	added constraint	action
a	true	—	—
b	false	—	—
$\forall$	true	—	$\$i := a$
$\exists F$	maybe	—	$\$i := a$

b) Selection with simple condition '$i > a$' as another example for '$i \theta a$' (Note that '$i > a$' evaluates to 'maybe' since 'a' might be the largest possible value).

value in column i	condition evaluates to	added constraint	action
a	false	—	—
$\forall$	maybe	$i > a$	—
$\exists F$	maybe	$i > a$	—

c) Selection with simple condition '$i = j$' (as an example for '$i \theta j$'). The entries show the value to which the condition evaluates plus the added constraint and the taken action. Actions are possible in this case, since equality enables us to replace variables with other variables or with constants. However, if we perform a replacement in some tuple, we must also adapt the constraints associated with this tuple

	value of j		
value of i	a	$\forall$	$\exists F$
a	true — —	true — $j := a$	maybe — $j := a$
$\forall$	true — $i := a$	true $i = j$ —	true $i = j$ $i := \exists F$
$\exists F$	maybe — $i := a$	true $i = j$ $j := \exists F$	true $i = j$ —
$\exists G$	maybe — $i := a$	true $i = j$ $j := \exists G$	maybe $i = j$ —

The following table shows the status changes that can be caused by applying a selection.

condition evaluates to

		true	mixed	maybe	
old tuple	true	true	mixed	maybe	new tuple
status	mixed	mixed	mixed	maybe	status
	maybe	maybe	maybe	maybe	

Of course, this table looks like the definition of $\wedge$ in some three-valued logic.

Note that a condition may only be evaluated to true as long as it is guarantied, that the resulting tuple does not represent an empty set of facts. So ($\forall = \exists F$) can only be evaluated to 'true' if the range of F is not restricted by any added constraints.

7.3 Cross Product

There is not much to be said about the cross product. If two tuples t1 and t2 are combined into a new one, the weaker status will become the status of the resulting tuple.

status of t1

		true	mixed	maybe	
		true	mixed	maybe	
status	true	true	mixed	maybe	status
of t2	mixed	mixed	mixed	maybe	of t1 × t2
	maybe	maybe	maybe	maybe	

Let C1 and C2 be the constraints of t1 and t2, then C1 ∧ C2 will become the constraint of t1 × t2.

7.4 Union

The union operator is a further source for redundancy, that can be handled in the usual way.

As already mentioned earlier, if we want to apply a selection with a condition like $(($i = a) \lor ($j = b))$, we have to apply two simple selections followed by a union. However, this does not automatically imply the need for constraints that are disjunctions of conjunctions. This still depends on what strategies we use for reducing redundant representations.

A union does not change the status of a tuple. However, a subsequent reduction of the representational redundancy might in some cases lead to a status change.

Note, that so far we have introduced all operators of the monotonous relational algebra, i.e. all operators needed for the implementation of Datalog without recursion and negation.

The introduction of a fixpoint operator only enables the arbitrarily repeated execution of the operators introduced so far and does not lead to new problems in the context of variables. Hence, we are now also able to implement Datalog with recursion.

To reach the full power of recursive Datalog with negation additionally the difference operator is needed.

7.5 Difference

The difference $R \setminus S$ can be computed either directly or via a natural join between R and the complement of S. For the following discussions we prefer the direct computation.

Let us start with an example. Assume that R includes the tuple

$$t1 = (\forall, a, b).true$$

and that S includes

$$t2 = (\exists G, \exists H, b).\text{mixed}$$

Obviously there is a chance that the intersection of the two sets of facts represented by these tuples is not empty. However, since the two sets are not directly comparable, it is not immediately clear how to compute a result.

Our approach is to assume 'best' and 'worst' cases. In order to determine the tuple that describes the facts that are guarantied to be true in all possible worlds, we take the 'best' case of the second tuple, i.e. we replace the $\exists$-variables by $\forall$-variables, the status 'mixed' by 'true' and then get

$$t2 = (\forall, \forall, b).\text{true}$$

If we now compute the difference, we easily get the tuple which denotes the empty set, i.e. no facts are guarantied to be true.

In order to get the tuple that describes the facts that may be true in some of the possible worlds, we consider the 'worst' case of the second tuple, i.e. the case where only one fact is described. We then have to consider whether this fact is in any case included in the set described by the first tuple. In our example this is not the case. So we get as a result

$$t1 \setminus t2 = (\forall, a, b).\text{maybe}, (\emptyset).\text{true}$$

Of course, $(\emptyset)$.true would not be included in the resulting relation. Now assume, that R further includes

$$t3 = (a, \forall, b).\text{true}$$

and that S also includes

$$t4 = (a, \exists H, b).\text{mixed}$$

then the computation again leads to

$$(\emptyset).\text{true}$$

However, we have problems to correctly express the result we get when computing the tuple with status 'maybe'. The second tuple represents at least one true fact that is guarantied to be represented by the first tuple as well. What we should be able to express is something like 'for all but at least one'. For this purpose we introduce a new kind of quantifier $\forall_{-\exists}$ with exactly this meaning. So we get

$$t3 \setminus t4 = (\emptyset).\text{true}, (a, \forall_{-\exists}, b).\text{maybe}$$

The advantage of introducing this new quantifier is, that we are able to preserve some additional information. If for instance later on we want to compute

$$(a, \forall, b).\text{true} \setminus (a, \forall_{-\exists}, b).\text{maybe}$$

then we are able to reconstruct

$$t4 = (a, \exists, b).\text{mixed}$$

which otherwise would have been impossible. However, we loose some information since now we use an anonymous $\exists$-variable. Note also that $\forall_{-\exists}$ will not change when during another difference operation a further $\exists$-variable is 'subtracted'.

In fact we can keep more information if we remember all the 'subtracted' $\exists$-variables, i.e. we could then write

$$t3 \setminus t4 = (\emptyset).\text{true}, (a, \forall_{-\{H\}}, b).\text{maybe}$$

where the later computation of

$$(a, \forall, b).\text{true} \setminus (a, \forall_{-\{H\}}, b).\text{maybe}$$

would lead to

$$t4 = (a, \exists H, b).\text{mixed}$$

which otherwise is not possible. Note that now in the case of further difference operations we could get something like

$$(a, \forall_{-\{H,G,K,F,I\}}, b).\text{maybe}$$

i.e. as in the case of keeping all constraints applied to variables that where projected out, now expressions can get arbitrarily complex.

The general procedure for computing the difference $R \setminus S$ in our context can roughly be given as follows:

1. Scan S for tuples that potentially 'overlap' with tuples in R. Let $t2$ in S be a tuple that 'overlaps' $t1$ in R.
2. (Skip if the status of $t1$ is maybe) Compute the 'best' case of $t2$ by replacing all $\exists$-variables with $\forall$-variables and by changing the status to 'true'. Then compute $t1 \setminus t2$, which can always be done, even in the presence of constraints. Set the status of (part 1 of) the result to the original status of $t1$.
3. Try to interpret $t1$ and $t2$ in a way such that $t1$ represents only facts not presented by $t2$. If this succeeds, then (part 2 of) the result can be given by $t1$ with the status being changed to 'maybe'.
4. (Skip if step 3 was successful) Compare $t1$ and $t2$ position by position. Whenever for some i $t1(i)$ is a $\forall$-variable and $t2(i)$ is an $\exists$-variable, say H, then replace $\forall$ by $\forall_{-\exists}$. Set the status of $t1$ to 'maybe' and take $t1$ as (part 2 of) the result.

8   Open Property Sets

So far we have followed the traditional database philosophy that all objects of the same type can uniquely be described by the same well known set of properties.

However, in the real world, two speakers describing objects of the same type will usually name differing sets of properties. Also, if we consider a dictionary, we will not be able to use a fixed set of properties for a given type of words.

Natural language applications usually require not only differing property sets for objects of the same type but also the ability to add additional properties at later points of time.

Assume the following collection of tuples

> (Name:jack, Age:30, Job:programmer)
> (Name:mary, Job:manager)
> (Name:john, Age:41, Hobby:tennis)

then the support of open property sets would not only allow the insertion of a tuple like

> (Name:jane, City:london)

but also to process queries like the following

> ?- (Name:X, Job:manager, Hair:red).

questioning for all managers with red hairs. Obviously, there is no tuple describing a person that is guarantied to be manager with red hair. But since we have open property sets, there is a certain possibility that Mary being already a manager could also have red hair. Additionally John or Jane may be managers with red hair. So if we remember our discussion of variables a suitable answer could be

> (Name:mary, Job:manager).maybe
> (Name:john, Age:41, Hobby:tennis).maybe
> (Name:jane, City:london).maybe

If we try to relate the concept of open property sets to our approach of handling variables, we can first state that an open property set (sometimes called a feature tuple) is a tuple, where each value is explicitly associated with a name. Such names closely correspond to the column names (attribute names) in relational databases. In fact, if we take a snapshot of a collection of open property sets we can construct a relation with a column for any property occurring in the given property sets. The property sets can then be modelled by tuples where all undefined properties are described by $\exists$-variables. For the above example we get

Name	Age	Job	City	Hobby
jack	30	programmer	$\exists F$	$\exists G$
mary	$\exists H$	manager	$\exists I$	$\exists J$
john	41	$\exists K$	$\exists L$	tennis
jane	$\exists M$	$\exists N$	london	$\exists O$

If we further adopt the usual database strategy of strongly separating between update operation and queries, we can now formulate a static situation for each individual query. The only thing we have to do, is to add a column for any property mentioned in the query. So now we get

Name	Age	Job	City	Hobby	Hair
jack	30	programmer	$\exists$F	$\exists$G	$\exists$P
mary	$\exists$H	manager	$\exists$I	$\exists$J	$\exists$Q
john	41	$\exists$K	$\exists$L	tennis	$\exists$R
jane	$\exists$M	$\exists$N	london	$\exists$O	$\exists$S

Of course, it would be inefficient to really store a relation like this and in reality one would certainly use more compact representation not representing any properties included in queries. The point is, that this approach does enable us to apply the same modified versions of relational algebra operators introduced for handling of variables.

However, so far we have not yet captured the complete intended semantics. So an $\exists$-variable denotes the existence of at least one value, whereas we might already know that there is exactly one value. For instance we do know that any person does have just one age.

Additionally, for some tuples it might be known, that no value does exist for some property, so it can be known that Jack has a bald head and hence no hair color does apply. Finally, it is possible that we do not know whether the head of John is hairy or bald.

The problem of presenting the information 'no value' can easily be solved by introducing a special value, $\perp$ which is incomparable with any other value.

If we do not know whether a value exists, we can continue to use $\exists$-variables but we must explicitly include the value $\perp$ into the domain of this variable, for instance by writing $\exists_\perp$. Note that there is no necessity to include the value $\perp$ into the domain of $\forall$-variables, since if needed we can just copy this tuple and then in the copy replace $\forall$ by $\perp$.

Finally, if we know that exactly one value does exist, we can keep this information for instance by simply writing $\exists 1$.

The interesting point about this proposal is, that we can perform practically all computations in the same way as introduced for handling variables.

9   Conclusion

We have discussed the problem of handling variables in (deductive) databases. The results can roughly be summarized as follows:

- Naming. It was shown that $\forall$-variables can be handled anonymously, whereas it is necessary to use individual names for $\exists$-variables. Although we use first order syntax, a second order semantics is used for $\exists$-variables. This could be done, since in none of the discussed operations we made any assumptions about the internal structure of the set of values associated with $\exists$-variables. For the same reason we could later on introduce special $\exists 1$-variables ($\exists$-variables with 'exactly one'–semantics), which in fact are handled exactly like normal $\exists$-variables (the differing semantics are only visible to the user when interpreting a result and to update operations).

- Status of certainty. If ∃-variables are used, computed result relations may contain tuples representing facts for which we can neither proof that they are 'true' nor can we show that they are 'false'. Thus the status 'maybe' was introduced. Since tuples in our approach usually represent sets of ground facts, which in the case of ∃-variables may individually be either 'true' or 'maybe', we further introduced 'mixed' in order to handle these mixed cases.
- Constraints. Since variables allow a tuple to represent a whole set of ground facts, it is necessary to use constraints in order to notate changes in these sets. If we follow the philosophy that 'maybe'–tuples cannot be used for reconstructing 'true'–tuples, then in the course of query processing constraints may be deleted whenever the corresponding variables are projected out. If however the reconstruction of 'true'-tuples is allowed, then in some cases we may get an explosion of constraints.
- Algebraic operations. Starting from those operators needed to implement languages like Datalog or SQL, we demonstrated that the handling of relations and tuples containing variables is possible. However, it is necessary to redefine the mathematical characteristics of these operators, especially if 'maybe'-tuples are regarded as being a point of no return.
- Open property sets. It was argued that open property sets require null values of the types 'no value' and 'no information'. It was demonstrated, that these can easily be integrated into our concept of supporting variables.

Due to space limitations we did not discuss any consequences for query languages. In fact, additional constructs are primarily needed for inspecting the structural inspection of tuples. Special predicates are needed in order to test tuple positions for the occurrence of ∀- and ∃-variables as well as for ∃1-variables and the for special value ⊥.

References

1. S. Abiteboul, P. Kannelakis, G. Grahne. *On the Representation and Querying of Sets of Possible Worlds.* Theoretical Computer Science 78 (1991) 159-187.
2. S. Abiteboul, P. C. Fischer, H.-J. Schek (Eds.). *Nested Relations and Complex Objects in Databases.* Lecture Notes in Computer Science 361, Springer–Verlag (1989).
3. H. Aït-Kaci, R. Nasr. *Login: A Logic Programming Language with Built-In Inheritance.* Journ. of Logic Programming 3(1986) 185–215.
4. F. Bancilhon, C. Delobel, P. Kanellakis (Eds.). *Building an Object–Oriented Database System: The Story of O_2.* Morgan Kaufmann Publishers 1992.
5. D. Beech. *Collection of Objects in SQL3.* Proc. 19th VLDB, Dublin (1993) 244–255.
6. S. Benzschawel. E. Gehlen, M. Ley, T. Ludwig, A. Maier, B. Walter. *LILOG-DB: Database Support for Knowledge Based Systems.* in: O. Herzog, C.-R. Rollinger (eds.): *Textunderstanding in LILOG.* Lecture Notes in Computer Science 546, Springer (1991) 501-594

7. C. Beri, R. Nasr, S. Tsur. *Embedding Ψ−Terms in a Horn−clause Logic Language.* Proc. 3rd Int. Conf. on Data and Knowledge Bases, Jerusalem, Morgan Kaufmann Publishers (1988) 347–359.

8. R. Demolombe, L. Farinas del Cerro. *An Algebraic Method for Deduction in Incomplete Data Bases.* Journal of Logic Programming 5 (1988) 183-205.

9. M. A. Derr, S. Morishita, G. Phipps. *Design and Implementation of the Glue-Nail Database System.* Proc. ACM SIGMOD'93 (1993) 147–156.

10. G. Gottlob, R. Zicari. *Closed World Databases Opened Through Null Values.* Proc. 14th VLDB, Los Angeles (1988) 50-61.

11. T. Imielinski, W. Lipski. *Incomplete Information in Relational Databases.* Journal of the ACM 31 (1984) 761-791.

12. W. Kim et al. *Architecture of the ORION Next−Generation Database System.* IEEE Transaction on Knowledge and Data Engineering 2(1990) 109–124.

13. M. Ley. *The Term Retrieval Machine.* Proc. ACM SIGMOD'92 (1992) 154-163.

14. M. Ley. *Ein Datenbankkern zur Speicherung variabel strukturierter Feature-Terme.* Dissertationen zur Künstlichen Intelligenz, Bd. 41, Infix (1993) 263 S.

15. T. Ludwig, B. Walter. *EFTA: A Database Retrieval Algebra for Feature Terms.* Data & Knowledge Engineering 6 (1991) 125-149.

16. R. Reiter. *A Sound and sometimes Complete Query Evaluation Algorithm for Relational Databases with Null Values.* Journal of the ACM 33 (1986) 349-370.

17. M. Roth, H. Korth, A. Silberschatz. *Null Values in Nested Relational Databases.* Acta Informatica 26 (1989) 615-642.

18. M. Vardi. *Querying Logical Databases.* Journal of Computer and System Sciences 33 (1986) 142-160.

19. C. Zaniolo. *Database Relations with Null Values.* Journal of Computer and System Sciences 28 (1984) 142-166.

Object–Oriented System Specification Using Defaults*

Udo W. Lipeck and Stefan Brass

Institut für Informatik, Universität Hannover, Lange Laube 22,
D-30159 Hannover, Germany,
{sb|ul}@informatik.uni-hannover.de

Abstract. This paper aims at integrating techniques of non-monotonic reasoning about updates and of object-oriented specification of information systems. We present how to utilize defaults in specifications of dynamic system behaviour. Thus overridable rules may be used in specifications which deal not only with state structures, but also with state transitions and sequences. Systems are viewed as societies of interacting objects.

The underlying object specification logic is based on temporal logic and allows to refer to the enabling and occurrence of actions. It is extended with prioritized defaults and module composition. By discussing a variety of examples, we study which default patterns should be used for typical problems of behavioural specification.

1 Introduction

In this paper, we consider the different uses defaults may have in object-oriented specifications of dynamic system behaviour. Systems are viewed as societies of interacting objects.

To this end, we define an object specification logic with defaults, called *OSD;* it is based on a temporal logic which allows to refer to the enabling and occurrence of actions in the style of OSL [SSC92, SS93]. OSD includes arbitrary default formulae with priorities and a simple composition of specification modules.

In [BRL91] we have already introduced a general (institutional) framework for extending arbitrary logics by prioritized defaults, and its application to a multi-modal object calculus [FM91] (with elements from dynamic and temporal logic). To support temporal specifications more specifically (e.g. to solve standard problems like the "Yale shooting" problem) we here add a temporal prioritization. The semantics of defaults is explained by giving a preference relation between models and by distinguishing minimal models with respect to that relation. Basically, such models are preferred that satisfy more default instances of higher priority.

---

* This work was partially supported by the CEC under the ESPRIT Working Group 6071 IS-CORE (Information Systems — COrrectness and REusability), coordinated by Amílcar Sernadas.

Here, we study which default patterns should be used for typical problems of behavioural specification. In how far some of these defaults should be built into the logic is subject to further discussion; we first want to make all needed defaults explicit, the standard as well as the application–specific ones.

Let us now consider some applications for defaults. Specifications (no matter in what logic) are often made much simpler by allowing to concentrate on the "interesting half" of "if and only if"–definitions and leaving the other direction as subject to an implicit completion default, e.g.:

1. A proposition is false unless it is explicitly specified to be true (the usual "closed world assumption" in databases).
2. An attribute can only change its value unless this is explicitly specified (the "minimal change" frame rule).
3. An action is enabled unless explicitly specified otherwise.
4. An action cannot occur unless it is explicitly called.
5. Rules for object classes are inherited by subclasses unless they are (partially) overridden by more specific rules (in a given hierarchy of object classes).

Each of these rules defines a default. Of course, the minimal change frame rule is especially interesting in the context of temporal specifications, and the inheritance rule is central to an object–oriented structuring of system specifications.

The minimal change frame rule has raised a lot of discussions whether defaults can be used to formalize it, e.g. [HM87, Rei92]. To understand that defaults can make the specification task much simpler, consider a simple example: Let us assume to have a set, represented by a predicate *is-in*, and two operations *insert* and *delete*. In OSD, we can concentrate on the effect the two actions have, i.e. it is sufficient to specify that if *insert(Y)* occurs, then *is-in(Y)* is true in the next state, and if *delete(Y)* occurs, then *is-in(Y)* is false afterwards:

$$\nabla insert(Y) \rightarrow \mathbf{X}\ is\text{-}in(Y)$$
$$\nabla delete(Y) \rightarrow \mathbf{X}\ \neg is\text{-}in(Y)$$

However, without an implicit frame rule, we need the following specification:

$$\big(\mathbf{X}\ is\text{-}in(Y)\big) \leftrightarrow \nabla insert(Y) \vee \big(is\text{-}in(Y) \wedge \neg\nabla delete(Y)\big)$$

Furthermore, suppose we later want to add an action *clear*, which makes *is-in* empty. Without the frame rule, we must rewrite the explicit specification of $\mathbf{X}\ is\text{-}in(Y)$ to

$$\big(\mathbf{X}\ is\text{-}in(Y)\big) \leftrightarrow \nabla insert(Y) \vee \big(is\text{-}in(Y) \wedge \neg\nabla delete(Y) \wedge \neg\nabla clear\big)\ .$$

In OSD, we do not have to change the existing rules, we simply add

$$\nabla clear \rightarrow \mathbf{X}\ \neg is\text{-}in(Y)\ .$$

The other main application of defaults is to formalize the overriding of inherited rules in object-oriented specifications; this direction has already been followed by us in [BL91, BRL91, BL93]. It allows, for example, to first specify an ideal counter, which works with arbitrary long integers, and later derive counters restricted to different word sizes from the general specification. Here we study the joint impacts of inheritance / overriding and behavioural defaults.

In general, defaults allow to write specifications in an incremental style, giving general principles first and adding exceptions later, without running into inconsistencies as they often occur in the course of writing specifications in the conventional way. This improves also the reusability of specifications.

The rest of the paper is structured as follows: In Sect. 2, we introduce the underlying temporal logic for object specification, then we define the syntax and semantics of specifications with defaults in Sect. 3. Section 4 contains quite a number of specification patterns which illustrate the use of defaults for different purposes, especially the interplay between the different defaults, but also their semantical limitations. In Sect. 5, we consider the composition of object specifications and discuss how such a modular structure can increase the expressiveness of specifications with defaults (e.g. to handle the standard "stolen car" problem). Finally, we give a short summary and outline directions for future research.

2 Temporal Logic

In this section, we present syntax and semantics of the underlying temporal logic. It contains the temporal quantifiers **I** (initially), **X** (next), **F** (sometime), **G** (always), **U** (until), and it allows to refer to the enabling ($\Diamond$) and the occurrence (∇) of actions.

2.1 Syntax

For the syntax, our goal is to define formulae, which are strings of symbols from an alphabet $\mathcal{A}$, partitioned into logical symbols $\mathcal{A}_L$ (like $\wedge$, $\neg$, **X** , **U**), variable symbols $\mathcal{A}_V$ (like X, Y, Z), and non-logical symbols $\mathcal{A}_N$ (like *is-in*, *insert*). The non-logical symbols which can be used in formulae depend on the application and are defined by means of a signature:

Definition 1 (Signature). A signature $\Sigma = \langle S, F, P, A \rangle$ consists of

1. S, a finite set of nonlogical symbols (sorts, type symbols),
2. F, an $S^* \times S$-indexed family of nonlogical symbols (function symbols),
3. P, an S^*-indexed family of nonlogical symbols (predicate symbols),
4. A, an S^*-indexed family of nonlogical symbols (action symbols).   □

This is the standard definition of a first-order signature, extended by action symbols. For simplicity, the function symbols will be assigned their "free" interpretation, so they can only be used as (time-independent) names or record constructors. Object attributes must be modelled by predicates.

Special built-in predicates are used to express the enabling and the occurrence of an action (as introduced by [SSC92] for OSL):

Definition 2 (Extended Predicates). We write E for the family

$$E_{s_1 \ldots s_n} := P_{s_1 \ldots s_n} \cup \{\nabla a \mid a \in A_{s_1 \ldots s_n}\} \cup \{\Diamond a \mid a \in A_{s_1 \ldots s_n}\}. \qquad \square$$

Beside the logical symbols and the application symbols, we need variables to build formulae. Each formula can have its own set of variables. The following definition is standard:

Definition 3 (Variable Declaration). A variable declaration is an S-indexed family V of subsets of $\mathcal{A}_V$. $\qquad \square$

As usual, objects in the universe are denoted by terms:

Definition 4 (Term). The set of (Σ, V)–terms $T_{\Sigma,V}^{(s)}$ of sort s is the smallest set with:

1. If $f \in F_{s_1 \ldots s_n, s}$, and $t_i \in T_{\Sigma,V}^{(s_i)}$ $(i = 1, \ldots, n)$, then $f(t_1, \ldots, t_n) \in T_{\Sigma,V}^{(s)}$.
2. If $v \in V_s$, then $v \in T_{\Sigma,V}^{(s)}$.

A Σ-ground term is a $(\Sigma, \emptyset)$-term (a variable-free term). $\qquad \square$

Now we can define the formulae of the logic:

Definition 5 (Formula). The set of (Σ, V)–formulae $\mathcal{L}_{\Sigma,V}$ is the smallest set with:

1. If $t_1, t_2 \in T_{\Sigma,V}^{(s)}$, then $t_1 = t_2 \in \mathcal{L}_{\Sigma,V}$.
2. If $e \in E_{s_1 \ldots s_n}$, and $t_i \in T_{\Sigma,V}^{(s_i)}$, then $e(t_1, \ldots, t_n) \in \mathcal{L}_{\Sigma,V}$.
3. If $L_1, L_2 \in \mathcal{L}_{\Sigma,V}$, then $(\neg L_1)$, $(L_1 \wedge L_2) \in \mathcal{L}_{\Sigma,V}$.
4. If $L \in \mathcal{L}_{\Sigma,V}$ and $v \in V_s$, then $(\exists v \, L) \in \mathcal{L}_{\Sigma,V}$.
5. If $L_1, L_2 \in \mathcal{L}_{\Sigma,V}$, then $\mathbf{I} L_1$, $\mathbf{X} L_1$, $L_1 \mathbf{U} L_2 \in \mathcal{L}_{\Sigma,V}$.

A Σ-formula is a pair consisting of a variable declaration V and a (Σ, V)–formula L. $\qquad \square$

In the examples, the sorts of symbols and terms will always be clear from the context so that we do not mention them explicitly. Other syntactic simplifications are adopted as well, for instance, dropping parentheses corresponding to usual binding rules or using infix notation for arithmetic operators. We usually do not mention variable declarations, since they can be determined from the formulae, and we also introduce the usual shorthands:

1. $t_1 \neq t_2$ for $\neg(t_1 = t_2)$,
2. *false* for $X \neq X$,
3. *true* for $X = X$,
4. $L_1 \vee L_2$ for $\neg(\neg L_1 \wedge \neg L_2)$,
5. $L_1 \to L_2$ for $\neg L_1 \vee L_2$,
6. $L_1 \leftarrow L_2$ for $L_1 \vee \neg L_2$,
7. $L_1 \leftrightarrow L_2$ for $(L_1 \leftarrow L_2) \wedge (L_1 \to L_2)$,
8. $\forall v \, L$ for $\neg \exists v \, (\neg L)$,
9. $\mathbf{G} \, L$ for $L \mathbf{U}$ *false*,
10. $\mathbf{F} \, L$ for $\neg \mathbf{G} \, \neg L$.

2.2   Semantics

We use a fixed domain (the Herbrand universe) for every sort in order to avoid problems with variable assignments referring to deleted objects. Since it is, however, possible to introduce a predicate for the current objects of some sort, the fixed domain is no restriction.

So we have a Herbrand interpretation for every point in the timeline:

Definition 6 (State). A state I defines a relation $I[e] \subseteq I[s_1] \times \cdots \times I[s_n]$ for every extended predicate symbol $e \in E_{s_1,\ldots,s_n}$, and it satisfies the additional condition for every action symbol a:

$$\text{if } (d_1, \ldots, d_n) \in I[\nabla a], \text{ then } (d_1, \ldots, d_n) \in I[\Diamond a] \ . \qquad \square$$

The latter requirement means that only enabled actions can occur. Formulae are interpreted in state sequences:

Definition 7 (Interpretation). An interpretation is a mapping $\mathcal{I}$, which assigns a state $\mathcal{I}(i)$ to every natural number $i \geq 1$. $\qquad \square$

The notions of variable assignment and term evaluation are again standard (since we consider only Herbrand interpretations, term evaluation merely consists of applying the substitution given by the variable assignment):

Definition 8 (Variable Assignment). Let a variable declaration V be given. A variable assignment α is an S-indexed family of mappings from V_S to $T_{\Sigma,\emptyset}^{(s)}$.

Definition 9 (Term Evaluation). The value $\alpha[t]$ of a term t given an assignment α is defined as follows:

1. If t has the form $f(t_1, \ldots, t_n)$, then $\alpha[t] := f(\alpha[t_1], \ldots, \alpha[t_n])$.
2. If t is a variable v, then $\alpha[t] := \alpha(v)$. $\qquad \square$

Definition 10 (Satisfaction of Formulae). The satisfaction of a formula L in an interpretation $\mathcal{I}$ for a variable assignment α and current state number $i \in \mathbb{N}$ is defined as follows:

1. $(\mathcal{I}, \alpha, i) \models t_1 = t_2 \;:\Longleftrightarrow\; \alpha[t_1] = \alpha[t_2]$.
2. $(\mathcal{I}, \alpha, i) \models e(t_1, \ldots, t_n) \;:\Longleftrightarrow\; (\alpha[t_1], \ldots, \alpha[t_n]) \in \mathcal{I}(i)[e]$.
3. $(\mathcal{I}, \alpha, i) \models \neg L \;:\Longleftrightarrow\;$ not $(\mathcal{I}, \alpha, i) \models L$.
4. $(\mathcal{I}, \alpha, i) \models L_1 \wedge L_2 \;:\Longleftrightarrow\; (\mathcal{I}, \alpha, i) \models L_1$ and $(\mathcal{I}, \alpha, i) \models L_2$.
5. $(\mathcal{I}, \alpha, i) \models \exists v \, L \;:\Longleftrightarrow\;$ there is α', $(\mathcal{I}, \alpha', i) \models L$, differing from α only in v.
6. $(\mathcal{I}, \alpha, i) \models \mathbf{I} \, L \;:\Longleftrightarrow\;$ if $i = 1$ then $(\mathcal{I}, \alpha, i) \models L$.
7. $(\mathcal{I}, \alpha, i) \models \mathbf{X} \, L \;:\Longleftrightarrow\; (\mathcal{I}, \alpha, i+1) \models L$.
8. $(\mathcal{I}, \alpha, i) \models L_1 \, \mathbf{U} \, L_2 \;:\Longleftrightarrow\; (\mathcal{I}, \alpha, j) \models L_1$ for all $j \in \mathbb{N}$ with $i \leq j \leq k$, where $k := \min\{j \in \mathbb{N} \mid j \geq i, (\mathcal{I}, \alpha, j) \models L_2\} \cup \{\infty\}$. $\qquad \square$

Definition 11 (Model). An interpretation $\mathcal{I}$ is a model of a formula L ($\mathcal{I} \models L$) iff $(\mathcal{I}, \alpha, i) \models L$ for all variable assignments α and all state numbers $i \in \mathbb{N}$. $\quad \square$

2.3 Examples

Let us now consider some typical formulae which might appear in specifications:

1. $counter(Y) \wedge succ(Y, Z) \wedge \nabla inc \rightarrow \mathbf{X}\, counter(Z)$. This rule defines the effect of an action (inc, i.e. increment) on the value of an attribute ($counter$).
2. $\mathbf{I}\, counter(0)$. This rule gives the initial value of the attribute.
3. $counter(Y) \wedge counter(Z) \rightarrow Y = Z$. This is a key constraint, which is needed since we only have predicates to model attributes.
4. $counter(Y) \wedge Y = 0 \rightarrow \neg\Diamond dec$. This rule requires that an action (dec) is not enabled (i.e. permitted to occur) when a certain condition is true.
5. $\mathbf{F}\,\nabla inc$. This requires that there is an infinite number of actions occurring (note that our logic treats this formula like $\mathbf{G}\,\mathbf{F}\,\nabla inc$). Such "liveness constraints" are only used for active objects, e.g. when turning the counter into a clock.
6. $\neg(\nabla dec \wedge \nabla inc)$. Our logic allows any number of actions to occur at the same time (in parallel), so that it is necessary to specify mutual exclusion explicitly.
7. $\nabla task \rightarrow \nabla inc$. This means that an external action $task$ calls the action inc (probably $task$ does some other things as well).
8. $(counter(Y) \wedge \mathbf{X}\, counter(Z) \wedge Y \neq Z) \rightarrow \nabla inc \vee \nabla dec$. This is a locality rule: the value of the attribute $counter$ is only changed by the actions inc and dec.
9. The formula $\nabla reset \rightarrow \mathbf{X}\,(counter(0)\,\mathbf{U}\,\nabla inc)$ might serve as a verification goal, here for checking that no undesired changes can be observed: Whenever $reset$ occurs, $counter(0)$ holds in the future until inc occurs for the first time.

3 Specifications with Defaults

In this section, we extend the logic by defaults. By defaults we mean supernormal defaults in the sense of REITER's default logic [Rei80] which would be represented as $true:\delta/\delta$. Although these defaults are very simple, surprisingly many examples can be formalized with them (especially if coupled with priorities). This type of defaults was suggested and investigated in [Poo88, BL89, Bre91, DJ91, Dix92, Bra93a, Bra93b].

3.1 Syntax

Let us now define the central notion of a specification:

Definition 12 (Specification). A specification $\mathcal{S} = \langle \Sigma, \Phi, \Delta, \ell \rangle$ consists of

1. Σ, a signature,
2. Φ, a consistent set of Σ-formulae, the axioms,
3. Δ, a set of Σ-formulae, the defaults,
4. ℓ, a mapping $\Delta \rightarrow \mathbb{N}_0$, assigning a priority level to each default. $\qquad\square$

First, a specification should contain a signature Σ to define names for the objects of interest in the application domain. Then Σ-formulae can be defined as axioms Φ, if they have to be fully satisfied and should be non-overridable, or as defaults Δ, if they should be satisfied only as much as possible given the axioms and other defaults. Different priorities ℓ can be assigned to defaults in order to solve conflicts between them, i.e. to determine which formulae should override other formulae. In this paper, we use higher numbers to denote higher priorities. In the concrete syntax, we attach the priority in brackets to the formula, e.g.

$$\neg p(Y_1, \ldots, Y_n) \quad [0]$$

would be the usual negation default (with minimal priority). Axioms are distinguished from defaults by specifying no priority, e.g.

$$p(c_1, \ldots, c_n).$$

3.2 Semantics

The next goal is of course to define the semantics of such specifications, i.e. their intended models. Surely an intended model of $\mathcal{S}$ should be a model of the axioms Φ. But it should also satisfy the defaults Δ "as much as possible". This is formalized by giving a preference relation on the models of Φ.

But first note that not the defaults themselves are the units of assumption or rejection. For instance, if the above negation default $p(Y_1, \ldots, Y_n)$ [0] could be assumed only on an "all or nothing" basis, then the single fact $p(c_1, \ldots, c_n)$ with constants $c_1, \ldots, c_n$ would block the default completely. So we need the notion of instances of a default, which define its granularity. (Different definitions of instances are possible; e.g., the natural consequences of [Rya91] have a finer granularity than our semantical instances.)

An instance of a default formulae is at least determined by specific values substituted for the variables of the default, i.e. by a variable assignment. But in the context of temporal logic (compare Def. 10), there is also an implicit state parameter that has to be instantiated:

Definition 13 (Default Instance). A default instance is a triple $\langle \delta, \alpha, i \rangle$ where

1. $\delta \in \Delta$ is a default,
2. α is a variable assignment for the variables of δ,
3. $i \in \mathbb{N}$ is a state number.

The set of all instances of Δ is denoted by Δ^*. □

Now we define the following preference relation. Intuitively, $\mathcal{I} \prec_{(\Delta, \ell)} \mathcal{I}'$ means that $\mathcal{I}$ is better in satisfying the defaults than $\mathcal{I}'$.

Definition 14 (Preference Relation). $\mathcal{I} \prec_{(\Delta, \ell)} \mathcal{I}'$ iff there are $i, l \in \mathbb{N}$ such that

1. $\big\{ \langle \delta, \alpha, i \rangle \in \varDelta^* \mid (\mathcal{I}, \alpha, i) \models \delta,\ \ell(\delta) = l \big\}$
   $\supset \big\{ \langle \delta, \alpha, i \rangle \in \varDelta^* \mid (\mathcal{I}', \alpha, i) \models \delta,\ \ell(\delta) = l \big\}$,

2. $\big\{ \langle \delta, \alpha, i \rangle \in \varDelta^* \mid (\mathcal{I}, \alpha, i) \models \delta,\ \ell(\delta) > l \big\}$
   $= \big\{ \langle \delta, \alpha, i \rangle \in \varDelta^* \mid (\mathcal{I}', \alpha, i) \models \delta,\ \ell(\delta) > l \big\}$,

3. $\big\{ \langle \delta, \alpha, j \rangle \in \varDelta^* \mid (\mathcal{I}, \alpha, j) \models \delta,\ j < i \big\}$
   $= \big\{ \langle \delta, \alpha, j \rangle \in \varDelta^* \mid (\mathcal{I}', \alpha, j) \models \delta,\ j < i \big\}$. $\qquad\square$

The first condition is the maximization of satisfied default instances: For some state number i and priority l, $\mathcal{I}$ has to satisfy a strict superset of the default instances true in $\mathcal{I}'$. The next two conditions are necessary to check that this state number i and this priority level l are the relevant ones for differentiating between the two models: they require that the two models satisfy the same defaults in earlier states and for higher priorities.

With respect to the priority level (the second condition), this is clear: If the two models differ with respect to higher priority defaults, that or a higher priority level will be used as a basis for the comparison.

The third condition represents the natural (as we believe) view that defaults should be assumed as early as possible in a state sequence; thus earlier default instances are implicitly given higher priority. Consequences will be discussed later.

Note that the temporal prioritization is considered as more important than the explicit prioritization of the default instances. So the defaults are considered in the following sequence:

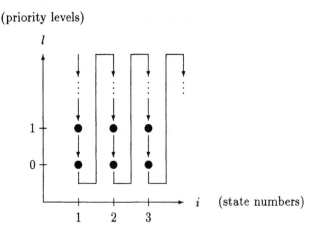

Once the two models differ in considered defaults, the comparison stops. If the set of satisfied default instances of the current priority level l and state number i in one model is a subset of those satisfied in the other model, then the latter model will be preferred. If no such subset relation holds, the two models are uncomparable.

Lemma 15. *The preference relation $\prec_{(\Delta,\ell)}$ is transitive and irreflexive, i.e. a strict partial order.* □

Proof.

1. "Irreflexivity": This follows directly from the required strict superset condition.

2. "Transitivity": Let $\mathcal{I}_1 \prec_{(\Delta,\ell)} \mathcal{I}_2$ and $\mathcal{I}_2 \prec_{(\Delta,\ell)} \mathcal{I}_3$. So there are i_{12} and l_{12} such that the conditions of Def. 14 are satisfied for $\mathcal{I}_1$ and $\mathcal{I}_2$, and there are i_{23} and l_{23} such that they are satisfied for $\mathcal{I}_2$ and $\mathcal{I}_3$.
   Now we have to define i_{13} and l_{13} in order to show that $\mathcal{I}_1 \prec_{(\Delta,\ell)} \mathcal{I}_3$ according to Def. 14. Consider the following three cases:
   (a) $i_{12} < i_{23}$: Choose $i_{13} := i_{12}$ and $l_{13} := l_{12}$.
   (b) $i_{12} = i_{23}$: Choose $i_{13} := i_{12}$ and $l_{13} := \max(l_{12}, l_{23})$.
   (c) $i_{12} > i_{23}$: Choose $i_{13} := i_{23}$ and $l_{13} := l_{23}$.
   In each of the three cases it is easy to see that the conditions of Def. 14 are satisfied, so $\mathcal{I}_1 \prec_{(\Delta,\ell)} \mathcal{I}_3$. □

Now the intended models should be the minimal models (minimal for historical reasons) with respect to the preference relation:

Definition 16 (Intended Model). Let $\mathcal{S} = \langle \Sigma, \Phi, \Delta, \ell \rangle$ be a specification. An intended model of $\mathcal{S}$ is a Σ-model $\mathcal{I}$ of Φ such that there is no Σ-model $\mathcal{I}'$ of Φ with $\mathcal{I}' \prec_{(\Delta,\ell)} \mathcal{I}$. □

4 Pragmatics

In this section, we study a number of examples to demonstrate typical application patterns of defaults. We are especially interested in the interplay of different kinds of defaults. Of course, many of the defaults used here should really be built into the semantics; this will be our next goal and the examples given here may act as "benchmark problems" to test different semantics.

4.1 Minimal Change

Of course, the most important application of defaults in temporal specifications is to formalize the frame rule: Predicates do not change unless explicitly required in the specification. Let us begin with a simple example, which nevertheless demonstrates some problems:

Example 17. Assume that we have a propositional variable p (i.e. a switch), which is initially false, and an action set_p for making it true:

$$\mathbf{I}\,\neg p$$
$$\nabla\,set\_p \rightarrow \mathbf{X}\,p$$

To represent other non-related actions (e.g. a set action for another switch), we have also an action *wait*, which does nothing. We explicitly specify that both actions are always enabled and mutually exclusive:

$$\Diamond set\_p$$
$$\Diamond wait$$
$$\neg(\nabla set\_p \wedge \nabla wait)$$

This is not strictly needed in the following, but it restricts the possible models we have to consider.

Now we would like to conclude from this specification that p remains false until *set_p* occurs:

$$\neg p \rightarrow (\neg p \ \mathbf{U} \ \nabla set\_p)$$

This formula, however, is not a logical consequence of the above axioms: For example, it is not excluded that p changes its value when *wait* occurs.

The solution is obviously to add a minimal change default. If possible, p should keep its value in the next state:

$$p \leftrightarrow \mathbf{X} p \ [0]$$

So the default really is a "no change" default, but since it may be overridden, it enforces a minimal change. Instead of the "if and only if" condition we could also write $p \rightarrow \mathbf{X} p \ [0]$ and $\neg p \rightarrow \mathbf{X} \neg p \ [0]$.

Now this specification has a trivial, but undesirable intended model, namely one without any *set_p* occurring! The reason is that nothing prevents us from assuming all default instances (surely the best possible model with respect to the defaults), but then p has to stay false forever.

In order to remedy this problem we must make two models uncomparable if they differ in the actions which occur. Therefore we have to declare the occurrence and non-occurrence of actions explicitly as defaults of equal priority:

$$\nabla set\_p, \ \neg\nabla set\_p \ [1]$$

(Such defaults should be added for all actions, i.e. also for *wait*, but this is not needed in this example.) The priority of these defaults must be greater or equal to the minimal change defaults.

Now the specification in fact has the desired semantics. Take any sequence of occurring actions as given, e.g. let *wait* occur in state 1, and *set_p* in state 2. No model with these actions occurring at other times is comparable, so we do not have to consider such models. It is also not possible to improve the set of satisfied default instances of priority [1] in any way, so we can concentrate on the default of priority [0] (the minimal change default).

The temporal prioritization requires that we give the earlier default instances their chance first. The minimal change default is assumed in state 1. So p is still false in state 2. Here *set_p* occurs, so the axiom $\nabla set\_p \rightarrow \mathbf{X} p$ requires that p is true in the next state, and we cannot assume $p \leftrightarrow \mathbf{X} p$. In state 3 and all following states we can again assume the minimal change default, so p remains true forever (as expected).

Since this reasoning can be generalized to arbitrary sequences of action occurrences, all intended models satisfy $\neg p \rightarrow (\neg p \mathbf{U} \nabla set\_p)$.

Note that the chronological minimization (earlier defaults have higher priority) is necessary for this example. If we treated all default instances as having the same priority, then models changing p to true before the set_p action would also be minimal. □

It is known that chronological minimization solves also the Yale shooting problem [HM87].

4.2 Incomplete Information

Example 18. Minimal change defaults interfere with incomplete information. Assume that we again have a propositional variable p which is initialized to true by the action set_p, but we do not know anything about its value before that (in contrast to Example 17):

$$\nabla set\_p \rightarrow \mathbf{X}\, p$$

As above, we introduce standard defaults for minimal change and arbitrary occurrences:

$$p \leftrightarrow \mathbf{X}\, p \qquad [0]$$
$$\nabla set\_p,\ \neg \nabla set\_p \quad [1]$$

But now again nothing prevents us from assuming all instances of the minimal change default, so that we can conclude that p was already true in the initial state, if set_p occurs sometime later:

$$(\mathbf{F}\, \nabla set\_p) \rightarrow \mathbf{I}\, p$$

This is not desirable since p should have been undefined before the setting. The solution is again to make models uncomparable by introducing pairs of defaults which offer both possibilities:

$$\mathbf{I}\, p,\ \mathbf{I}\, \neg p \quad [1]$$

Now the specification has the intended semantics. □

Example 19. Note that this works even if the incomplete information is generated later:

$$\nabla a \rightarrow \mathbf{X}\, (p \vee q)$$
$$\nabla set\_p \rightarrow \mathbf{X}\, p$$
$$\mathbf{I}\, \neg p$$
$$\mathbf{I}\, \neg q$$

We again have the standard defaults:

$$p \leftrightarrow \mathbf{X}\, p \qquad\qquad [0]$$
$$q \leftrightarrow \mathbf{X}\, q \qquad\qquad [0]$$
$$\nabla set\_p,\ \neg \nabla set\_p \quad [1]$$
$$\nabla a,\ \neg \nabla a \qquad\quad [1]$$

Now assume that a occurs in state 1 and set_p in state 2. Then the following two models are uncomparable:

	1	2	3	
$\mathcal{I}$	$\neg p, \neg q$	$p, \neg q$	$p, \neg q$	...
$\mathcal{I}'$	$\neg p, \neg q$	$\neg p, q$	p, q	...

(because they satisfy different minimal change defaults in state 1). So the defaults stating that both observations are possible are only needed in the initial state.

4.3 Implicit Negation

Example 20. The classical usage of defaults is implicit negation. As a first example let us consider the following specification:

$$
\begin{aligned}
& p(Y) \leftrightarrow \mathbf{X}\, p(Y) && [0] \\
& \nabla set\_p(Y),\ \neg \nabla set\_p(Y) && [1] \\
& \neg \mathbf{I}\, p(Y) && [2] \\
& \mathbf{I}\, p(c) && \\
& \nabla set\_p(Y) \rightarrow \mathbf{X}\, p(Y) &&
\end{aligned}
$$

This specification works as intended, i.e. in the beginning $p(c)$ is true and $p(Y)$ is false for all $Y \neq c$, and later $set\_p(Y)$ makes $p(Y)$ true.

Note that it is important that the negation default has higher priority than the minimal change default. Otherwise update rules with negative preconditions would not work, e.g.

$$
\neg p(d) \wedge \nabla set\_p(Y) \rightarrow \mathbf{X}\, p(Y) \ .
$$

Suppose that $set\_p(e)$ occurs. If $p(e) \leftrightarrow \mathbf{X}\, p(e)$ had higher priority than $\neg p(d)$, we would assume the minimal change default and not the negation default. This is obviously not intended.

With a similar argument it can be seen that the negation default must have higher priority than the possibility of ∇set_p, if the enabling of set_p depends on the negation default (see below). □

Example 21. In the preceding example, a negation default referring only to the first state was sufficient (and in fact the only convincing solution). But this is not always the case. Suppose that q is a derived predicate defined by

$$
q(Y) \leftarrow p(Y)
$$

plus a negation default. Now if a p-fact is deleted by some action, the negation of the corresponding q-fact should become derivable. So in this case the negation default must refer to all states:

$$
\neg q(Y) \quad [2]
$$

But as discussed above, we then cannot use minimal change defaults, and this means that it is impossible to specify actions which insert q-facts. Thus it seems to be conceptually clearer to distinguish between updatable predicates with minimal change defaults (and a negation default only for the first state), and derived predicates with full negation defaults (and no minimal change defaults). □

4.4 Disabling of Actions

Example 22. We have argued above that if we use minimal-change defaults it also will be important to explicitly ensure that the actions can happen:

$$p \leftrightarrow \mathbf{X}\, p \quad [0]$$
$$\nabla a,\ \neg\nabla a \quad [1]$$

But, of course, under certain conditions actions cannot occur, since they are disabled:

$$\mathbf{I}\, p$$
$$p \rightarrow \neg\Diamond a$$

It is easy to check that this specification works as intended, i.e. a is disabled all the time. □

Example 23. A practically very important default will be that an action a is enabled unless explicitly specified otherwise:

$$\Diamond a \quad [1].$$

Then only disabling conditions need to be specified in the form $p \rightarrow \neg\Diamond a$ or $\Diamond a \rightarrow \neg p$. Note that there may be a conflict with implicit negation defaults. In this case the enabling of the action depends on the truth value of $\neg p$, therefore the negation default for p should have higher priority, so that it is evaluated first. □

Example 24. It is useful to distinguish between actions which are only called internally in the specified system and actions which are called from the environment. For internal actions b we can assume that they only occur if explicitly called, so that we take the default $\neg\nabla b$. For instance, consider the case that *task* is an external action, which may occur or not arbitrarily, but *set_p* is an internal action called by *task*:

$$\neg\nabla set\_p \quad\qquad [0]$$
$$\nabla task,\ \neg\nabla task \quad [1]$$
$$\nabla task \rightarrow \nabla set\_p$$

We give $\neg\nabla set\_p$ a lower priority than $\nabla task$, because the occurrence of *set_p* depends on the occurrence of *task*. □

4.5 Overridable Rules

Example 25. The temporal minimization is not only adequate for minimal change defaults, but for every kind of default. Suppose we have a simple counter with only an increment action, but in order to make the specification reusable, we declare the main rule for the action effect as a default:

$$\mathbf{I}\ counter(0)$$
$$counter(Y) \wedge counter(Z) \rightarrow Y = Z$$
$$counter(Y) \wedge succ(Y, Z) \wedge \nabla inc \rightarrow \mathbf{X}\ counter(Z)\ \ [3]\ \ (*)$$

Of course, we need also the standard defaults:

$$counter(Y) \leftrightarrow \mathbf{X}\ counter(Y)\ \ [0]$$
$$\nabla inc,\ \neg\nabla inc\ \ [1]$$

This is an ideal counter, which is able to work with arbitrary large numbers. But usually the set of possible values is limited. For instance, to derive a 2-bit counter from this specification, we add the following rule (as an axiom or a default of higher priority):

$$counter(Y) \rightarrow Y \le 3\ \ [4]$$

Let us assume that four *inc*-actions occur, so it is not possible to assume all instances of (*). Now the first three *inc*-actions indeed have the expected effect, because the earlier default instances have priority. If we treated all default instances as of equal importance, we could choose to violate any of the four default instances in question, for instance, we could magically reset the counter after the second *inc*. □

4.6 Integrity Constraints

Example 26. In non-temporal default specifications, there is no difference between axioms and defaults of highest priority (if they are consistent). This does not hold for temporal default specifications, since earlier default instances are preferred even if they have a smaller explicit priority. For instance, assume the following variant of Example 17:

$$\nabla set\_p \rightarrow \mathbf{X}\ p\ \ [0]$$
$$\mathbf{I}\ \nabla set\_p$$
$$\neg p$$

Here the default defining the effect of the action cannot be assumed because the postcondition p contradicts the integrity constraint $\neg p$. If we, however, use a default of priority [1] instead of the second axiom, $\neg p$ will not be assumed in state 2. So it is crucial that constraints are really specified as axioms. □

Example 27. It may be useful to specify the effect of an action by means of defaults, if one is not sure that the action really preserves the integrity. If it violates a constraint, the default will not be assumed; so the minimal change defaults ensure that the state remains unchanged (corresponding to a "rollback"). Consider the following action specification which surely violates the integrity:

$$\neg p \wedge \nabla a \rightarrow \mathbf{X}\,false \quad [2]$$

Now of course the priorities of ∇a and $\neg p$ are interesting: It depends on the application whether one wants to conclude that a simply cannot happen (give ∇a priority < 2) or that ∇a has no effect (give ∇a priority ≥ 2). But it seems clear that the truth value of p is determined in the prestate before executing a. This means that the negation default for p should have priority > 2. $\quad\square$

4.7 Semantical Problems

Note that there are specifications without intended models:

Example 28. The classical example [EMR85] uses the natural numbers, i.e. a signature with a constant 0 and a function $succ$. The axioms formalize that a predicate p holds for all "big enough" numbers:

$$p(Y) \rightarrow p\big(succ(Y)\big)$$
$$\exists Y \,\big(p(Y)\big)$$

Then we add the usual negation default (nothing should be true unless required by the axioms):

$$\neg p(Y) \quad [0]$$

This results in an infinite descending chain of models, so there is no intended model. $\quad\square$

Example 29. Since we have the natural numbers "built-in" for the time axis, we can have the same problem with the "sometime" quantifier, which is needed for liveness requirements:

$$\neg p \quad [0]$$
$$\mathbf{F}\,p$$

Since we prefer to violate the default $\neg p$ as late as possible, and there is no deadline when p has to be true, we again get an infinite descending chain of models. $\quad\square$

Example 30. The preceding example may look a bit artificial, but the same trap lurks in the following specification of a propositional variable on constantly changing its value (perhaps a binary clock of some processor):

$$on \leftrightarrow \mathbf{X}\,on \quad [0]$$
$$\mathbf{I}\,\neg on$$
$$\neg on \wedge \nabla tick \rightarrow \mathbf{X}\,on$$
$$on \wedge \nabla tick \rightarrow \mathbf{X}\,\neg on$$
$$\mathbf{F}\,\nabla tick$$

Since the minimal change default is violated if *tick* occurs, the occurrence is delayed forever contradicting the liveness condition. It again helps to introduce the standard occurrence defaults:

$$\nabla tick, \ \neg \nabla tick \ [1]$$

Then the specification behaves as intended: $\mathbf{F}\nabla tick$ acts as a liveness requirement excluding models where tick does not happen infinitely often.

This simple solution, however, does not work for conditional liveness requirements. Moreover, it seems to be a bit counterintuitive that occurrence defaults are needed although there is an axiom controlling occurrences. Such situations have to be subject to further semantical analysis. $\qquad\qquad \Box$

4.8 Summary

In the examples above, we have proposed patterns of defaults which should be considered as standard elements of behaviour specifications.

For predicates, we have to distinguish the following cases:

1. If the predicate is initially undefined and explicitly set by actions, use the defaults

$$\mathbf{I}\,p(Y_1,\ldots,Y_n), \ \mathbf{I}\,\neg p(Y_1,\ldots,Y_n) \ [1]$$

   "Every value may be observed in the initial state unless something different is specified explicitly." In addition, the minimal change (or no change) default is needed:

$$p(Y_1,\ldots,Y_n) \leftrightarrow \mathbf{X}\,p(Y_1,\ldots,Y_n) \ [0]$$

   "A predicate (attribute) does not change its value unless explicitly required to do so."

2. If the positive information about the predicate is specified explicitly in the initial state, and the usual completion should be applied, use the negation default for the initial state:

$$\mathbf{I}\,\neg p(Y_1,\ldots,Y_n) \ [1]$$

   "The predicate extension contains only those tuples which are explicitly given." Again, we apply also the minimal change default:

$$p(Y_1,\ldots,Y_n) \leftrightarrow \mathbf{X}\,p(Y_1,\ldots,Y_n) \ [0]$$

3. If the predicate is a derived predicate, which is not directly updated (it changes only in order to reflect changes in other predicates), we need no minimal change default. Instead, we use a negation default for all states:

$$\neg p(Y_1,\ldots,Y_n) \ [1]$$

4. In the next section, we will introduce "volatile" predicates, which are changed from the outside. They need the following defaults:

$$p(Y_1, \ldots, Y_n), \ \neg p(Y_1, \ldots, Y_n) \ [1]$$

"In every state, every value may be observed." Of course, no minimal change default is applied.

For actions, it seems useful to assume by default that "an action is enabled unless explicitly specified otherwise":

$$\Diamond a(Y_1, \ldots, Y_n) \ [1]$$

Then we have to distinguish between the following cases:

1. Usually we assume by default that there may be arbitrary sequences of actions, i.e. "every action may occur in an arbitrary state or not", depending on the environment (e.g., the user) and only restricted by axioms (or higher prioritized defaults) on enabling conditions.:

$$\nabla a(Y_1, \ldots, Y_n), \ \neg \nabla a(Y_1, \ldots, Y_n) \ [1]$$

2. For a passive object, we assume by default that "every action does not occur unless explicitly called":

$$\neg \nabla a(Y_1, \ldots, Y_n) \ [1]$$

3. On principle, the fully active counterpart $\nabla a(...)$ could be specified as well, but it seems to be unusual as a default at least in conventional systems, and it, of course, would lead to a different style of the remaining specification.

4. No defaults on occurrences usually do not make sense, since then typical specifications are ideally satisfied when nothing happens in the system.

Cases 1 and 2 can be understood as differentiating between external (externally accessible) and internal (only internally called) actions of a system. But note that actions with liveness requirements have to be treated like external actions to solve the problem of infinitely delaying the liveness condition (Example 30).

Finally, some hints on the right selection of the priorities can be given. Here the idea of a stratification is useful: If A depends on B, then the defaults defining A should have higher priority.

A specific instance is that the future depends on the past, and usually not vice versa. To some degree, this is already built into the logic. But it further helps to give the defaults defining the current state priority over the defaults defining the next state. For instance, the negation defaults for the predicates can be given higher priority than the rules defining the effects of actions (see Example 27). And of course, the minimal change default should be given the lowest possible priority.

Finally, it is clear that if overridable rules are used, the more specific definitions (from the subclasses) should have higher priority than the more general definitions (from the superclasses).

5 Module Composition

Up to now, we have specified only single objects. Now the goal is to extend our approach to the specification of object societies. To this end, we introduce a simple module system. This is needed because the specified objects usually should have some locality — the interaction with other objects may select one of the intended models, but the global model should contain an isomorphic copy of one of the intended models of the object specification considered in isolation. Otherwise local reasoning becomes impossible, and we have to consult always the complete specification of the object society.

5.1 Local and Global Signatures

Of course, to allow the objects to interact, they have to share some symbols: actions, functions, and predicates. Probably a true object-oriented approach would allow to share only actions (methods), but then we would at least have to make a distinction between update and query methods.

But at the moment we take a rather simple approach. We assume that the shared symbols are named the same and the local symbols are named differently in the single object specifications. In large applications it is surely a simplistic assumption that any overlap of the signatures is intended, i.e. the same name in different modules really means the same thing and is not simply by accident. So of course, the concrete syntax would have to support local names and name mappings for interface couplings.

Definition 31 (Compatible Signatures). Let Σ_i, $i = 1, \ldots, n$, be signatures, and $\Sigma_i = \langle S^{(i)}, F^{(i)}, P^{(i)}, A^{(i)} \rangle$. The signatures are called compatible iff

If $s_1, \ldots, s_m, s \in S^{(i)}$, $F^{(i)}_{s_1 \ldots s_m, s} \neq \emptyset$, and $s \in S^{(j)}$, then $s_1, \ldots, s_m \in S^{(j)}$
and $F^{(i)}_{s_1 \ldots s_m, s} = F^{(j)}_{s_1, \ldots, s_m, s}$. □

Since we allow arbitrary overloading of symbols, we only need to ensure that the Herbrand universe of shared sorts is equal. Then we can simply take the union of the local signatures to construct a global signature:

Definition 32 (Global Signature). Let $\Sigma_i = \langle S^{(i)}, F^{(i)}, P^{(i)}, A^{(i)} \rangle$, $i = 1, \ldots, n$ be signatures. The global signature of the Σ_i is $\Sigma = \langle S, F, P, A \rangle$ with

1. $S := \bigcup_{i=1}^n S^{(i)}$,
2. $F_{s_1 \ldots s_m, s} := \bigcup_{i=1}^n F^{(i)}_{s_1 \ldots s_m, s}$,
3. $P_{s_1 \ldots s_m} := \bigcup_{i=1}^n P^{(i)}_{s_1 \ldots s_m}$,
4. $A_{s_1 \ldots s_m} := \bigcup_{i=1}^n A^{(i)}_{s_1 \ldots s_m}$. □

With this definition of global signature, a Σ-interpretation $\mathcal{I}$ obviously contains Σ_i-interpretations, called the Σ_i-reducts of $\mathcal{I}$. Now a global model of a modular specification is one which is also an intended model of the single specifications:

Definition 33 (Globally Intended Model). Let $\mathcal{S}_i = \langle \Sigma_i, \Phi_i, \Delta_i, \ell_i \rangle$, $i = 1, ..., n$, be specifications such that the Σ_i are compatible. Let Σ be the global signature. Then a globally intended model of $\{\mathcal{S}_1, ..., \mathcal{S}_n\}$ is a Σ-interpretation $\mathcal{I}$ such that each Σ_i-reduct $\mathcal{I}_i$ of $\mathcal{I}$ is an intended model of $\mathcal{S}_i$. $\quad\square$

5.2 Tolerance with Respect to Imports

The above definitions only refer to "shared symbols". But usually a symbol is defined (exported) in one module and used (imported) in another module. Then it is important that a module can live with any interpretation of the imported symbols. We call such a module tolerant [BL91].

Example 34. First suppose that module 1 defines the proposition p, initially false, but it can be set by set_p:

$$p \leftrightarrow \mathbf{X}\,p \qquad [0]$$
$$\nabla set\_p, \ \neg \nabla set\_p \quad [1]$$
$$\mathbf{I}\,p$$
$$\nabla set\_p \rightarrow \mathbf{X}\,p$$

It remains true because of the usual minimal change default.

Now module 2 defines p', which is initially false, but it copies the value of p if $tick$ occurs (so it acts as a delay element.)

$$p' \leftrightarrow \mathbf{X}\,p' \qquad [0]$$
$$\nabla tick, \ \neg \nabla tick \quad [1]$$
$$\mathbf{I}\,\neg p'$$
$$p \wedge \nabla tick \rightarrow \mathbf{X}\,p'$$
$$\neg p \wedge \nabla tick \rightarrow \mathbf{X}\,\neg p'$$

In module 2 the minimal change default is assumed, so p' remains false forever, and this implies that p also is false all the time. Thus a specification consisting of these two modules would have only intended models without set_p ever occurring. We should, however, ensure that module 2 assumes every value of the imported attribute to be observable. Therefore, we introduce a pair of defaults:

$$p, \ \neg p \quad [2]$$

It would also be possible to use priority [1], but only as long as the value of p has no influence on the occurrence of $tick$. $\quad\square$

5.3 The Stolen Car Problem

In the examples of Sect. 4, we have heavily used the temporal prioritization: Violations of defaults are assumed to happen as late as possible.

In the literature, it is argued that this is not always intended. For instance, if somebody returns to the place where he/she has parked his/her car, and does not find it, he/she will not conclude that the car was moved (stolen) just in the second before this observation.

This problem can also be explained using a variant of Example 17:

Example 35. Let the following specification of a propositional variable (here *stolen*) with a set-action (here *steal*) be given:

$$stolen \leftrightarrow \mathbf{X}\, stolen \quad [0]$$
$$\nabla steal,\ \neg\nabla steal \quad [1]$$
$$\Diamond steal$$
$$\mathbf{I}\,\neg stolen$$
$$\nabla steal \rightarrow \mathbf{X}\, stolen$$

Additionally, we have the observation that *stolen* is true in the third state:

$$\mathbf{I}\,\mathbf{X}\,\mathbf{X}\, stolen$$

This can also be viewed as a planning task: Which actions have to be executed in order to make *stolen* true in the third state?

Of course, this specification does not behave as expected. As in the above mentioned stolen car problem, *stolen* becomes true exactly from the second to the third state. And worse, *steal* does not even have to happen in the second state! □

Our proposal is to give a better specification of this scenario: The owner looking at the parking place should have no effect on the movement of the car. So we really should use a modular specification: First we define the car with the possible movement actions, then close the specification with respect to the defaults, i.e. determine the intended models, and only after that use the car in the specification of the world with the car owner coming back and not finding his/her car.

Example 36. So the correct formulation of Example 35 consists of two modules: One is the specification of *stolen* depending on *steal* as given above. Note that in the intended models of this specification, *stolen* can only become true if *steal* happens, and *steal* can happen at any time.

The other module treats *stolen* as defined elsewhere, but contains the observation that *stolen* is true in the third state:

$$stolen,\ \neg stolen \quad [1]$$
$$\mathbf{I}\,\mathbf{X}\,\mathbf{X}\, stolen$$

In the intended models of this specification, *stolen* is sometimes true and sometimes false, but surely true in the third state.

If we now compose the two specifications, we get models in which *stolen* is true in the third state, and *stolen* only becomes true because of *steal* occurring, and *steal* may occur in the first or the second state. So this modular specification behaves as intended. □

6 Conclusions

In this paper we have demonstrated how defaults with priorities can be utilized in specifications of dynamic system behaviour. The work is based on the object specification logic OSL, which basically is a temporal logic enriched by enabling/occurrence predicates for actions. Its extension by defaults to OSD can be explained semantically by a preferential model approach for prioritized defaults plus temporal prioritization. With defaults available in such a non-standard logic, typical requirements on dynamic behaviour can be expressed easily and combined flexibly; this will be helpful for designing systems composed of active and passive objects, and maintaining stored and deduced information.

To this end, we have already identified quite a number of standard default patterns. The class of liveness and fairness requirements, however, still needs deeper analysis, since careless usage of defaults can here lead to semantical limits, when specifications have no intended model (since typically mandatory actions are delayed infinitely). In this context, we will also consider an alternative semantics which prefers models on the basis of counting default satisfactions/violations instead of comparing sets of default satisfactions. It has to be checked when the two semantics differ, in which specification cases one or the other logic proves more appropriate.

Another direction on the way to a specification language will of course be to offer default-based requirements as built-in constructions of the logic itself, so that specifications become simpler and shorter. In particular, it might be interesting to automatically derive the needed priorities from a stratification and an inheritance hierarchy.

For composition purposes, we have used here a very simple module concept, which assumes a syntactic overlapping of modules, and which semantically closes the single specifications by evaluating the defaults, and then amalgamates intended models (if possible). Instead of composing object specifications on the model level, it might be desirable to compose the specifications themselves by keeping the defaults open for overriding by later defaults and axioms, which refer to the composed objects. The most general approach would be an arbitrary interleaving of closed and open module composition. Finally, we should obviously support local name spaces and renaming on composition.

Acknowledgement

We are grateful to PEDRO RESENDE for his comments on an earlier version of this paper, and we would like to thank him, MIGUEL DIONÍSIO, MARK RYAN, AMÍLCAR SERNADAS, and CRISTINA SERNADAS for helpful discussions.

References

[BL89]   S. Brass, U. W. Lipeck: Specifying closed world assumptions for logic databases. In J. Demetrovics, B. Thalheim (eds.), *2nd Symp. on Mathematical Fundamentals of Database Systems (MFDBS'89)*, 68–84, LNCS 364, Springer-Verlag, 1989.

[BL91]   S. Brass, U. W. Lipeck: Semantics of inheritance in logical object specifications. In C. Delobel, M. Kifer, Y. Masunaga (eds.), *Deductive and Object-Oriented Databases, 2nd Int. Conf. (DOOD'91)*, 411–430, LNCS 566, Springer-Verlag, 1991.

[BL93]   S. Brass, U. W. Lipeck: Bottom-up query evaluation with partially ordered defaults. In S. Ceri, K. Tanaka, S. Tsur (eds.), *Deductive and Object-Oriented Databases, 3rd Int. Conf. (DOOD'93)*, 252–266, LNCS 760, Springer, 1993.

[Bra93a] S. Brass: Deduction with supernormal defaults. In G. Brewka, K. P. Jantke, P. H. Schmitt (eds.), *Nonmonotonic and Inductive Logics, 2nd Int. Workshop (NIL'91)*, 153–174, LNAI 659, Springer-Verlag, 1993.

[Bra93b] S. Brass: On the semantics of supernormal defaults. In R. Bajcsy (ed.), *Proc. of the 13th Int. Joint Conf. on Artificial Intelligence (IJCAI'93)*, Morgan Kaufmann, 1993.

[Bre91] G. Brewka: *Nonmonotonic Reasoning: Logical Foundations of Commonsense.* Cambridge University Press, 1991.

[BRL91] S. Brass, M. Ryan, U. W. Lipeck: Hierarchical defaults in specifications. In G. Saake, A. Sernadas (eds.), *Information Systems — Correctness and Reusability, Workshop IS-CORE '91*, 179–201, Informatik-Bericht 91-03, TU Braunschweig, 1991.

[Dix92] J. Dix: Default theories of Poole-type and a method for constructing cumulative versions of default logic. In B. Neumann (ed.), *Proc. of the 10th Europ. Conf. on Artificial Intelligence (ECAI 92)*, 289–293, John Wiley & Sons, 1992.

[DJ91]   J. P. Delgrande, W. K. Jackson: Default logic revisited. In J. Allen, R. Fikes, E. Sandewall (eds.), *Principles of Knowledge Representation and Reasoning, 2nd Int. Conf. (KR'91)*, 118–127, Morgan Kaufmann, 1991.

[EMR85] D. W. Etherington, R. E. Mercer, R. Reiter: On the adequacy of predicate circumscription for closed-world reasoning. *Computational Intelligence 1 (1985)*, 11–15.

[FM91]   J. Fiadeiro, T. Maibaum: Towards object calculi. In G. Saake, A. Sernadas (eds.), *Information Systems — Correctness and Reusability, Workshop IS-CORE '91*, 129–178, Informatik-Bericht 91-03, TU Braunschweig, 1991.

[HM87]   S. Hanks, D. McDermott: Nonmonotonic logic and temporal projection. *Artificial Intelligence 33 (1987)*, 379–412.

[Poo88] D. Poole: A logical framework for default reasoning. *Artificial Intelligence 36 (1988)*, 27–47.

[Rei80] R. Reiter: A logic for default reasoning. *Artif. Intelligence 13 (1980)*, 81–132.

[Rei92] R. Reiter: On formalizing database updates – preliminary report. In A. Pirotte, C. Delobel, G. Gottlob (eds.), *Advances in Database Technology – EDBT'92, 3rd Int. Conf.*, 10–20, LNCS 580, Springer-Verlag, 1992.

[Rya91] M. Ryan: Defaults and revision in structured theories. In *Proc. of the IEEE Symposium on Logic in Computer Science (LICS'91)*, 362–373, 1991.

[SS93]   A. Sernadas, C. Sernadas. Denotational semantics of object specification within an arbitrary temporal logic institution. In U.W.Lipeck, G.Koschorreck (eds.), *Information Systems — Correctness and Reusability, Workshop IS-CORE '93*, 61-89, Informatik-Bericht 93-01, Univ. Hannover, 1993.

[SSC92] A. Sernadas, C. Sernadas, J. F. Costa: Object specification logic. Technical report, INESC, Lisbon, June 1992.

Terminologies and Rules

Hans-Jürgen Bürckert

Deutsches Forschungszentrum für Künstliche Intelligenz (DFKI)
Stuhlsatzenhausweg 3
66123 Saarbrücken
e-mail: hjb@dfki.uni-sb.de

Abstract. Terminological logics have become a well understood formal basis for taxonomic knowledge representation, both for the semantics (classically by Tarski models) and for the inference services (like concept subsumption, instantiation, classification, and realization) of terminological systems of the KL-ONE family. It has been demonstrated that terminological reasoning can be realized by efficient and logically complete algorithms based on tableaux style calculi.

However, representation of and reasoning with terminological information supports just a rather static form of knowledge representation. Only a fixed description of a domain can be represented: There is the schematic description of concepts in the socalled TBox and the instantiation of concepts by individuals and objects in the ABox of such systems. Terminological inferences can retrieve implicit information, but cannot be used for deriving new data.

In order to overcome this restriction terminological systems often allow for additional rule based formalisms. Those, however, are missing a clear declarative semantics. In this paper we will sketch several declarative forms of rule based extensions of terminological systems that have been developed recently.

1 Introduction

Concept description languages are widely accepted formalisms for taxonomic knowledge representation (KR) systems of the KL-ONE family (cf. [34] for an overview of such terminological systems). During the last few years terminological logics or description logics [27] have become a well understood formal basis for those systems, both for the semantics (classically by Tarski models) and for the inference services (like concept subsumption, instantiation, classification, and realization). It has been demonstrated that terminological reasoning can be realized by *efficient* and logically *complete* algorithms based on tableaux style calculi.

However, representation of and reasoning with terminological information supports only the static, purely representational part of knowledge processing. Pure terminological logics allow only for a fixed description of a domain: There is the schematic specification of concepts in a socalled terminology and there is the instantiation of those concepts by individuals and objects. Terminological inferences can just retrieve implicit information, but cannot be used for deriving new data. In order to overcome this restriction terminological systems often allow for additional rule based formalisms or for a direct access to the host language.

Thus terminological KR systems usually offer (at least) the following three different formalisms for representing knowledge: There is the *TBox formalism* for defining and structuring the *terminology* of the domain knowledge through a concept or class hierarchy that states the subconcept and superconcept relations mainly based on intensional descriptions of concepts. In the *ABox formalism* one can *assert* individuals and objects as instances of those concepts or one can assert relations and attributes of individuals or objects. Terminological logics provide declarative semantics for these two subformalisms and for their inference services. Finally, in the *RBox formalism* we can specify rules for the derivation of additional, often extensional relations between concepts or any other form of new information about concepts or their instances. This third subformalism, however, is mostly missing a clear declarative semantics.

Let us a brief, first look at a sample knowledge base (KB) from a shipping domain, that will accompany us during this paper, in order to demonstrate the different formalisms (cf. Section 2). In its TBox, for instance, we may have the information that furniture trucks are a subconcept of trucks, namely exactly those trucks that are used for transporting furnitures. That means every possible or real instance of a furniture truck is also an instance of a truck. In its ABox we may have assertions about some specific objects that are trucks. Other objects may be stated to have the property that they are used for the transportation of certain objects that are asserted to be furnitures. Thus we could infer the implicit information that these transporting objects must be furniture trucks. With rules it might be expressed in our KB that in some context—say for a specific transportation agency—the only trucks that exist are furniture trucks. Thus we could derive in this specific context that all other mentioned trucks are furniture trucks, too.

The rule based formalism of many terminological systems is often based on an informal extension of the pure descriptional formalism in the TBox and ABox, realized, for instance, through a direct access to the host language. Recently there are several approaches to give a clean, declarative basis for the integration of pure terminological KR and rule based formalisms.

One approach—we have called concept logics elsewhere—is based on constrained logics. Here the TBox and ABox formalisms are attached as constraint language into constrained logic (programming) schemes [19,1,7]. Such an approach provides essentially a classical first order semantics for the integration of rules (definite Horn clauses) and terminologies, where concept descriptions play the role of constraints for the variables occurring in the rules. They are allowed to occur only in the body of rules and they are interpreted with respect to a constraint theory given by a TBox and ABox. We will describe this approach in Section 3

A different way can be taken by using Levesque's K-Operator [21] together with a suitable possible world semantics, in order to model socalled trigger rules, where both in the body and the head of a rule consist of a single concept expression. Interpreting the K-Operator as "what the knowledge base knows about the world" the variables in the rules can be seen as quantifying over all named, i.e., "known" instances in an underlying ABox, but not over implicit objects (e.g., hidden by an existential quantifier in existential role restrictions or number restrictions.) For similar reasons this form of rule based reasoning lacks, for example, for case distinction or contraposition (if we allow for disjunction or negation in the underlying concept description language.) We will consider this in Section 4.

Quite recently trigger rules have been generalized to arbitrary rules mixing terminological and non-terminological expressions without the separation of the two formalisms as in the constraint logic approach: Here we obtain an integration of rules via definite clauses, where terminological literals, which are like schemes of ABox assertions, are allowed in both the body and the head of rule (cf. Section 5).

Finally we sketch how non-monotonic extensions of terminological reasoning with default rules can be achieved. Here the default rules may have concept expressions in the assumption, the justification, and the conclusion. Again the variables in those rules are interpreted as quantifying over all named instances in the ABox, but not the implicit ones. This non-monotonic rule extension is based on Reiter's Default Logic. We discuss this idea in Section 6.

2 Terminological Logics

In this section we will briefly recall the basics of terminological logics. Terminological logics are syntactic variants of certain fragments of predicate logics, which usually subsume propositional logics. Its semantics is an adapted version of the usual Tarski semantics, i.e., interpretations are given as structures $\mathcal{I}$ with a universe $\Delta^{\mathcal{I}}$ and a denotation function $.^{\mathcal{I}}$ for the primitives of the underlying language.

Terminological logics provide two formalisms to describe a problem domain, the terminological part or TBox formalism and the assertional part or ABox formalism.

The terminological part can be seen as an extension of class logics. Its basic language is a class or concept description language, which consists of a set of primitives called *concept symbols* A, B, ... semantically denoting subsets $A^{\mathcal{I}}$, $B^{\mathcal{I}}$,... of the universe of any interpreting structure $\mathcal{I}$. It goes beyond class logics in that it provides also a special form of relational extension. That means that there are in addition *role symbols* denoting binary relations of the universe.

Starting with these atomic symbols we can build complex concept expressions with a number of concept forming operators. These contain the Boolean operators ($\sqcap$, $\sqcup$, $\neg$) taking concept expressions C, D and forming new concept expressions $C \sqcap D$, $C \sqcup D$, and $\neg C$ which denote intersection, union, and complement, respectively, of the denoted sets $C^{\mathcal{I}}$ and $D^{\mathcal{I}}$. Then there are two quantifiers ($\forall$ and $\exists$) that can be used to combine role symbols R and concept expressions C to new concept expressions $\forall R.C$ and $\exists R.C$ denoting the sets

$$\{o \in \Delta^{\mathcal{I}} \mid \forall o' : (o, o') \in R^{\mathcal{I}} \Rightarrow o' \in C^{\mathcal{I}}\}$$

and

$$\{o \in \Delta^{\mathcal{I}} \mid \exists o' : (o, o') \in R^{\mathcal{I}} \wedge o' \in C^{\mathcal{I}}\},$$

repectively.

With these and usually further concept forming operators[1] the TBox formalism now allows for introducing new (atomic) concepts A to be subconcepts of or to be defined through other (compound) concepts C by *subconcept declarations* $A \sqsubseteq C$ or by *concept definitions* $A = C$. Models of such subconcept declarations and definitions are structures that satisfy the according subset relations and set equations. A *terminology* or a *TBox*, now, consists of a set of unique and acyclic concept definitions and subconcept declarations.[2]

Let us demonstrate the TBox formalism by an example. Suppose we want to model some knowledge base of a transportation agency. This must contain knowledge about goods, say furnitures etc., about vehicles like trucks, freighters, freight trains, and transport planes that can be used for transporting some kinds of goods. Depending on the needs we have to model some of those concepts by specifying necessary conditions or by completely defining them. We also might have some knowledge about locations depending on which kind of transport vehicles could be used to transport the cargo between them. Of course, much more information is needed, but we will restrict our example to the following simplified terminology:

$Furniture \sqsubseteq Goods$
$Vehicle = MotorVehicle \sqcup Ship \sqcup Train \sqcup Plane$
$Transporter = Vehicle \sqcap \exists transport.Goods$
$Truck = MotorVehicle \sqcap \exists transport.Goods$
$Freighter = Ship \sqcap \exists transport.Goods$
$FreightTrain = Train \sqcap \exists transport.Goods$
$TransportPlane = Plane \sqcap \exists transport.Goods$
$FurnitureTruck = Truck \sqcap \forall transport.Furniture$
$Town \sqsubseteq Location$
$PortTown = Town \sqcap \exists equipped\_with.Port$
$StationTown = Town \sqcap \exists equipped\_with.Station$
$AirportTown = Town \sqcap \exists equipped\_with.Airport$

---

[1] Some languages also have role forming operators, cf. [27] for the syntax and semantics of a proposed language standard for terminological systems.

[2] Some recent paper proposes a stronger separation of subconcept declarations and concept definitions into different boxes with different description languages [6]. Influenced by database systems here the idea is to take a box of subconcept declarations as a kind of *knowledge base schema*, which is instantiated by concrete ABoxes, while concept definitions are used to define *views* on those concrete KBs.

Notice that there is some hidden information, for instance, that trucks are transporters, since they are motor vehicles—and hence vehicles—, which transport some goods.

Depending on which concept forming operators are allowed—some languages only take subsets or variants of the above ones others take further operators—we distinguish different languages of terminological logics with different expressive power and different computational behaviour for the basic inferences. The above one is known as $\mathcal{ALC}$. In some languages some of the role symbols are interpreted as functional relations (or partial unary functions), socalled *features*, and some further concept forming operators with feature symbols are allowed (cf. [27]).

The assertional part or *ABox* of concept description formalism provides, in addition, *constant symbols* denoting elements of the universe in an interpreting structure. In the ABox, now, we can introduce instance relations between constants a and compound concepts C through *instance assertions* $a:C$ and role relations between constants through *role assertions* $R(a, b)$. Models of an ABox are structures (satisfying the TBox), for which the corresponding element relations $a^{\mathcal{I}} \in C^{\mathcal{I}}$ and binary relations $(a^{\mathcal{I}}, b^{\mathcal{I}}) \in R^{\mathcal{I}}$ hold.

Let us continue our above example with some assertions that may realize some part of the data of a specific transport agency concerning its transport facilities, locations, and transportation tasks. There might be specific transporters, knowledge about towns, say Hamburg (HH) and Saarbrücken (SB), and some specific goods:

> $truck\_1{:}FurnitureTruck$
> $truck\_2{:}Truck$
> $couch\_1{:}Furniture$
> $board\_1{:}Goods$
> $transport(truck\_1, board\_1)$
> $transport(truck\_2, couch\_1)$
> $HH{:}PortTown \sqcap StationTown \sqcap AirportTown$
> $SB{:}StationTown$
> $equipped\_with(SB, Ensheim\_Airport)$
> $Ensheim\_Airport{:}Airport$

Again, we may see possible inferences of implicit information, for instance, that Saarbrücken is an AirportTown; or that he board must be a piece of furniture, since otherwise the second truck could not transport it according to our definition of furniture trucks.

Both the TBox and the ABox formalism of a terminological KR system provide several inference services for retrieving explicit and implicit information. According to our declarative semantics these inference services can be described independetly of any possible implementation:

- Proving whether all concepts in the TBox are meaningful, i.e., testing whether every concept can be interpreted as non-empty set in at least one interpretation (*concept satisfiability*).

- Finding implicit subconcept relations, i.e., finding out whether a concept is interpreted as subset of the denotation of another concept in all models of the TBox (*subsumption*); and based on this, computing the implicit subconcept hierarchy of all the concept names used in the TBox or finding the place in that hierarchy for any further given compound concept expression (*classification*).
- Checking consistency of the whole knowledge base, i.e., testing whether there exists a common model of the TBox and ABox (*KB satisfiability*).
- Testing implicit instance relations, i.e., finding out whether in all models of the TBox and ABox a given constant denotes an element of the denotation of a given concept (*instance test*); and based on this, computing all instances of a given concept (*retrieval*) or computing the lowest concepts in the hierarchy that have a given constant as instance (*realization*).

In the past there was put some emphasis on finding logically complete algorithms for that inference services and figuring out the complexity of that algorithms (cf. [22,14,15,29,13]). The fundament for most of the algorithms is the fact that—essentially since the language contains negation—these services can be reduced to each other, say to the consistency test for an ABox.[3] Thus they can be reduced to the question whether or not there exists an interpretations for a set of instance and role assertions. The following transformation rules on ABoxes provide a correct and complete algorithm for that test for the language $\mathcal{ALC}$:[4]

(1) Expand an ABox containing $a{:}C \sqcap D$ by the assertions $a{:}C, a{:}D$
    if the ABox contains neither $a{:}C$ nor $a{:}D$.
(2) Expand an ABox containing $a{:}C \sqcup D$ by the assertion $a{:}E$
    if the ABox does not contain $a{:}E$, where E is either C or D.
(3) Expand an ABox containing $a{:}\exists R.C$ by the assertions $R(a, x), x{:}C$
    if x is a fresh constant and
    there is no z, such that $R(a, z)$ and $z{:}C$ are in the ABox.
(4) Expand an ABox containing $a{:}\forall R.C, R(a, b)$ by the assertion $b{:}C$
    if the ABox does not yet contain $b{:}C$.

If we apply those rules to any ABox, rule application will terminate—in all branches opened by the *nondeterministic* rule (2)—and the original ABox is unsatisfiable if every expansion leads to an ABox containing an obvious contradiction, i.e., a *clash* of two complementary assertions $a{:}A, a{:}\neg A$. The original ABox is satisfiable, if there is at least one expansion without a clash. In that case the resulting ABox can be used to construct a model of the original one.

---

[3] For instance, the satisfiability test of a concept C is just equivalent to the satisfiability test of the ABox with a single instance assertion $\{a{:}C\}$ with a fresh constant a. The instance test whether $a{:}C$ holds in all models of the KB is equivalent to the satisfiability test of the ABox extended with the instance assertion $a{:}\neg C$.

[4] Introduced fresh constants are not interpreted under the unique name assumption. One might think of them equivalently as existantially quantified variables.

The consistency test of an ABox with respect to a TBox can be obtained by replacing every defined concept by its definitions and by replacing every concepts with subconcept declaration by the conjunction of its superconcept and a fresh concept symbol. If this is done recursively in the ABox as long as possible the resulting ABox is consistent iff the original one together with the TBox is consistent.[5]

If we want to implement a terminological system, these inference rules have to be realized by an algorithm with a sophisticated control mechanism. Of course, in such a system it would not be a good idea to realize all other inferences trough a reduction of the consistency check. Instead one must provide more direct realizations of the services. Also reasoning with respect to a TBox should not be reduced to reasoning without TBoxes as mentioned above, but by incremental expansion of the concept definitions and subconcept declarations. Thus the description given here can only be a principal view onto terminological systems and their inference services.

3 Concept Logics

The knowledge we have specified in our example of the transportation agency consists only of very static parts of the domain description. What we might need further is knowledge about how transportation tasks could be managed. For instance, we might need some general rules such as: Trucks can be used to transport goods between any two towns, while trains only may be used between towns that have a station; or, transportation by ships requires port towns and, in addition, they must be connected through some waterway.

A natural way to integrate terminological formalisms and rules of that kind is available, since general constrained logic programming schemes like the Höhfeld-Smolka scheme [19] and constrained logic schemes [7,8] came up. These formalisms provide a separation of background information through constraint systems and foreground information through first order formulae enhanced with constraints.

In these approaches constraint systems consist of a constraint language, a constraint theory, and a constraint solver. The constraint language is essentially a distinguished set of (syntactic variants of) open first order formulae, the *constraints*. This set has to be closed under conjunction and variable instantiation of constraints. The constraint theory is any specification of a set of first order models for the constraint language.[6] The constraint solver is at least a test calculus for satisfiability of constraints. That is, given any constraint the constraint solver has to find out whether there is some constraint model and an assignment of the free variables of that constraint, such that the constraint becomes true in

---

[5] This replacement terminates since we did not allow cyclic definition or subconcept declarations.

[6] This is more general then common constrained logic programming schemes, where the constraint theory is given as a complete specification of just a single model (cf. [20,25])

that model. Such a pair of a constraint model and an assignment is also called a solution of that constraint. The constraint solver may in addition transform the constraints into simpler ones, socalled solved forms (cf. [19,8]).

In the foreground part we have first order formulae enhanced with constraints. The Höhfeld-Smolka scheme just allows for Horn formulae and attaches constraints as part of the body.[7] General constrained logics have arbitrary first order formulae with *restricted quantifiers* where the constraints are used as quantifier restriction—similar as in sorted logics, but restricting sets of variables instead of single variables. Notice that the constraints in constrained logic programming schemes can also be seen as quantifier restriction, namely of the (implicit) universal quantifiers of the Horn clauses.

Recalling that concept expressions are open formulae with one free variable we can take concepts as constraints (or quantifier restrictions) for single variables. We also can be slightly more general and take pairs of a concepts and a variable (written $x:C$) with the meaning x is constrained by C, i.e., the variable can only be assigned by objects that are elements of the set denoted by C. This, however, is like an instance assertion (without unique name assumption), quite the same as the fresh constants introduced in our consistency algorithm for ABoxes. In fact, we could be still more general and allow for arbitrary ABoxes (with variables and constants) as constraints.[8] In [1] such a general scheme for an integration of concept constraints and predicate logics, called concept logics, is described.

In concept logics the background description of some domain modelling is given in terms of a terminological constraint theory, i.e., specified by a TBox and an ABox. In the foreground we have facts and rules (or general clauses) in a different first order language, but with additional terminological constraints in their bodies. Hence we have constrained formulae of the form

$$Head \Leftarrow Body \| Constraint$$

where *Head* is a first order atom, *Body* is a possibly empty conjunction of first order atoms, and *Constraint* is a possibly empty terminological constraint. Notice that the first order language for *Head* and *Body* and the terminological language for the constraints are disjoint except for the variables and the constants, which are shared.[9]

---

[7] Notice, that this might lead to non-Horn formulae, if the constraint language allows for negation. Moreover, the constraint theory can be non-Horn or even not axiomatizable in first order logics, since we allow for an arbitrary specification of the constraint theory.

[8] One of the instances of the Höhfeld-Smolka scheme is socalled feature logics. Here feature constraints are exactly such ABoxes for a concept language with atomic concepts and functional roles (features) only and certain concept forming operators [30].

[9] There could be arbitrary first order terms in the foreground language. In that case, however, the constraint language must also be extended for terms and in addition for equations. It causes not much problems to extend the ABox formalism by terms

Like in logic programming a KB consists of a set of such rules and facts (i.e., rules with empty body and empty constraint) and in addition a TBox and an ABox as constraint language.[10] Given a query, i.e., a rule clause without head, the interpreter of our rules proceeds by constrained SLD-resolution. It selects some of the goal literals and a suitable rule. By a generalization of the unification process between the goal and the head literal a new goal is derived. This generalization replaces (or extends) unification by constraint solving: After a match of the argument variables the combined set of constraints of the goal and the selected rule has to be solved or at least has to be tested for solvability with respect to the constraint theory. This test can, for instance, be done by the consistency algorithm through testing the union of the ABox of the constraint theory and the constraint (with respect to the TBox.) Thus we have the following procedure transforming goal clauses into new goal clauses until we reach a goal clause without body literals, but with the collected constraint:

1. Select a literal $p(s_1, ..., s_n)$ in the goal clause.
2. Find a rule (or fact) clause with suitable head $p(t_1, ..., t_n)$.
3. Match the argument terms and test the constraint combined by that of the goal clause and that of the rule clause (under the argument match) for solvability.
4. If this is solvable, replace the selected goal literal by the body of the rule clause and the goal constraint by the combined constraint (or any solved form).

The collected constraint of the final goal clause (or its solved form) is returned as an answer to the query. If the constraint solver fails, backtracking has to take place as in common SLD-resolution procedures.

Let us briefly exemplify this. We assume that our constraint theory is given as the TBox and ABox of the former example. With our constrained rules we now can model the general rules above. We may use an new predicate for specifying a four-place deliver relation for vehicles and goods between two locations:

$$deliver(x, y, u, v) \Leftarrow \quad \| x{:}Truck, y{:}Goods, u, v{:}Town$$
$$deliver(x, y, u, v) \Leftarrow \quad \| x{:}FreightTrain, y{:}Goods, u, v{:}StationTown$$
$$deliver(x, y, u, v) \Leftarrow waterway(u, v) \| x{:}Freighter, y{:}Goods, u, v{:}PortTown$$

In order to solve a transportation task the system has to find out whether there are any vehicles and if so, which of them can be used for transporting the cargo from one location to the other. Thus the following query might be posed to the knowledge base:

$$? \Leftarrow deliver(x, couch\_1, HH, SB) \| x{:}Vehicle$$

---

and equations, but only by ground terms and ground equations. As constraints have to be tested for satisfiability, all variables can be considered as (Skolem) constants— without unique name assumption. This is similar to the fresh introduced constants in the ABox consistency algorithm.

[10] In [16] concept logics is instantiated to a DATALOG style language with terminological constraints.

That is, we have the query whether there are some vehicles that can be used tpodeliver the couch from Hamburg to Saarbrücken. The system has then to extract, for instance, the answer that $truck\_1$ can do that job. This can be done by a constrained resolution procedure above.

A first step, for instance, could be, to choose the third *deliver* clause. In that case, we obtain the new goal clause (its constraint is already simplified and is obviously satisfiable)

$$\Leftarrow waterway(HH, SB) \| x{:}Freighter, couch\_1{:}Goods, HH, SB{:}PortTown$$

Notice that this will lead to backtracking, since there exists no information about a waterway between the two locations. The other two rules, however, will result in answers.

Slightly different as usual for constraints, our terminological constraint theory need not describe a single constraint model. Instead, our TBox and ABox may be an incomplete world description. Therefore it usually will have more than one model and solvability of a constraint means that there is at least one model, such that the constraint can be solved in that model.

Of course this gives us some further nondeterminism for the selection of the models. In the end of an answer computation we cannot be sure that we have chosen the correct model. Still worse, it can be shown that none of the models alone need to guarantee the answer. It might be necessary that we need to do some case distinction, in order to find the answer. For instance, in our transportation example we might need a case distinction between the different kinds of transporters we have there. This might lead to different cases for answering the query, for example, if we had an object in our knowledge base, of which we only know that it is a transporter. Thus, depending of which kind of transporter it really is, we can give the answer that it could be used. That means we will get conditional answers. For instance, a derivation that takes the second clause only provides such a conditional answer: There are models with or without freight trains. The answer, hence, would be here "Yes, the couch can be delivered, if there is a freight train." Only if we result in a complete case distinction, we can combine those cases to a complete answer.[11]

In the example, however, we have the nice case that there is also an answer without any condition, if we choose the first clause. In that case $truck\_1$ is a complete solution, since it will solve the constraint in all possible models.

Here we just want to contrast once more some advantages and disadvantages of that approach to integrate terminological and rule based formalisms for knowledge representation. As main advantage we would like to pose the almost classical declarative semantics and the natural way of that integration. Related to this is a third advantage of the more or less straightforward extension of well-known inference machines that can be used to realize the inference services for the integrated formalisms. Disadvantages are the inefficiencies of resolution

---

[11] See [7,8] for more details on constrained resolution and [11] for a discussion of the problems and the logical nature of conditional and indefinit answers in constrained logic programming languages with open constraint theories.

based inference procedures, which are extended here with an additional non-determinism for that combination. A further disadvantage is the fact that if we allow function symbols and terms in the formalism the test whether or not our case distinction is complete becomes undecidable—thus this is a source for further inefficiences (cf. [9,9]).

Let us close that section with a reference to an older approach of integrating a rule based formalism with terminological logics. This has been proposed in [4], where Stickel's theory resolution approach [33] was used, such that a terminological formalism plays the role of a special theory. Rules could be modelled here also as Horn clauses, where some literals are concept or role assertions (again with variables instead of constants in the case of non-ground literals). However, this approach has also been shown to suffer from the very inefficient behaviour of general purpose reasoners.[12]

4   Simple Trigger Rules

As usual system designers of terminological systems have taken a more pragmatic way to integrate rule based formalisms. For several reasons the systems have to offer the direct access of functions and procedures of the host language. One way to integrate something like rules is to implement these just through host language calls. More elaborated approaches, however, provide a proper rule formalism—they use a rule interpreter for a special class of rules.

In many cases these rules are relatively simple, socalled *trigger rules*. The condition and consequence of those rules are single concept expressions:

$$C \longrightarrow D$$

They are used as patterns of concept instances operating like domain specific inference rules on the ABox. This means that they can be seen as consisting of a concept description and a variable for possible objects:

$$x{:}C \longrightarrow x{:}D.$$

Such a trigger rule fires, whenever the system can derive for any constant a that it is an instance of the concept expression C. In that case it is concluded that a has to be an instance of D, too, and technically the assertion $a{:}D$ may be added dynamically to the ABox. Hence trigger rules are, in fact, handled as (partially instantiated) inference rules. Thus this rule mechanism is purely operational and depends on the realization of the instance test of the ABox formalism. Declarative semantics have been missed until recently.

A first idea might be to consider trigger rules as additional subconcept relations—similar as those in the TBox, but with compound concepts on left hand sides, too. However, the operational usage of trigger rules is different from that view, for three reasons: Trigger rules fire only for explicit objects, i.e., only

---

[12] In [7] we show some closer connection between theory resolution and constrained resolution.

for constants that occur explicitly in the ABox. Subconcept relations would hold for all objects, i.e., also for implicit objects, e.g., those hidden by existential role restrictions. A second difference is that for a subconcept relation $C \sqsubseteq D$ the contraposition must hold also: $\neg D \sqsubseteq \neg C$. For trigger rules this need not be the case, since there need not be an instance of $\neg D$ in the ABox. The third difference is that trigger rules do not allow for reasoning by case distinction, i.e., a rule with disjunctive precondition, $C \sqcup D \rightarrow E$, is not equivalent to the two rules $C \rightarrow E$ and $D \rightarrow E$. The reason is that there might be an instance of $C \sqcup D$ in the ABox, such that the disjunctive rule can fire. But, of course, none of the two alternative rules need do so.

In [21] H. Levesque considers ASK and TELL operations on knowledge bases. According to this, trigger rules can be taken as part of the query language of a terminological KR system: The precondition is an ASK operation to the system querying the ABox for (actual) instances of the concept description C, while the postcondition is a TELL operation on the ABox asserting the further property D about those instances.

In his paper Levesque presents a declarative semantics for the query language. This is based on the idea that an ASK operation asks for what the knowledge base (KB) knows about (objects of) the world and a TELL operation asserts new such knowledge to the KB. Therefore he expands the KR language by a K-*operator* representing the KB's knowledge and gives a possible world semantics for the extended language.

Under this view a trigger rule is like a universally closed implication using an additional modal operator K:

$$\forall x \; \mathsf{K}(x{:}C) \Rightarrow \mathsf{K}(x{:}D),$$

where C and D are concept expressions.

In order to remain closer to the syntax of terminological logics, we will attach—similar as in [17]—the terminological language with the K-operator in allowing additional concept descriptions KC with the intuitive meaning that it denotes the class of all known objects of C.[13] With these epistemic concepts a trigger rule gets the form[14]

$$\mathsf{K}C \sqsubseteq \mathsf{K}D.$$

Notice that we allow no recursive nesting of the K-operator and that we will allow epistemic concepts only in trigger rules, but neither in the TBox nor in the ABox. If we compare trigger rules with our TBox language it turns out that trigger rules are like subconcept declarations but with arbitrary compound (epistemic) concept expressions on *both* sides.

---

[13] Notice that from a philosophical point of view one might argue that there is a difference between the two expressions $x{:}\mathsf{K}C$ and $\mathsf{K}(x{:}C)$. While the first states a fact about known objects of the class C, the second asserts knowledge of the fact $x{:}C$. This is related the difference between *de re* and *de dicto* interpretation of epistemic operators.

[14] The semantics allow also to take, equivalently, the form $\mathsf{K}C \sqsubseteq D$.

For the semantics we introduce epistemic interpretations for the language with K-operator. An *epistemic interpretation* is given as a pair $(\mathcal{I}, \mathcal{W})$ of a distinguished interpretation $\mathcal{I}$ and a set of interpretations $\mathcal{W}$ all with the same universe. An epistemic interpretation $(\mathcal{I}, \mathcal{W})$ interprets non-epistemic concept expressions C as its distinguished interpretation $\mathcal{I}$ does: $C^{\mathcal{I}, \mathcal{W}} = C^{\mathcal{I}}$, if C is without K-operator. It interprets an epistemic concept expression KC by an intersection over the interpretations in $\mathcal{W}$, i.e.,[15]

$$(KC)^{\mathcal{I}, \mathcal{W}} = \bigcap_{\mathcal{J} \in \mathcal{W}} C^{\mathcal{J}}.$$

As one would require, an epistemic interpretation satisfies TBox and ABox expressions iff its distinguished interpretation does. It satisfies a trigger rule $KC \sqsubseteq KD$ iff $(KC)^{\mathcal{I}, \mathcal{W}} \subseteq (KD)^{\mathcal{I}, \mathcal{W}}$. It is not dificult to verify that the K-operator is essentially an S5-modal operator (if we would have allowed recursive nesting of K-operators), cf. [12]: It satisfies all common properties of S5-modal operators, e.g., $KC \sqsubseteq C$, $KC \sqsubseteq KKC$, $\neg KC \sqsubseteq K\neg KC$ (with the expected semantics of these expressions). However, differently as in S5-modal logics we will only consider maximal models of a KB—that means we minimize the *knowledge* of a KB.

Given a KB consisting of a TBox, an ABox, and a set of trigger rules, called *RBox* in the sequel, an epistemic interpretation $(\mathcal{I}, \mathcal{W})$ is called an *epistemic model* of that KB iff $\mathcal{I} \in \mathcal{W}$ and $\mathcal{W}$ is any maximal set of interpretations such that for each $\mathcal{J} \in \mathcal{W}$ the epistemic interpretaion $(\mathcal{J}, \mathcal{W})$ satisfies every formula in the KB. Notice that this means that for a pure terminological KB, i.e., a TBox and an ABox only, the epistemic models are just the epistemic interpretations $(\mathcal{I}, \mathcal{W})$ such that $\mathcal{I} \in \mathcal{W}$ and $\mathcal{W}$ is the set of all models of the KB. We say an instance assertion $a{:}C$ is an *epistemic consequence* of the KB iff it is satisfied by every epistemic model of the KB. Notice that role assertions are not effected by the epistemic operator.

With that semantics both the universal meaning of the quantification and the material meaning of the implication for trigger rules in the expanded language is correct. E.g., we get the intended difference between the contraposition of the trigger rule in that extended language

$$\forall x \, \neg K(x{:}D) \Rightarrow \neg K(x{:}C)$$

and a reformulation of the contraposition of the original trigger rule

$$\forall x \, K(x{:}\neg D) \Rightarrow K(x{:}\neg C).$$

Similarily, this holds for disjunctive triggers. The fact, that quantification is restricted to named objects only, is reflected by the maximality requirement of epistemic models.

---

[15] Notice that, since it is not needed for simple trigger rules, we will not use recursive epistemic concept expressions here as in [17]. If we would have done this, the semantics had to be according to that recursion $(KC)^{\mathcal{I}, \mathcal{W}} = \bigcap_{\mathcal{J} \in \mathcal{W}} C^{\mathcal{J}, \mathcal{W}}$.

A typical usage for trigger rules could be as in the following example. Suppose we had in addition to our given TBox of the transportation domain the definition of a gasoline truck

$$GasolineTruck = Truck \sqcap \exists transport.Gasoline$$

Now, gasoline trucks should not be used to carry any liquid food. One might take this as part of the definition of a gasoline truck, but it seems to be more adequate to add this as a rule: Whenever the KB knows about an object to be a gasoline truck it also should know that it cannot use that truck to transport liquid food, i.e., we should have the rule

$$\mathsf{K}GasolineTruck \sqsubseteq \mathsf{K}\neg\exists transport.LiquidFood$$

According to the operational reading of trigger rules we will have the following inference rule for an expanded instance test, i.e., a test whether an instance assertion is an epistemic consequence of our KB. As earlier we assume that our inference rules operate on an ABox, where all concept expressions are expanded with respect to the TBox, and take into account the RBox, where also all concept expressions are expanded. Thus the inference rule is

$$ABox \longrightarrow ABox \cup \{a{:}D\}$$
if there is a trigger rule $\mathsf{K}C \sqsubseteq \mathsf{K}D$ in the RBox
and $a{:}C$ is a consequence of ABox.

The reader is referred to [17] for a more detailed description of reasoning with simple trigger rules and their semantics. That paper contains also some other interesting applications of Levesque's K-operator for queries to terminological systems.

5   More General Rules

The two integrations of concept descriptions and rules discussed in the former sections remained more or less unsatisfactory. Concept logics, on the one hand side, has the disadvantages that its reasoning is rather untractable, especially, if one is interested in complete answers. It has, however, the nice feature that it seems to be a very natural integration of a logic programming style of rule based knowledge processing and of the class and object oriented form of structuring the knowledge base in terminological logics. What is missed further here is a form of rules that allow for dynamic modification of that structured part of the knowledge. Constrained rules can only be used to express additional, but non-terminological information about the objects of a modelled domain. Trigger rules, on the other hand side, have been proven useful for that kind of processing on the domain's concepts. However, trigger rules are still not expressive enough.

Quite recently something like a combination of the two rule based formalisms has been proposed [18]. Recall that trigger rules are universal rules that talk about named objects only. On the other hand the usual least Herbrand semantics of definite rules in logic programming has exactly the same effect. Logic programs talk about the objects that are named by ground terms—of course this is only possible since they do not have existential quantifiers, which refer to implicit objects.[16]

Now, the idea of that combination is to expand the definite rule language of logic programming by allowing both in the bodies and heads of rules instance and role assertions (with variables). Differently as in the constrained logic approach, however, the variables of such extended rules are quantifying over named objects, i.e., over ground terms only.

Thus we have the following language now: There are concept symbols, role symbols and non-terminological predicate symbols as well as arbitrary function symbols and constant symbols. We have a TBox and an ABox as before, but with arbitrary ground terms as object denoting expressions in the ABox—as in pure terminological languages one might assume that for (some of the) constants we still have unique name assumption, but not for arbitrary ground terms. In addition we have a fact base, i.e., a set of ground atoms as in logic programming, and a set of general rules, where both body and head literals are allowed to be instance or role assertions with variables (or non-ground terms) or first order atoms with non-terminological predicate symbol.

The procedural semantics one gets is a combination of the fixed point semantics of logic programs (cf. [24]) and of trigger rules. Thus a forward chaining version is as follows: A rule fires, whenever the ABox and fact base together entail an instantiation of the body of the rule. Then we derive the accordingly instantiated head of the rule either as an ABox assertion, if it is a terminological head, or as a non-terminological fact, otherwise. In order to guarantee that the derived assertion or fact is ground we need the requirement that the body of a rule contains at least all the variables of the head.[17]

The declarative semantics of that combination is also not really difficult. We just have to recognize that for an extension of pure Horn logic programs with Levesque's K-operator we do not get anything new: If we replace any literal in a common Horn logic program by the same literal but preceeded with a K-operator the above possible world semantics for the K-operator together with our maximality requirement is equivalent to the least Herbrand semantics of the program without K-operator (cf. [23]). Thus we can expand our language accordingly with the K-operator to be used in the rules—it is enough to use it for the terminological part of the rules. We will not describe this in more detail, but it should be clear how we had to proceed. With that semantics we can show correctness and completeness of the procedural semantics sketched above. The reader is refered to [18] for further details—but notice that there a backward

---

[16] Notice that in pure Horn logic programming to some extent rules are neither contrapositive and nor allow for case distinction, since the language does not support negation or disjunction.

[17] This could be weakened, if we allow for some further nondeterminism: Variables in the head that do not occur in the body have to be instantiated by arbitrary ground terms.

chaining variant of the description here has been given.

We also might think of a further backward chaining form of rule interpretation like in the usual SLD-resolution style of logic programs—but this has not been worked out yet:[18] In that case we might start with a query, i.e., a rule without head. Computation could proceed by selecting a body literal and depending on whether the selected literal is terminological or non-terminological we have three cases. If the selected literal is an instance assertion $s{:}C$, we have to find a suitable rule with any instance assertion $t{:}D$ as head, such that there exists a common instance of the two concept expressions, i.e., the terms s and t have to be unifiable by some ground substitution σ and for the instantiated term $r = \sigma s = \sigma t$ we must be able to derive that it is an instance of $C \sqcap D$. A similar case happens if we have selected a role assertion. If the selected literal is non-terminological, a suitable rule with non-terminological unifying head has to be chosen. In all three cases the selected literal of the query has to be replaced by the body of the chosen rule and the new query has to instantiated by the unifier. It should be clear that this is a very first idea, that has to be worked out further—and, of course, it has to be checked for correctness and completeness according to the above semantics.

Let us conclude that section by a further remark. It has been shown that terms and non-terminological atoms can be modelled by certain concept expressions with functional roles as in feature logics (cf. [31,32]). Thus it should be possible to get the same expressive power as with the above general rules, if we only allow for terminological literals in that rules—but with a terminological language that contains functional roles with socalled agreements and disagreements. An according proposal for a rule based extension of terminological logics is under development.

6 Default Rules

Several terminological systems also provide a non-monotonic rule formalism. According to the operational view of trigger rules (or the general rules of the last section) as additional domain specific inference rules, it seems to be quite natural to extend them also to default rules. One view of trigger rules could be to take them as a method for propagating properties to objects—additional to the properties that are inherited by the subconcept relations entailed by the TBox.

Let us consider an example. We might want to weaken our definition of a furniture truck somewhat by saying that it can be used to transport furnitures:

$$FurnitureTruck = Truck \sqcap \exists transport.Furniture$$

We might, however, have as a default rule for our specific agency that it usually should be used to transport furnitures only.

---

[18] The backward chaining interpretation in [18] is different from the one sketched in the sequel.

This could be modeled with Reiter's default rules [28]. Since Reiter introduced his default logics as a non-monotonic extension of predicate logics, we directly can adapt it for terminological logics. Recall that Reiter's default rules consist of three parts, the condition, the justification and the consequence, which are all (open) formulae of first order logics

$$Condition : Justification \longrightarrow Consequence.$$

The indended meaning of such a default rule is that if the condition holds then the consequence must be true, too, provided the justification can consistently be assumed. If these formulae contain free variables, a rule represents schematically all possible instantiations by named objects, i.e., by ground terms.[19]

Since concept expressions are open first order formulae, it is straightforward to extend terminological formalisms with default rules, such that all parts consist of concept expressions. Thus terminological default rules have the form

$$C : D \longrightarrow E$$

where C, D, and E are any concept expressions of the underlying concept language (cf. [3]). Due to problems with skolemization we assume that such terminological default rules are schemes for all named, explicit objects of the terminological KB, i.e., for constants of the language only.[20] Thus the reading of such a default is: If there is a constant a that can be derived to be an instance of C then we can conclude that a is an instance of E provided it will not lead to a contradiction to assume that a is an instance of D.

The reader may have recognized that close relation to trigger rules: The intuitive reading of trigger rules is like default rules without a justification part (i.e., with the trivially assumable justification that a is in the universe.) In fact, this close connection exists also formally. This connection also suggests that we might be able to expand defaults to the more general rules of the former section. In fact, the minimal knowledge logics with negation as failure in [23] may be used for a semantical formalization of such an expanded form of default reasoning.

7 Conclusion

We have given an overview of several ways for integrating terminological reasoning in a clean declarative way. Some of the sketched approaches—like the general trigger rules or general default rules—still need some further elaboration

---

[19] Reiter assumes that both in the fact base and in the rules all existential quantifiers are eliminated by skolemization. This means that there are no implicit objects at all. However, it has been shown that this reading of open defaults causes a number of problems, e.g., syntactically different, but logically equivalent fact bases could lead to different default consequences, if they are skolemized (cf. [3]).

[20] A further reason for that restriction is that this restricted form of default reasoning is decidable, since the underlying logic is decidable and there are only finitely many default rules.

also with respect to their operationalization. Others have been proven useful, such as the simple trigger rules, which have been included into the proposal for a standardiazation of description logics (cf. [27]).

We would like to argue that these integrations will be extremely useful in the future of knowledge representation systems, also since they may allow for further logic based extensions with several epistemic operators, e.g., for knowledge based multi-agent systems, or with reasoning under uncertainty. First proposals in that direction have been made for the pure terminological formalisms. Such extensions might also be fruitful for non-standard approaches to database systems, e.g., for deductive, object-oriented, or federated database systems, and of course, also for integrating knowledge base and database approaches.

Main parts of the formal, logical bases of the approaches sketched in this paper have been developed or elaborated at DFKI and there exist prototypical implementations (based on the terminological system KRIS, cf. [2]) that can be used to play with those different ways of modelling. First sample applications from shipping domains, from mechanical engineering domains, or for knowledge based information presentation have been modeled with the system.

Acknowledgements: I would like to thank my colleagues Franz Baader, Martin Buchheit, Philipp Hanschke, Bernhard Hollunder, Armin Laux, Werner Nutt, and Klaus Schild for several discussions on the topics of this paper. This work has been supported by the German Research Ministry under grant ITR 9201.

References

1. F. Baader, H.-J. Bürckert, B. Hollunder, W. Nutt, J.H. Siekmann. Concept Logics. In: *Computational Logic*, J.W. Lloyd (ed.). ESPRIT Basic Research Series, Springer, 1990.
2. F. Baader and B. Hollunder. KRIS: Knowledge Representation and Inference System. *SIGART Bulletin*, 2(3), 1991, pp. 8–14.
3. F. Baader and B. Hollunder. Embedding Defaults into Terminological Knowledge Representation Formalisms. *Proc. of 3rd Conference on Principles of Knowledge Representation and Reasoning*, 1992, pp. 306–317.
4. R.J. Brachman, R.E. Fikes, H.J. Levesque. KRYPTON: Integrating Terminology and Assertion. *Proc. of 3rd National Conference on Artifial Intelligence*, 1983, pp. 31–35.
5. M. Buchheit, F.M. Donini, A. Schaerf. Decidable Reasoning in Terminological Knowledge Representation Systems. *J. of Artificial Intelligence Research*, 1, 1993, 109–138.
6. M. Buchheit, M.A. Jeusfeld, W. Nutt, M. Staudt. *Subsumption between Queries to Object-Oriented Databases*. DFKI Research Report RR-93-44, Saarbrücken, 1993. To appear also in *Information Systems*, 1994.
7. H.-J. Bürckert. *A Resolution Principle for a Logic with Restricted Quantifiers*. Lecture Notes in Artificial Intelligence 568, Springer, 1991.
8. H.-J. Bürckert. A Resolution Principle for Constrained Logics. *Artificial Intelligence*, to appear.

9. H.-J. Bürckert, B. Hollunder, A. Laux: On Skolemization in Constrained Logics. DFKI-Research-Report RR-93-06, Saarbrücken, 1993

10. H.-J. Bürckert, B. Hollunder, A. Laux: Concept Logics with Function Symbols. DFKI-Research-Report RR-93-07, Saarbrücken, 1993

11. H.-J. Bürckert and W. Nutt. On Abduction and Answer Generation through Constrained Resolution. DFKI Research Report RR-92-51, Saarbrücken, 1992.

12. B.F. Chellas. *Modal Logic: An Introduction.* Cambridge University Press, 1980.

13. F.M. Donini, B. Hollunder, M. Lenzerini, A. Marchetti Spaccamela, D. Nardi, W. Nutt. The Complexity of Existential Quantification in Concept Languages. *Artificial Intelligence,* **55**, 1992, pp. 309–327.

14. F.M. Donini, M. Lenzerini, D. Nardi, W. Nutt. The Complexity of Concept Languages. *Proc. of 2nd International Conference on Pronciples of Knowledge Representation and Reasoning,* 1991, pp. 151–162.

15. F.M. Donini, M. Lenzerini, D. Nardi, W. Nutt. Tractable Concept Languages. *Proc. of 12th International Joint Conference on Artificial Intelligence,* 1991

16. F.M. Donini, M. Lenzerini, D. Nardi, A. Schaerf. A Hybrid System Integrating DATALOG and Concept Languages. *Proc. of 2nd Conf. of Italian Association for Artificial Intelligence.* Lecture Notes in Artificial Intelligence **549**, 1991.

17. F.M. Donini, M. Lenzerini, D. Nardi, A. Schaerf, W. Nutt. *Queries and Rules as Epistemic Sentences in Concept Languages.* DFKI Research Report RR-93-40, Saarbrücken, 1993.

18. P. Hanschke. *A Declarative Integration of Terminological, Constraint-based, Data-driven, and Goal-directed Reasoning.* Dissertation, Universität Kaiserslautern, 1993.

19. M. Höhfeld and G. Smolka. *Definite Relations over Constraint Languages.* LILOG-Report 53, IBM Deutschland, 1988.

20. J. Jaffar, J.-L. Lassez. Constrained Logic Programming. *Proc. of ACM Symposium on Principles of Programming Languages,* 1987, pp. 111–119.

21. H. Levesque. Foundations of a Functional Approach to Knowledge Representation. *Artificial Intelligence,* 1984, pp. 195–212.

22. H.J. Levesque and R.J. Brachman. Expressivity and Tractability in Knowledge Representation and Reasoning. *Computational Intelligence,* **3**, 1987, pp. 78–93.

23. W. Lifschitz. Minimal Beliefs and Negation as Failure. *Proc. of 12th International Joint Conference on Artificial Intelligence,* 1991.

24. J.W. Lloyd. *Foundations of Logic Programming.* Springer, 1987.

25. M. Maher. Logic Semantics for a Class of Committed-choice Programs. *Proc. of 4th International Conference on Logic Programming,* 1987, pp. 858–876.

26. B. Nebel. *Reasoning and Revision in Hybrid Representation Systems.* Lecture Notes in Computer Science **422**, Springer, 1990.

27. P.F. Patel-Schneider and B. Swartout. Description Logic Specification from the KRSS Effort. Working version, 1993.

28. R. Reiter. A Logic for Default Reasoning. *Artificial Intelligence,* **13**, 1980, pp. 81–132.

29. M. Schmidt-Schauss and G. Smolka. Attributive Concept Descriptions with Complements. *Artificial Intelligence,* **48**, 1991, pp.1–26.

30. G. Smolka. *Feature Logics with Subsorts.* LILOG-Report 33, IBM Deutschland, 1988.

31. G. Smolka. *Logic Programming over Polymorphically Order-sorted Types.* Dissertation, Kaiserslautern, 1989.

32. G. Smolka and R. Treinen. Records for Logic Programming. *J. of Logic Programming*, to appear.
33. M.E. Stickel. Automated Deduction by Theory Resolution. *J. of Automated Reasoning*, 1(4), 1985, pp. 333-357.
34. W.A. Woods and J.G. Schmolze. The KL-ONE Family. In: *Semantic Networks in Artificial Intelligence*, F.W. Lehmann (ed.), Pergamon Press, 1992, pp. 133–178.

Evolution towards, in, and beyond
Object Databases

Marc H. Scholl and Markus Tresch

Faculty of Computer Science
Databases and Information Systems
University of Ulm, D-89069 Ulm, Germany
{scholl,tresch}@informatik.uni-ulm.de

Abstract. There is a manifold of meanings we could associate with the term "evolution" in the database arena. This paper tries to categorize some of these into a unique framework, showing similarities and differences. Among the topics touched upon are: extending traditional data models to become "object-oriented", migrating existing data to (not necessarily OO) databases, schema extension and modification in a populated database, integration of federated systems, and the use of "external services" to enrich DBMS functionalities. The following are presented in more detail: first, we describe the necessity of object evolution over time; second, we discuss schema evolution; and third, we present evolutionary database interoperability by identifying different coupling levels. A few basic mechanisms, such as views (derived information) and a uniform treatment of data and meta data, and type and/or class hierarchies, allow for a formal description of (most of) the relevant problems. Beyond presenting our own approach, we try to provide a platform to solicit further discussion.

1   Introduction

The term evolution is used in this paper in a very broad sense to denote several kinds of dynamics that occur in the context of database systems and database applications. We will identify three main lines of evolution that are addressed in the title:

- *Evolution towards object databases:*
  Here we address the advance of database technology in terms of data models. Data models have evolved from flat files via first generation DBMSs (network, hierarchical), second generation DBMSs (relational) to third generation DBMSs (extended relational, object-oriented, ...) [30]. It has been the primary concern of our prior work [21] to point out that particularly the latter advance can in fact be evolutionary, i.e., preserve the advantages of relational technology, such as powerful descriptive query and update languages.
- *Evolution in object databases:*
  This covers all aspects of the life-cycle of database objects. Traditional issues such as database updates (including maintenance of DB consistency),

more advanced issues such as dynamic type changes of existing objects (often called "objects in different roles") or automatic classification of objects into subclasses (as known from AI systems), and finally dynamic schema modification in populated databases are addressed under this topic.

- *Evolution beyond object databases:*
This third meaning of the term is the most challenging, both from an academic as well as from a practical point of view. Here we talk about interoperability among several data management tools (not all of which are necessarily database systems). Stepwise integration of preexisting autonomous databases into a federated system, (smooth) migration of file-based or relational data-intensive applications into ODBMSs, and the integration of external services into a DBMS are the problem areas we are aiming at here.

Clearly, the points mentioned above are relevant, important and difficult to solve. We can not provide complete solutions, rather we have tried over the last few years to address some specific technical questions within this framework. Most of the problems have two parts: policy and mechanisms. We have concentrated on the necessary mechanisms, and have not concerned ourselves with policy issues, such as, for example, *how* to resolve conflicts in schema integration, rather we provide a platform that can implement any conflict resolution strategy by means of formally defined schema transformation primitives (including instance conversion, when necessary). The main focus has been on the exploitation of query and update languages in the presence of a semantically rich (object) data model as an underlying formal mechanism.

The first line of evolution (the advances of the technology of DBMSs and of data models) is mentioned in this paper only in passing. It has turned out that the essentials of relational DB languages, together with ingredients from other fields (most prominently, AI knowledge representation languages and programming languages), can be carried over to ODB languages. The most important feature — as far as evolution *in* object databases is concerned — is to provide all kinds of derived information (e.g., computed attributes, views, subschemas, type inferencing, automatic classification). We have designed a prototype object database language, COOL, to prove the concepts and as an experimentation platform [25, 24, 23, 11]. Update operations of this COOL language respect all the integrity constraints, that is, they automatically propagate to all the derived concepts.

The second line of evolution (database dynamics) profits from those language properties described above. Once database updates are defined formally in such a way that integrity constraints and derivation rules are automatically maintained, there remain only a few modifications of data objects to be discussed. Among them are dynamic changes of the types of existing objects, a functionality that will be described below. The next level of complexity is changes to the structure, i.e., the schema of a database. Object databases typically have a meta schema that contains types/classes that describe the schema. Consequently, the database language can be used to query (data dictionary functionality, also present in most relational DBMSs) and update (schema modification functionality, typically prohibited in most DBMSs) those schema objects. We will show that the COOL language can be used to implement schema evolution by means of schema modification primitives that include propagation to the instance level (automatic database reorganization due to schema changes) [33, 34, 31].

Finally, the third line of evolution leaves the context of a single system and considers schema changes in the context of a stepwise integration of previously independent databases. It turns out that with very small extensions to the language semantics (mainly the introduction of an application-defined object identity predicate to unify objects across databases), the schema modification operations can be used to implement the integration strategies. We identify five levels of increasingly tight database interoperation that are distinguished by the language features they need to exploit. These levels can be observed in other approaches to ODBS integration, too. Hence, the results obtained here are not limited to the COOL language. An even wider interpretation of this last evolutionary line includes migration paths from file-based or RDBMS applications to ODBMSs, an issue that we will not elaborate in this paper, though. Some preliminary considerations are presented in [19]. Ultimately, database systems and other service providers in a cooperation of interoperable systems may interact in more subtle ways, for example, a DBMS may import computation services from other systems, in the sense of externally defined data types [22].

The paper gives a tour through several aspects of this framework. Particular focus lies on evolution mechanisms within a single DBMS and beyond single DBMSs for DB integration. Section 2 shows the basic evolution mechanisms provided by the COOL language. In Section 3, we discuss schema modification within a single database, and Section 4 presents the five levels of database interoperability, together with the COOL mechanisms that can be used to realize them. We conclude with a comparison with related approaches and a summary.

2 Fundamental Evolution Mechanisms

There are a couple of fundamental mechanisms in ODBSs, that are prerequisites for such systems to support dynamic evolution. We identify some of them, using the object model COCOON [23] as a platform.

2.1 Object Evolution

Object evolution describes the problem that a real world entity may be represented by a database object in several roles over time. Thus, we need the possibility in ODBSs to change dynamically type instantiation and class membership of objects. Furthermore, objects may be instances of multiple types and classes at a time.

Example 1. Consider an object *john*, being instance of object type *student*. It may be necessary that this object loses the properties (attributes) of *student* and should be removed from class *UniUlmStuds*.

lose[*student*](*john*); **remove**[*john*](*UniUlmStuds*);
gain[*employee*](*john*); **add**[*john*](*CompanyX*)

Later on, *john* may gain properties of *employee* instead, and should be added to class *CompanyX*.

Unfortunately, this kind of object evolution is a neglected concept in object database systems, and is supported by only a few data models, e.g. Iris [7]. Especially C++ based databases either ignore such mechanisms, or need costly off-line reorganizations to do so, e.g. ObjectStore [16], ONTOS [17].

One main reason is an implementation reason, namely that such systems do not manage OIDs with location transparency, but either consider an object's virtual memory address as its OID, e.g. ObjectStore, or encode class identifiers into the OID, e.g. ORION [10].

2.2   Logical Data Independence

Logical data independence is commonly established by defining external schemata, i.e., schemata that are derived (computed) from the logical level. Although there is no widely accepted concept of views in object databases [32], they are often understood as virtual (derived) classes, declared for example as

define view *v* **as** *e*

where *e* is a query expression. Our language supports logical data independence, i.e. it offers possibilities to define derived class extents, derived object types, and derived object properties (refer to [24] for a comprehensive discussion of the view mechanism).

We now argue that data independence in object database systems is a first attempt to realize database evolution. In fact, views can be used straight forward to simulate some schema evolutions.

Example 2. Consider an ODBS schema with two classes *Boys* and *Girls*, and a schema evolution, integrating these two classes into one unified class *Persons*. The following view definition is a first approach

define view *Persons*
as   extend[*sex*:= (*o* ∈ *Boys*)](*Boys* **union** *Girls*)

The extent of view *Persons* holds the union of all objects from *Boys* and *Girls*. The object type of the view consists of the intersection of the functions from the classes *Boys* and *Girls*, plus an additional boolean function *sex*, distinguishing male (*sex* = *true*) and female (*sex* = *false*) persons.

The above example does not yet fully simulate the desired schema evolution. Although many updates of and into views are already managed by the system, update propagation rules must be added for non-standard transformation of view updates into base class updates. E.g., because *sex* is a derived function, any attempt to assign a new value to it, would be rejected by the parser already.

Example 3. We complete the previous example by adding update transformation rules. It shows, how assigning a new value to *sex* and adding/removing person objects is propagated into updates of base classes:

> **define view** *Persons*
> **as** extend[*sex*:= (*o* ∈ *Boys*)](*Boys* **union** *Girls*)
> **on** set[*sex*:= *x*](*o*) **do if** *x* **then** add[*o*](*Boys*); **remove**[*o*](*Girls*)
>   **else** add[*o*](*Girls*); **remove**[*o*](*Boys*)
> **on** **add**[*o*](*Persons*) **do if** *sex*(*o*) **then** **add**[*o*](*Boys*)
>   **else** **add**[*o*](*Girls*)
> **on** **remove**[*o*](*Persons*) **do** **remove**[*o*](*Boys*); **remove**[*o*](*Girls*)
> ⋮

Finally, this is now a fully equivalent simulation of the desired schema evolution.

After view classes have been defined and positioned in the schema, a subset of existing classes and views can be collected in a subschema. Subschemata describe a part of the base schema (extended with views) that should be made available to external users. Typically, we have to require that subschemata are closed [20, 34].

Since external schema cannot be used to simulate all desired schema evolutions, some must be physically performed, because they augment the information content of the database. In the sequel, we search for a formal handle of that difference.

2.3   Uniform Treatment of Data and Meta Data Objects

In ODBSs, data and meta data are often treated uniformly as objects. That is, an object database can be partitioned into three disjoint sets of objects: (i) primary objects, representing user data, (ii) secondary objects, representing the user's application schema, and (iii) tertiary objects, representing the data model itself. Since all of these are "ordinary" objects, generic query and updates operations should be applicable as usual on any kind of object.

Whereas querying the meta database is quite common (cf. data dictionary), updating meta databases is usually only allowed through a special data definition language. However, meta databases should be updatable for schema evolution purposes.

Example 4. Consider the following generic update sequence, creating a new variable *a*, adding it to class *Variables*, and assigning values to its attributes, e.g. the variable name:

> **create**[*variable*](*a*); **add**[*a*](*Variables*); **set**[*name* := *n*; . . .](*a*)

Direct updates to meta databases may cause several side effects that must be handled: (i) to ensure that no incorrect database schemata are produced, a set of integrity constraints must be modeled in the meta database; (ii) to ensure that no inconsistency between the schema and the instance level arises, schema updates must be propagated to existing objects; (iii) to ensure that no run-time errors occur in existing (compiled) applications, these programs must be recompiled.

3 Schema Evolution

In this section, we follow our second line and consider evolution issues within one independent object database. First, we show, how external schemata can be used as a first attempt for schema evolution and why this is not yet satisfactory. Then, we develop a formal evolution model, which is independent from any concrete object model. Based on that, a set of elementary schema updates is presented and global database restructuring is discussed.

3.1 A Formal Evolution Model

In order to be able to characterize schema evolution (i.e. to determine, whether it can be simulated), we define a formal description of database evolution, which is independent of any concrete data model. The notion of *information capacity* [8, 1] in object databases forms the basis for our evolution model:

Definition 1. Let S be a given object database schema. The information capacity $\mathcal{DB}_S$ is the set of all potential states, a database can have with that schema.

The definition of schema evolution follows directly:

Definition 2. Let S, S' be schemata of two object databases with database states $\sigma \in \mathcal{DB}_S$ and $\sigma' \in \mathcal{DB}_{S'}$ respectively. A schema evolution as a pair

$$< u : S \mapsto S', r : \sigma \mapsto \sigma' > ,$$

with schema update u and database reorganization r.

Schema update u is an update of the meta-database, mapping one database schema $S \in \mathcal{S}$ into another schema $S' \in \mathcal{S}$, with $\mathcal{S}$ the set of all correct schemata of a particular data model. Database reorganization r is an update of the (primary) database, mapping the actual database state $\sigma \in \mathcal{DB}_S$ fitting schema S into another database state $\sigma' \in \mathcal{DB}_{S'}$, fitting new schema S'.

In general, schema evolution changes the capacity of an ODBS, which follows from that information capacity of an object database is determined by its schema. We use this fact to classify schema evolution:

Definition 3. Schema evolution $< u : S \mapsto S', r : \sigma \mapsto \sigma' >$ is called

- capacity preserving (CP), iff mapping r is bijective;
- capacity augmenting (CA), iff mapping r is injective, but not surjective;

- capacity reducing (CR), iff mapping r is surjective, but not injective;
- capacity changing (CC), otherwise;

From the mathematical definition of database reorganization it follows: (1) CP and CR schema evolutions can be simulated, that is, there exists an external schema of S (a view definition) that is equal to S'. (2) CP and CA schema evolutions are lossless and can therefore be compensated, that is, there exists an external schema of S' that is equal to S.

3.2   A Set of Local Schema Updates

Based on this formal evolution model, a set of elementary schema updates can be defined for any concrete data model. Such a set of operations must fulfill the following formal conditions:

- **Locality:** Each schema update must be local in the sense, that one particular variable, function, type, class, or view is changed at a time.
- **Correctness:** Each schema update must be correct, such that (i) only correct database schemata are produced[1], and (ii) existing instances are correct w.r.t the new schema.
- **Capacity:** The change of information capacity by each schema update must be well defined, that is CP, CR, or CA, and never CC.
- **Minimality:** The set of schema updates must be minimal, such that no operation can be replaced by others.
- **Completeness:** The set of schema updates must be complete, such that all desired local schema changes can be performed.

The resulting set of elementary schema updates is given by the semantic concepts of the considered data model. Such sets of elementary schema updates can also be found for ORION [4], O_2 [35], and GemStone [18]. For COCOON, these are changes of variables, functions, types, classes, and views. An exhaustive enumeration can be found in [33], here, we focus on the technique, how they are implemented.

As we know, any elementary schema update is described as a tuple, consisting of a schema update and a database reorganization. We understand that u and r are performed as an atom, that is, both together or none of them are executed. They are realized as follows:

1. Schema updates $(u : S \mapsto S')$ are (sequences of) update operations, applied to the meta database, and thus changing schema information.
2. Database reorganizations $(r : \sigma \mapsto \sigma')$ are (sequences of) update operations, applied to the ordinary database, and thus updating instances.

Consider the following example:

---

[1] Correctness of database schemata is usually described by a set of schema invariants, that must not be violated.

Example 5. Consider an elementary schema update, specializing the type of variable **var** p : *person* into a subtype *employee* $\preceq$ *person*. Assume, every schema object is represented by an object in the meta database: i.e. there is a meta object p, representing variable "p" in the meta database, and object *employee*, representing object type "employee". To change the schema, a simple meta database update is performed, that updates value *ran* (range type) of meta object p to new value *employee*:

u : **set**$[ran := employee](p)$

Afterwards, instances of the database may be invalid w.r.t the new schema. E.g. the actual value of p may be not an instance of type *employee*. There are several possibilities to reorganize the database. One can either make p to an instance of employee (see $r1$), or alternatively check, whether p is already of type *employee*, and if not, p is set to undefined (see $r2$):

$r1$: **gain**$[employee](p)$
$r2$: **if not** $employee(p)$ **then** $p :=$ *"undefined"*

Notice that both reorganizations are not injective, and therefore not lossless. With $r1$, the information is lost, whether new p has already been instance of p before or not, and with $r1$, the value of p may be lost (set to undefined). Thus, schema updates $< u, r1 >$ and $< u, r2 >$ are both capacity reducing.

To be complete, elementary schema operations should not only exist for schema changes, but also for schema definition and deletion. To build a user interface on top of the elementary schema updates, the data definition language (DDL) must be extended towards a schema manipulation language (SML).

To do so, in addition to the DDL statement **define**, three new statements must be introduced: **redefine** to change existing schema objects, **rename** to change the name of schema objects, and **undefine** to delete schema objects. The formal semantics of the SML is now given by its mapping into elementary schema updates (e.g. implemented as a SML parser/interpreter).

Example 6. Reconsider the above example of variable p, that is defined by the following SML statement (in fact, it is a DDL statement):

define var p : *person*

The definition is mapped into the elementary schema update "define variable". Later, the type of the variable can be specialized. To to redefine p, we use the following SML statement:

redefine var p : *employee*

The SML parser compares this redefinition with the actual definition in the meta database (see section 2.3) and identifies the differences. Here, the only difference is that the new definition uses a more special instance type *employee*. Thus, this statement is mapped into elementary schema update "specialize variable type", as implemented in Example 5.

3.3 Global Database Restructuring

The SML presented so far, forms an interface to the elementary operations for local schema updates. However, not only local changes, but also global database restructurings ere desired. We show, what must be added to the SML to perform such evolution as well.

Simulated schema evolution is just a new view on top of the existing (unchanged) databases. In some cases, simulation is not yet sufficient. Capacity augmenting schema evolutions, for example, cannot be simulated, since they enlarge the information contents of an ODBS.

Thus, we need in addition the possibility to really perform schema evolution. The corresponding language mechanism follows directly from the above simulation. It mainly consist of "conceptually materializing" the schema definition as a "snapshot".

Example 7. Persons is now defined as a class (not anymore a view). The class is initialized using the same query as in the previous example. However, to really perform the desired schema evolution, the query is now materialized by adding all objects to class *Persons*. Again, the object type of the new class is implicitly derived.

> **redefine database** *PersDB;*
>   **define class** *Persons*
>   **from extend**[*sex*:= ($o \in Boys$)](*Boys* **union** *Girls*);
>   **undefine class** *Boys, Girls;*
> **end** .

After that, base classes *Boys, Girls* can be deleted from the schema. Notice that update transformation rules are not required, since after the schema evolution is performed, updates are evaluated on the new schema.

Obviously, global database restructurings may need a sequence of SML statements that must be encapsulated in schema evolution transactions. Such transactions are as usual performed completely or not at all. **redefine database** ... **end** show begin and end of transaction.

To be more flexible in defining database restructuring transactions, the meta database must be queried at run-time.

Example 8. Consider a more general variant of Example 7, where class *articles* with a variable, but at any time finite number of subclasses *screws, bolts, nails, ...* is given, and it is further assumed that every article is in exactly one subclass (cf. Figure 1). This database should be reorganized, such that only class *articles* exists, but with an additional attribute *kind* : **string**, such that every article holds as value *kind* the name of the subclass it belongs to.

> **define function** *kind* : *article* → **string**
> **from** $a : cname($**pick**(**select**[$a \in extent(c)$](*c* : *subclasses*(*Articles*)))))

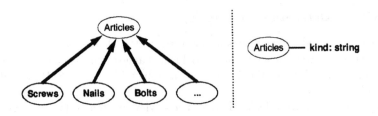

Fig. 1. Dynamic Function Definition

This SML statement shows the desired function definition. For each article a, $kind(a)$ is set to the name of that class c, that holds a in its extent. The number of subclasses of *Articles* and its names are evaluated at run-time.

4 Evolutionary Interoperability

In this section, we follow our third line and consider evolution issues between multiple cooperating object databases.

Our point of view of evolutionary database interoperability is as follows: So far isolated database systems are starting cooperating with other systems very loosely, e.g., by global transactions. Later, global schemata (views and "others") are defined, such that systems are getting more tightly coupled, until they are finally completely integrated.

To classify multi-databases according to their form of cooperation, we distinguish five integration levels with increasing strength of coupling. Consider Figure 2. This refines the known classification of [28], distinguishing between losely and tightly coupled federated database systems.

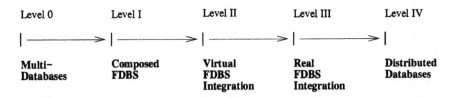

Fig. 2. Evolutionary Cooperation of Multi-Database Systems

At the left most end, level 0 represents non-integrated multi-database systems. This is the weakest form of database coupling, where component systems are completely independent of each other. Cooperation is established ad hoc, by transactions, using objects from multiple databases. Within a transaction, each operation is uniquely mapped to one component ODBS.

At the right most end, level IV represents fully integrated distributed databases. Either, there exists only one single global database management system, or participating component systems don't have any local autonomy. Hence, objects can physically be distributed, although there exists only one logical database.

Levels I to III are known as federated database systems (FDBS), where component ODBSs are integrated up to some degree, whereas some autonomy is lost. In the sequel, we focus on these three levels of FDBS.

4.1 Level I: Composed FDBS

Interoperability of this level is called schema composition. It is the elementary process to combine schemata of multiple local ODBS into one *composed schema*, and is therefore the foundation for establishing a federated database system. Schema composition places only minimal requirements on the degree of integration between participating systems. In fact, it basically just imports the names of all schema elements (variables, functions, types, classes, views) from component ODBSs and makes them globally available [26].

Example 9. The following statement composes two ODBSs, the library database *LibDB* and the student database *StudDB*:

define database *GDB*
     import *LibDB, StudDB*
end .

More precisely, composition of component systems DB_i into a federated system GDB combines the class and type systems of the local databases. First, the basic data types (integer, string, ...) of the different systems are unified. Second, the class and type hierarchies of the local ODBS are put together on the schema level AND on the meta-schema level in the following (so far trivial) way:[2]

Schema Level: A global schema is created with a new top type **object@**GDB, a new bottom type **bottom@**GDB, and a new global top class **Objects@**GDB. The global type hierarchy is established, where all top types of the local ODBSs (**object@**DB_i) are made direct subtypes of the new global top element **object@**GDB. The new bottom type **bottom@**GDB is made common subtype of all local bottom types. No further subtype relationships are established.

Similar, a global subclass hierarchy is composed, with the new top element **Objects@**GDB as common superclass to all local top classes **Objects@**DB_i.

---

[2] In the sequel, we use the naming convention that schema components are suffixed by "@" and the name of the local schema. For example, class *Books* in *LibDB* has as globally unique name "*Books@LibDB*".

Meta Schema Level: A global meta schema is created as well. This is the meta schema of the *GDB*. The meta schema of each DB_i contains meta types *variables, functions, types, class, views* and meta classes *Variables, Functions, Types, Classes, Views*, respectively (a detailed discussion of the COCOON meta schema is contained in [33]).

A global meta schema is created with types *variable@GDB, function@GDB, type@GDB*, etc. as well as new meta classes *Variables@GDB, Functions@GDB, Types@GDB* etc. The *GDB* meta schema has therefore exactly the same structure as that of each DB_i. Then, the local meta classes and meta types are made subclass/subtype of their global counterparts.

Furthermore, meta functions are unified during the composition process, e.g., in each DB_i there is a meta function *super_types(t)@DB_i* finding all supertypes of a given type t. These functions are all automatically unified over all DB_i.

Schema composition is not yet real "database integration". In particular, no instance of **object@GDB** is instance of more than one component type **object@DB_i**. Furthermore, the extent of **Objects@GDB** is partitioned into **disjoint** subsets **Objects@DB_i**. As a consequence, no two objects in **Objects@DB** can be the same (identical), unless they originate from the same DB_i and are identical in DB_i.

Querying Composed Schemata Once two (or more) schemata are composed, we are ready to formulate queries that involve multiple LOBs. Recall composition *GDB* and assume we want to question, which customers are students as well. Since composition made basic data types and name spaces globally available, we can compare names of customers with names of students:

$$\mathbf{select}[\emptyset = \mathbf{select}[name(c) = name(s)](s : Students)](c : Customers)$$

Unfortunately, the possibilities of inter-objectbase queries are very limited. E.g., the following more elegant solution of the same problem is illegal:

$$\mathbf{select}[c \in Students](c : Customers)$$

Since the type of class *Students* is "student" and the type of c is "customer" and the two types customer and student are not related, this selection predicate would be rejected by the type checker.

The extend query operator defines new functions, derived by a query expression. We can already use this possibility to establish connections between ODBs. Suppose, we want to store together with each student (of *StudDB*) the books (of *LibDB*), that he lent:

$$\mathbf{extend}[lentbooks := \mathbf{select}[name(s) = name(lent(b))](b : Books)]$$
$$(s : Students)$$

The new function *lentbooks* is an inter-objectbase link, from *StudDB* to *LibDB*.

4.2 Level II: Virtual FDBS Integration

Virtual integration of schemata is the next step in the process of evolutionary cooperation of database systems. It is based on the idea that views can be used to build a uniform, virtual interface over multiple databases (cf. e.g. [12, 14, 27]).

Since database integration is not the main topic of this paper, but should just be discussed in the context of evolutionary cooperation, we refer for more formal details on the mechanism (i.e., *same*-functions, global identity, solving structural and semantic conflicts) to [26]. We recall here some of the results, as far as they are necessary to understand differences between coupling levels.

Unifying Objects. Since component databases have been used independently of each other, one real world (entity) object may be represented by different database (proxy) objects in different component databases. The fundamental assumption of object-oriented models, namely that one real world object is represented by exactly one database object, is therefore no longer true in FDBSs [9]. We therefore need an additional notion: we say that two local proxy objects are *the same*, iff they represent the same real world (entity) object.

Same objects are identified in FDBSs by extending the composed schema using extend views to define so called *same*-functions. Formally, we require that for any two component databases DB_i and DB_j, the instances of which shall be unified, we are giving a query expression that determines, for a given DB_i-object, what the corresponding DB_j-object is (if any), and vice versa. This query expression is used to define a derived function $same_{i,j}$ from DB_i to DB_j. Obviously, these query expressions are application dependent and can, in general, not be derived automatically.

Example 10. To state that objects of class *Customers* of *LibDB* are identical with objects of class *Students* of *StudDB*, if they have identical names, for example, we have to defined the following *same*-functions:

extend [$same_{\text{LibDB,StudDB}}$:=
$\qquad\qquad$ **pick**(**select**[$name(c) = name(s)$]($s : Students$))]
$\qquad$ ($c : Customers$);
extend [$same_{\text{StudDB,LibDB}}$:=
$\qquad\qquad$ **pick**(**select**[$name(s) = name(c)$]($c : Customers$))]
$\qquad$ ($s : Students$);

Notice that the **pick** operator does a set collapse, that is, it takes a single object out of a set of objects (**pick**($\emptyset$) = "undefined").

Unifying Meta Objects. After unifying proxy objects in different ODBS, we now focus on schema integration, that is, to find out, what the common parts in the local schemata are, and to define a correspondence among them.

We already mentioned that schema composition also constructs a global meta schema. To define correspondences between functions from different ODBSs, we make use of the fact that every function is represented by a meta object. Thus, integrating functions from DB_i and DB_j is now straightforward: we unify the objects that represent the functions in the meta schema by defining a *same*-function from meta type *function@DB$_i$* to meta type *function@DB$_j$*.

Example 11. To unify for example the functions *name@LibDB* and *name@StudDB*, the following *same*-function is defined on the meta schema of *GOB*:

$$\textbf{extend } [same_{\text{LibDB,StudDB}} :=$$
$$\textbf{pick}(\textbf{select } [name(f) = "name" \wedge name(g) = "name"]$$
$$(g : Functions@LibDB))]$$
$$(f : Functions@StudDB);$$

In contrast to most other schema integration approaches that emphasis on solving semantic and structural conflicts among different systems [5, 29], we concentrate here on reducing schema integration to unifying meta objects.

We have now defined all prerequisites for virtual ODBS integration: we showed how to find "same" objects over multiple systems and discussed schema integration as unification of meta-objects.

Example 12. Following to the above method, we first compose the local schemata by importing *LibDB* and *StudDB*. Then, we extend the classes *Customers* and *Students* with *same*-functions. Finally, the meta class *Functions@LibDB* is extended to integrate *name@LibDB* and *name@StudDB* properties.

> **define schema** *GDB* **as**
>   **import** *LibDB, StudDB* ;
>   **define view** *Customers'@LibDB* **as extend** ... ;   *// see Example 10*
>   **define view** *Students'@StudDB* **as extend** ... ;   *// see Example 10*
>   **define view** *Functions'@LibDB* **as extend** ... ;   *// see Example 11*
>   **define view** *Persons* **as** *Customers'@LibDB* **union** *Students'@StudDB* ;
> **end** ;

Now, we are ready to define views that span multiple ODBS, e.g., a view *Persons* as the union over the extended classes *Customers'@Lib* and *Students'@Stud*. The extent of this union view is defined to be the union of the objects of the base classes. However, if there would be a customer object and a student object, having equal names, they are defined through the *same*-function to represent the same real world object, and will therefore appear only once in the union view. The type of a union view is defined as intersection of the functions of the base classes. Thus, since the type of *Customer'* and of *Students'* are disjoint, except of *name@LibDB* and *name@StudDB* functions that are defined to be the same, the type of the view is [*name*].

4.3 Level III: Real FDBS Integration

So far, component ODBSs are virtually integrated by unifying views, spanning over multiple component systems. We now show, how ODBSs can be further integrated, without completely giving up their local autonomy.

There are several disadvantages of virtual integration at level II, since cooperation was restricted to views only. E.g. functions with domain and range type in different component ODBSs, let's say DB_i and DB_j (cf. *same*-Functions), have only been allowed, if they are **derived** from a query expression. The state (values) of a **stored** inter-database functions can be formalized as a set of tuples $< argument, value >$, with *argument* as objects from DB_i and *value* as objects from DB_j. Consequently, such functions have not been possible, because their state could not be stored exclusively in one of these ODBSs. Furthermore, variables of a supertype of types of multiple ODBSs are not allowed at level II, since they can store objects of multiple databases, such that its state could not be hold in one specific ODBS. Level III removes this inadequacy.

The federation dictionary (FD). The main difference to the previous level is that real integration is not completely virtual, but yields a real global database state, which is store in the federation dictionary (FD). Whereas till now, the FD was exclusively used to store meta information (e.g. the view definitions of level II), from now on, we allow to store primary object data as well. We therefore enhance the possibilities of the federation dictionary.

From the technical point of view, the FDBS must be able to handle OIDs, that are extended (colored) by the identification of its original ODBS. This qualification becomes necessary, since for autonomy reasons, the component ODBSs must not be restricted in the way how they generate OIDs. The FD, being managed by the FDBS, must be able to store such colored OIDs. Notice that this does not mean that all objects from ODBSs are copied into the FD. However, if needed, local OIDs are store in the FD.

Cooperation level III now allows for global schema augmentation, which can be understood as capacity augmenting changes to the federated schema.

Example 13. Consider again the above example. It is now possible to define an inter-database function *favourite_book* from *StudDB* to *LibDB*, which is typically not derived, but stored:

define function $favourite\_book : student@StudDB \rightarrow book@LibDB$

The state of this function can neither be stored in *StudDB* nor in *LibDB*. A special case of that are stored *same*-Functions, like e.g.

define function $same_{LibDB,StudDB} : customer@LibDB \rightarrow student@StudDB$

Notice that we really get advanced possibilities, since we do not need to know a query, to retrieve *same* objects from other ODBSs. Assume variable c, holding a customer object from *LibDB* and s, holding a student object from *StudDB*. We can now directly assign these object as being the same:

define var c : *customer@LibDB;*
define var s : *student@StudDB;*
$\mathrm{set}[same_{LibDB,StudDB} := s](c)$

In general, schema augmentation at level III is not limited to views. Additional possibilities to augment the global schema are: (i) to define global object types, that are subtypes of different ODBSs and therefore contain functions from muliple ODBS, (ii) classes that are subclasses from different ODBSs, and (iii) variables that can hold objects from multiple ODBSs as values. Notice that these global schema objects are only visible to the FDBS and are not known to a local ODBS.

Example 14. Consider the following type, which is a subtype of *customer* and *student*, both of which are from different ODBSs:

define type *emplstud* **isa** *customer@LibDB, student@StudDB*

The following variables are not visible to one of the component ODBSs. *o* can store any object from any system, and *A* can hold objects from different ODBSs at the same time.

define var o : **object**@GDB;
define var A : **set of** *emplstud*

5 Conclusion

We have discussed selected issues of evolution in and beyond database systems. We identified a number of elementary evolution mechanisms, that support adaptation and integration of ODBSs.

Dynamic object evolution provides the possibility that a database object can represent real world objects in different roles over time. Logical data independence allows for definition of views and subschemata, forming the possibility to simulate some schema updates. Uniform treatment of data and meta data objects, and the possibility to apply generic query and update operations on all levels of objects, can be used to perform schema evolution.

5.1 Evolution in Object Databases

First, on single ODBS is considered. Based on a formal evolution model, we showed, how the above mechansims are used to build a schema manipulation languages (SML). This language differs in two points from most other database systems supporting schema evolution, e.g. ORION [4], O_2 [35], and GemStone [18]:

- We did not invent special purpose schema update methods, but built elementary operations on top of our update language. Thus, the semantics of local schema changes is formally defined.

– We considered local schema changes as well as global database restructurings. We used snapshots to define new schema objects from existing ones.

Information capacity is shown to be a very important issue in context of database evolution, because it characterizes the impact of schema changes on existing instances as well as application programs, using the changed database.

5.2 Evolution beyond Object Databases

Second, consideration of one single ODBS is extended towards evolutionary cooperation between multiple autonomous object databases. Five levels of federated database systems (FDBS) with increasing strength of cooperation are described. Each coupling level is characterized by the use fundamental evolution mechanisms.

These five evolutionary levels of multi-database interoperability are well suited to compare multi-database system approaches among each other:

– Level I: we presented schema composition as the main mechanism of level I cooperation. This corresponds to the *connect to*-facility of existing relational multi-database systems, like e.g. Oracle SQL*Net or Ingres/Star.
– Level II: virtual database integration via views and other CP-schema evolutions is the main characteristics of cooperation level II. So in addition to the presented view mechanism, also the systems SuperViews [14] and Multibase [12] perform integration of this level, as well as the generalization constructs of VODAK [27, 15] and derived *unifier-/image*-Functions in Pegasus [3, 2].
– Level III: real integration of databases is done by CA-schema evolutions. Although this level is not considered in many systems, stored *image*-functions in Pegasus and the *merge*-operation of O*SQL [13] are additional mechanism of cooperation level III.

Acknowledgement

The authors wish to thank Hans-Jörg Schek who has been working with them for years on the topics described here. Many of the ideas worked out over that time have been inspired by him.

References

1. S. Abiteboul and R. Hull. Restructuring hierarchical database objects. *Theoretical Computer Science*, 62(1,2), December 1988.
2. R. Ahmed, J. Albert, W. Du, W. Kent, W.A. Litwin, and M.-C. Shan. An overview of Pegasus. In *Proc. 3st Int'l Workshop on Research Issues on Data Engineering: Interoperability in Multidatabase Systems (RIDE-IMS)*, Vienna, Austria, April 1993. IEEE Computer Society Press.
3. R. Ahmed, P. De Smedt, W. Du, W. Kent, M.A. Ketabchi, W.A. Litwin, A. Rafii, and M.-C. Shan. The Pegasus heterogeneous multidatabase system. *IEEE Computer*, 24(12), December 1991.

4. J. Banerjee, W. Kim, H.J. Kim, and H.F. Korth. Semantics and implementation of schema evolution in object-oriented databases. *ACM SIGMOD Record*, 15(4), February 1987.

5. C. Batini, M. Lenzerini, and S.B. Navathe. A comparative analysis of methodologies for database schema integration. *ACM Computing Surveys*, 18(4), December 1986.

6. *Proc. IFIP DS–5 Semantics of Interoperable Database Systems*, Lorne, Australien, November 1992.

7. D.H. Fishman et al. Overview of the Iris DBMS. In W. Kim and F.H. Lochovsky, editors, *Object-Oriented Concepts, Databases, and Applications*. ACM Press, New York, 1989.

8. R. Hull. Relative information capacity of simple relational database schemata. *SIAM Journal of Computing*, 15(3), August 1986.

9. W. Kent. The breakdown of the information model in multi-database systems. *ACM SIGMOD Record*, 20(4), December 1991.

10. W. Kim. *Introduction to Object-Oriented Databases*. MIT Press, Cambridge, MA, 1990.

11. C. Laasch and M. H. Scholl. A functional object database language. In *Proc. 4th Int'l Workshop on Database Programming Languages (DBPL-4)*, Manhatten, New York, August 1993.

12. T. Landers and R.L. Rosenberg. An overview of multibase. In *Proc. 2nd Int'l Symp. on Distributed Data Bases*, Berlin, Germany, September 1982. North-Holland.

13. W. Litwin. O*SQL: a language for multidatabase interoperability. In DS5 [6].

14. A. Motro. Superviews: virtual integration of multiple databases. *IEEE Trans. on Software Engineering*, 13(7), July 1987.

15. E.J. Neuhold and M. Schrefl. Dynamic derivation of personalized views. In *Proc. 14th Int'l Conf. on Very Large Data Bases (VLDB)*, Los Angeles, California, September 1988. Morgan Kaufmann.

16. Object Design Inc., Burlington, MA. *ObjectStore Rel. 2.0, Reference Manual*, October 1992.

17. ONTOS Inc., Burlington, MA. *ONTOS DB 2.2 – Reference Manual*, February 1992.

18. D.J. Penney and J. Stein. Class modification in the GemStone object-oriented DBMS. In *Proc. Int'l Conf. on Object-Oriented Programming Systems and Languages (OOPSLA)*. ACM Press, October 1987.

19. E. Radeke. Object management in federated database systems. Internal report, CADLAB, Paderborn, Geramny, 1993.

20. E.A. Rundensteiner. MultiView: a methodology for supporting multiple views in object-oriented databases. In *Proc. 18th Int'l Conf. on Very Large Data Bases (VLDB)*, Vancouver, Canada, August 1992.

21. H.-J. Schek and M.H. Scholl. Evolution of data models. In A. Blaser, editor, *Proc. Int'l Symposium on Database Systems for the 90's*, Berlin, Germany, November 1990. LNCS 466, Springer Verlag, Heidelberg.

22. H.-J. Schek and A. Wolf. Cooperation between autonomous operation services and object database systems in a heterogeneous environment. In DS5 [6].

23. M.H. Scholl, C. Laasch, C. Rich, H.-J. Schek, and M. Tresch. The COCOON object model. Technical Report 193, ETH Zurich, Dept. of Computer Science, December 1992.

24. M.H. Scholl, C. Laasch, and M. Tresch. Updatable views in object-oriented databases. In *Proc. 2nd Int'l Conf. on Deductive and Object-Oriented Databases (DOOD)*, Munich, Deutschland, December 1991. Springer, LNCS 566.

25. M.H. Scholl and H.-J. Schek. A relational object model. In *Proc. 3rd Int'l Conf. on Database Theory (ICDT)*, Paris, France, December 1990. Springer, LNCS 470.

26. M.H. Scholl, H.-J. Schek, and M. Tresch. Object algebra and views for multiobjectbases. In M.T. Özsu, U. Dayal, and P. Valduriez, editors, *Distributed Object Management*. Morgan Kaufmann, San Mateo, California, 1993.

27. M. Schrefl. *Object-oriented database integration*. PhD thesis, Technische Universität Wien, June 1988.

28. A.P. Sheth and J.A. Larson. Federated database systems for managing distributed, heterogeneuos, and autonomous databases. *ACM Computing Surveys*, 22(3), September 1990.

29. S. Spaccapietra, C. Parent, and Y. Dupont. Model independent assertions for integration of heterogeneous schemas. *The VLDB Journal*, 1(1), July 1992.

30. M.R. Stonebraker. The 3rd generation database system manifesto. In *Proc. IFIP TC2 DS-4 Conf. on Object-Oriented Databases – Analysis, Design & Construction*, Windermere, UK, November 1990. North-Holland.

31. M. Tresch. *Dynamic evolution of independent and cooperating object databases*. PhD thesis, University of Ulm, Germany, 1994.

32. M. Tresch and M. H. Scholl. Schema transformation without database reorganization. *ACM SIGMOD Record*, 22(1), March 1993.

33. M. Tresch and M.H. Scholl. Meta object management and its application to database evolution. In *Proc. 11th Int'l Conf. on Entity-Relationship Approach*, Karlsruhe, Germany, October 1992. Springer, LNCS 645.

34. M. Tresch and M.H. Scholl. Schema transformation processors for federated objectbases. In *Proc. 3rd Int'l Symp. on Database Systems for Advanced Applications (DASFAA)*, Daejon, Korea, April 1993.

35. R. Zicari. A framework for schema updates in an object-oriented database system. In *Proc. 7th Int'l IEEE Conf. on Data Engineering (ICDE)*, Kobe, Japan, April 1991.

Expressive Power and Complexity of Disjunctive Datalog under the Stable Model Semantics

Thomas Eiter, Georg Gottlob, Heikki Mannila*

Christian Doppler Labor für Expertensysteme
Institut für Informationssysteme
Technische Universität Wien
Paniglgasse 16, 1040 Wien, Austria.

E-mail: gottlob@vexpert.dbai.tuwien.ac.at

Abstract. DATALOG¬ is a well-known logical query language, whose expressive power and data complexity under the stable model semantics has been recently determined. In this paper we consider the extension of DATALOG¬ to disjunctive DATALOG¬ (DDL¬), which allows disjunction in the head of program clauses, under the stable model semantics. We investigate and determine the expressiveness and the data complexity of DDL¬, as well as the expression complexity. The main findings of this paper are that disjunctive datalog captures precisely the class of all Σ_2^P-recognizable queries under the brave version of reasoning, and symmetrically the class of all Π_2^P-recognizable queries under the cautious version; the data complexity is Σ_2^P-completeness in the brave version, and Π_2^P-complete in the cautious version, while the expression complexity is NEXPTIME^{NP}-complete in the brave version and co-NEXPTIME^{NP}-complete in the cautious version.

1 Introduction

DATALOG is an important logical query language which is theoretically quite well-understood [3, 34]. We denote by DATALOG¬ the extension of DATALOG which allows negation in rule bodies. Recently the data complexity and the expressive power of DATALOG¬ under the stable model semantics and variants thereof have been investigated [22, 23, 30, 29]. It was shown that the data complexity of cautious reasoning with DATALOG¬ under this semantics is co-NP-complete, and, moreover, that this language exactly captures co-NP [30]. Complexity results for stable models of first-order programs with function symbols have been derived in [30, 20, 21, 31] (cf. [31]).

In the present paper we are interested in disjunctive DATALOG¬ (DDL¬). A DDL¬-program is a DATALOG¬-program admitting disjunction in the clause heads. The generalization of the stable model semantics to DDL¬-programs

---

* The main part of this work has been carried out while this author, on leave from the University of Helsinki, was spending a sabbatical at the TU Vienna in spring 1993.

is straightforward, following Przymusinski's approach for disjunctive logic programs [28]. In this setting, we investigate and answer the following questions:

- *What is the expressive power of* DDL$^\neg$? We show that DDL$^\neg$ *exactly captures* Π_2^P. Thus, unless the polynomial hierarchy collapses to its first level, DDL$^\neg$ is strictly more expressive than DATALOG$^\neg$ under the stable model semantics.
- *What is the data-complexity of* DDL$^\neg$? We show that the data complexity of DDL$^\neg$ under the cautious (resp. brave) stable model semantics is Π_2^P (resp. Σ_2^P), and that the complexity of deciding whether a fixed DDL$^\neg$-program has a stable model is Σ_2^P.
- *What is the expression complexity of* DDL$^\neg$? We show that the expression complexity of DDL$^\neg$ under the cautious (resp. brave) stable model semantics is co-NEXPTIME^{NP} (resp. NEXPTIME^{NP}), and that the complexity of deciding whether a DDL$^\neg$-program has a stable model, measured by the program size, is NEXPTIME^{NP}.

We have thus completely determined the expressive power and complexity of disjunctive DDL under the stable semantics. We mention that similar results hold for the minimal model semantics [25] and the perfect model semantics [27] (cf. Section 6).

The rest of the paper is organized as follows. Section 2 provides basic concepts. In Section 3, we define DDL$^\neg$-programs and the stable model semantics for DDL$^\neg$queries. In Section 4, we determine the expressive power of this query language, while in Section 5 we analyze its complexity. Section 6 briefly addresses an extension of the expressiveness and complexity analysis to other semantics for disjunctive datalog. To alleviate the burden of technical details, some auxiliary results are separated from the main material and relegated to the appendix, which is organized into two sections.

2 Preliminaries and basic definitions

Complexity Classes

For basic concepts of complexity theory, cf. [1, 14]. We assume some knowledge about the classes NP $= \Sigma_1^P$, co-NP $= \Pi_1^P$, Σ_2^P, Π_2^P, ... of the polynomial hierarchy. Let NTIME$(f(n))$ denote the problems decidable by a nondeterministic Turing machine within time $f(n)$. Then, NP $= \bigcup_{k \in N} \text{NTIME}(n^k)$, NETIME $= \bigcup_{k \in N} \text{NTIME}(2^{k \cdot n})$, and NEXPTIME $= \bigcup_{k \in N} \text{NTIME}(2^{n^k})$. Similarly, let for any complexity class **C** denote NTIME$(f(n), \mathbf{C})$ the problems decidable by a nondeterministic oracle Turing machine within time $f(n)$ using an oracle for some problem in **C**. Then, $\Sigma_2^P = \bigcup_{k \in N} \text{NTIME}(n^k, \text{NP})$, NETIME$^{NP} = \bigcup_{k \in N} \text{NTIME}(2^{k \cdot n}, \text{NP})$, and NEXPTIME$^{NP} = \bigcup_{k \in N} \text{NTIME}(2^{n^k}, \text{NP})$. Unless stated otherwise, the notion of completeness refers to polynomial-time transformability ($\leq_m^p$).

Relational databases

We use upper case letters $R, S, \ldots$ to denote relation symbols. A *relational scheme* over a domain *Dom* is a list $\overline{R} = R_1, \ldots, R_k$ of relation symbols R_i, $i = 1, \ldots, k$ of arity $a_i \geq 0$. An *instance* of $\overline{R}$ *(relational database over $\overline{R}$)* is a tuple $D = (U, R_1, \ldots, R_k)$ of a finite universe, $U \subseteq Dom$, and relations $R_i \subseteq D^{a_i}$. (As common, we use relation symbols also to denote relation instances.) We assume a fixed domain which will not be explicitly mentioned. The universe of D is denoted by $U(D)$ and any projection of D to a subscheme $\overline{R}'$ of $\overline{R}$ by $D[\overline{R}']$. The set of all instances of $\overline{R}$ is denoted by $\mathcal{D}(\overline{R})$.

For a given relational scheme $\overline{R}$, a *database property* is a predicate **P** which associates with every instance D of $\overline{R}$ a truth value $\mathbf{P}(D)$ from {*true, false*} and which is closed under isomorphisms.

A *database mapping* or *query* is a (partial) recursive function $q : \mathcal{D}(\overline{R}) \rightarrow \mathcal{D}(\overline{S})$, i.e. which maps every instance D of $\overline{R}$ (intuitively, the input relations) to an instance $q(D)$ of $\overline{S}$ (the output relations) where $U(D) = U(q(D))$ and q is invariant under isomorphisms.[2] The pair $(\overline{R}, \overline{S})$ is called the *input/output scheme of q* and denoted by $IO(q)$; we will always assume that $\overline{R}$ and $\overline{S}$ are disjoint. A query q is *Boolean* if $\overline{S}$ consists of a single 0-ary relation symbol P, i.e., a propositional letter. Notice that each Boolean query corresponds to a database property $\mathbf{P}_q$ in the obvious way. A *query language* is a set $\mathcal{L}$ of query expressions E and a function μ such that for each $E \in \mathcal{L}$, $\mu(E)$ is a query.

The close relation between second order definability over finite structures and NP computability is well-known by Fagin's result [9], which generalizes to the polynomial hierarchy [33, 18]; say that a database property **P** is **C**-*recognizable* (or, *in* **C**) if deciding $\mathbf{P}(D) = true$ is in **C**.

Proposition 1. *A database property* **P** *over $\overline{R}$ is in* NP *(resp., Σ_k^P, $k \geq 1$) iff there exists a second order sentence Ψ over vocabulary $\sigma = \overline{R}$ of the form $(\exists \overline{S})\varphi(\overline{S})$ (resp. $(\exists \overline{S}_1)(\forall \overline{S}_2) \cdots \varphi(\overline{S}_1, \ldots, \overline{S}_k)$), where φ is first order, such that for each $D \in \mathcal{D}(\overline{R})$, $D \in \mathcal{C}$ iff* $\mathbf{P}(D) = true$.

Expressive power and complexity of query languages

We define the expressive power $E(\mathcal{L})$ of a query language $\mathcal{L}$ to be the class of all queries definable by query expressions from $\mathcal{L}$, i.e., $E(\mathcal{L}) = \{q : q = \mu(E), E \in \mathcal{L}\}$. We say that $\mathcal{L}_1$ is *at least as expressive as* $\mathcal{L}_2$ iff $E(\mathcal{L}_2) \subseteq E(\mathcal{L}_1)$, and that $\mathcal{L}_1$ is *more expressive than* $\mathcal{L}_2$ if the inclusion is strict.

For any query $q : \overline{R} \rightarrow \overline{S}$, the *query output tuple (QOT) problem* is as follows: Given $D \in \mathcal{D}(\overline{R})$ and a tuple $\overline{a}$ matching the format of $S_i \in \overline{S}$, decide whether $\overline{a}$ belongs to S_i in $q(D)[S_i]$. Let **C** be a complexity class. A database mapping $q : \overline{R} \rightarrow \overline{S}$ is **C**-*recognizable* (cf. [13]; or, *in* **C**) iff the QOT-problem is in **C**. (In [19], the term **C**-computable is used.)

---

[2] Other authors use a single output relation (cf. [35, 4, 5]); our results would be the same. The queries are computable in the sense of [4], generalized to multiple output relations.

The *data* (resp. *expression, data/expression*) *complexity* of a query language $\mathcal{L}$ is defined as the complexity of the QOT-problem for the queries defined by expressions $E \in \mathcal{L}$, where E is part of the input and E (resp. D, neither E nor D) is *fixed*.

We say that a query language $\mathcal{L}$ is *data-complete* (resp. *expression-complete, data/ expression-complete*) for complexity class $\mathbf{C}$ iff the data complexity (resp. expression complexity, data/expression complexity) of $\mathcal{L}$ is $\mathbf{C}$-completeness under $\leq_m^p$-transformation. Notice that in [35] the concept was proposed using logspace-reduction instead of $\leq_m^p$-reduction.

3 Disjunctive datalog

A disjunctive DATALOG$^\neg$ (or, DDL$^\neg$) program π is a finite collection of rules

$$l_1 \vee \cdots \vee l_n \leftarrow l_{n+1}, \cdots, l_m, \qquad 1 \leq n \leq m,$$

where the l_i's are literals. The literals $l_1, \ldots, l_n$, which form the *head* of the clause, are atomic formulas $S(x_1, \ldots, x_a)$, where each x_j, $j = 1, \ldots, a$ is a variable. The literals $l_{n+1}, \ldots, l_m$ constitute the *body* of the clause; each of them may state an equality $x_i = x_j$, an inequality $x_i \neq x_j$, an atomic formula $P(x_1, \ldots, x_a)$, or a negated atomic formula $\neg P(x_1, \ldots, x_a)$. For convenience, we allow that literals involve 0-ary relation symbols (i.e., propositional letters). Note that constants are not provided in the language; the formalism can be easily extended to this case.

A simple example is the following program π, where informally $P(x, y)$ means that x is parent of y, $S(x, y)$ that x is a sibling of y, $A(x, y)$ that x is an aunt of y, and $U(x, y)$ that x is an uncle of y.

$$S(y, z) \leftarrow P(x, y), P(x, z), y \neq z.$$
$$A(x, z) \vee U(x, z) \leftarrow S(x, y), \neg P(x, z), P(y, z).$$

Notice that such a program is reasonable if evaluated over a (most likely) incomplete database of ancient Egyptian dynasties, say.

Denote by $RS(\pi)$ the relation schema consisting of the relation symbols in π. In the literature, it is common to distinguish between *extensional database (EDB) relations*, which provide explicitly stored data, and *intensional database (IDB) relations*, which are defined by the data and the program. The EDB relation symbols are those which may appear in the body but not in the head of any rule, while the IDB relation symbols are those which appear in the head of at least one rule. We define the *input/output schema* $IO(\pi)$ of a DDL$^\neg$-program π as a pair $(\overline{R}, \overline{S})$ of relation schemata such that $\overline{R}$ consists of the EDB relation symbols and $\overline{S}$ of a *subset* of the IDB relation symbols; the relation symbols which do not occur in $\overline{R}, \overline{S}$ are called *auxiliary relation symbols*.

The tuple $(IO(\pi), \pi)$ defines a query expression (a DDL$^\neg$-*query*), whose semantics has yet to be defined.

We deal with DDL$^\neg$-programs over finite structures; this is not the standard logic programming environment, but is common in the context of logical databases [3, 34, 15], where database instances are regarded as finite structures.

Logic programs over finite structures

Given a DDL⁻program π where $IO(\pi) = (\overline{R}, \overline{S})$ and a finite structure D for vocabulary $\sigma = RS(\pi)$, (i.e., an instance of $RS(\pi)$), we define the *interpretation of π* as the following logic program $LP_D(\pi)$. The universe $U(D)$ of D is the set of constant symbols. The *interpretation* $\mathcal{I}_D(r)$ of a rule r of π is the collection of logic program rules obtained if every variable x in r is substituted by an arbitrary element $a \in U(D)$. Then,

$$LP_D(\pi) = \bigcup_{r \in \pi} \mathcal{I}_D(r) \cup E(D),$$

where $E(D)$ is the collection of rules

$$R(\overline{a}) \leftarrow .$$

such that $R \in \overline{R}$ and $D \models R(\overline{a})$. Notice that $LP_D(\pi)$ is grounded, i.e., it is a propositional logic program.

First order view

Alternatively, there is a pure logical view of DDL⁻-programs. Each rule

$$l_1 \vee \cdots \vee l_n \leftarrow l_{n+1}, \cdots, l_m,$$

of a DDL⁻-program π can be seen as the universally closed first order formula

$$(\forall \overline{x})(l_{n+1} \wedge \cdots \wedge l_m \rightarrow l_1 \vee \cdots \vee l_n)$$

and π as the conjunction of all these formulae. A *model* of π is any finite structure M for vocabulary $\sigma = RS(\pi)$ such that $M \models \pi$. We denote by $M(\pi)$ the set of all models of π.

3.1 Stable model semantics

We define now the stable model semantics of DDL⁻-queries over finite databases.

Given a grounded logic program LP and a Herbrand interpretation I, the Gelfond-Lifschitz transformation on LP, LP^I, is the logic program obtained from LP as follows (cf. [28]):

(*i*)   Remove every rule such that for some literal $\neg P(\overline{a})$ from the body, $P(\overline{a}) \in I$;

(*ii*) cancel in the remaining rules all negated atoms $\neg P(\overline{a})$ from the body.

A stable model of LP is then any Herbrand interpretation M such that M is a minimal Herbrand model of LP^M.

The *stable models of π for an instance D of $\overline{R}$ (stable models on D)* are the finite structures M over vocabulary $\sigma = RS(\pi)$ such that the H-interpretation corresponding to M is a stable model of $LP_D(\pi)$. As can be easily seen, every stable model of π is a model of π. Note that there may be one stable model, several stable models, or even no stable model.

The meaning of the DDL$^\neg$-query $((\overline{R}, \overline{S}), \pi)$ under the *brave stable model semantics (BSM)* (resp. *cautious stable model semantics (CSM)*) is defined as the database mapping $q : \mathcal{D}(\overline{R}) \rightarrow \mathcal{D}(\overline{S})$, such that for each $S_i \in \overline{S}$ and each tuple $\overline{a}$, $\overline{a}$ belongs to $q(D)[S_i]$ iff $M \models S_i(\overline{a})$ for some (resp. every) stable model M of π on D.

Logical characterization of stable models

The stable models of a DDL$^\neg$-program π on instance D of $\overline{R}$ can be characterized as follows. Define the binary relation $\sqsubseteq$ on the databases over $RS(\pi)$ as follows: $D_1 \sqsubseteq D_2$ iff $U(D_1) = U(D_2)$, $D_1[\overline{R}] = D_2[\overline{R}]$, and for every S in $RS(\pi) - \overline{R}$, it holds that $D_1[S] \subseteq D_2[S]$. A model M of π is *minimal* iff there exists no distinct model M' of π such that $M' \sqsubseteq M$; the set of minimal models of π is denoted by $MM(\pi)$.

Now define that a model M of π has the *s-property* iff for each database $D \in \mathcal{D}(RS(\pi))$ such that $D \neq M$ and $D \sqsubseteq M$, there exists a rule r in π and a tuple $\overline{a}$ such that

(i) $M \models l(\overline{a})$ for each l of the form $\neg P(x_1, \ldots, x_a)$ in the body of r, and
(ii) $D \not\models r(\overline{a})$.

Then, we have the following.

Proposition 2. *Let π be a DDL$^\neg$-program, where $IO(\pi) = (\overline{R}, \overline{S})$, and let $D \in \mathcal{D}(\overline{R})$. A model M of π with $M[\overline{R}] = D$ is a stable model on D iff M has the s-property.*

Notice that from this proposition, it follows immediately that each stable model of π is a minimal model of π, and that the stable models and the minimal models of π coincide if negation in π occurs only in front of the input predicates $\overline{R}$.

4 Expressiveness of stable models

In this section, we analyze the expressive power of DDL$^\neg$ under the stable model semantics. We refer in the proofs of our results to a useful normal form for second order sentences with second order quantifier prefix of type $\exists\forall$, which is derived in Theorem 20 (see Appendix A).

Theorem 3. *The Boolean DDL$^\neg$-queries under the brave stable model semantics precisely capture the class of all database properties in Σ_2^P.*

Proof. (Sketch) First we show that the database mapping defined by a Boolean DDL$^\neg$-query $((\overline{R}, W), \pi)$ under the BSM-semantics is Σ_2^P-recognizable. It holds that W is true for an instance D of $\overline{R}$ iff there exists a stable model M of π

over D such that $M \models W$. Notice that for fixed π, the size of any such M is polynomial in the size of π and D. A guess for M can be verified with an NP oracle in polynomial time; hence, the desired follows.

Let us now show that every Σ_2^P-recognizable database property $\mathbf{P}(\overline{R})$ can be expressed by a Boolean DDL¬-query under the BSM-semantics.

From Proposition 1 and Theorem 20, we know that $\mathbf{P}$ can be expressed by a second order sentence Ψ over vocabulary $\sigma = \overline{R}$ of the form

$$(\exists \overline{S})(\forall \overline{T})[\,(\forall \overline{y})(T_m(\overline{y})) \vee (\exists \overline{x})(\vartheta_1(\overline{x}) \vee \cdots \vee \vartheta_k(\overline{x}))\,], \tag{1}$$

where $\overline{S} = (S_1, \ldots, S_l)$ and $\overline{T} = (T_1, \ldots, T_m)$, $m \geq 1$. We will define a DDL¬-program π with $IO(\pi) = (\overline{R}, W)$, where W is a new 0-ary predicate symbol (i.e., a propositional letter), such that the defined Boolean DDL¬-query, $(IO(\pi), \pi)$, computes under BSM-semantics W true on every input database D if and only if $D \models \Psi$.

Program π consists of two parts π_ℓ and π_r and intuitively works as follows. Given any interpretation of the $\overline{S}$ predicates, it checks whether for each interpretation of the $\overline{T}$ predicates the first order part of (1) is true; the first part, π_ℓ, checks whether the left disjunct is true and the second part, π_r, whether the right disjunct is true. The common predicates of π_ℓ and π_r are W, which intuitively is derived in π_ℓ resp. π_r if the respective disjunct is true, and T_m. We describe first π_r and then π_ℓ.

Program π_r consists of the following clauses (the arities of predicates and tuple variables are obvious):

$$
\begin{array}{lll}
(1) & S_i(\overline{x}) \vee S_i^*(\overline{x}) \leftarrow, & \text{for } i = 1, \ldots, l; \\
(2) & T_j(\overline{x}) \vee T_j^*(\overline{x}) \leftarrow, & \text{for } j = 1, \ldots, m; \\
(3) & T_j(\overline{x}) \leftarrow W, & \text{for } j = 1, \ldots, m; \\
(4) & T_j^*(\overline{x}) \leftarrow W, & \text{for } j = 1, \ldots, m; \\
(5) & W \leftarrow T_j(\overline{x}), T_j^*(\overline{x}), & \text{for } j = 1, \ldots, m; \\
(6) & W \leftarrow \eta_i(\overline{x}), & \text{for } i = 1, \ldots, k;
\end{array}
$$

In this program, the S_i^* and T_j^* are new predicate symbols of the same arity as S_i and T_j, respectively, intended to be interpreted as the complements of those relations. Furthermore, for each $i = 1, \ldots, k$

$$\eta_i = L'_{i,1}, \ldots, L'_{i,n_i} \qquad \text{where} \qquad \vartheta_i = L_{i,1} \wedge \cdots \wedge L_{i,n_i}$$

and each $L'_{i,j}$ is the literal resulting from $L_{i,j}$ if any $\neg S_g$ and $\neg T_h$ are replaced by the positive predicates S_g^* and T_h^*, respectively. Notice that negation occurs in π_r only in front of input predicates.

Now we describe program π_ℓ. Denote the arity of T_m by s. Intuitively, the test whether $\forall \overline{x}(T_m(\overline{x}))$ is true is done by induction along a linear order $<^s$ of all s-tuples over the universe $U(D)$ of the input database D. To do so, π_ℓ uses predicates F^s, S^s and L^s which are interpreted as the relations associated with $<^s$ describing the first element of $<^s$, the successor element ($S^s(\overline{x}, \overline{x}')$ means that $\overline{x}'$ is the successor of $\overline{x}$), and the last element of $<^s$, respectively. These predicates are defined in stable semantics from predicates F^{s*}, S^{s*}, and L^{s*}

that describe their complements. In addition, π_ℓ uses an s-ary predicate $I^s(\overline{x})$ which intuitively states that T_m is true for $\overline{x}$ and for all tuples $\overline{x}'$ ordered before $\overline{x}$.

Program π_ℓ consists of the following clauses ($\overline{x} = (x_1, \ldots, x_s)$ etc):

$$
\begin{aligned}
&(01) && \overline{x} <^s \overline{y} \vee \overline{y} <^s \overline{x} \leftarrow x_i \neq y_i, && \text{for } i = 1, \ldots, s; \\
&(02) && \overline{x} <^s \overline{y} \leftarrow \overline{x} <^s \overline{z}, \overline{z} <^s \overline{y}; \\
&(03) && F^{s*}(\overline{x}) \leftarrow \overline{y} <^s \overline{x}; \\
&(04) && F^s(\overline{x}) \leftarrow \neg F^{s*}(\overline{x}); \\
&(05) && S^{s*}(\overline{x}, \overline{y}) \leftarrow \overline{y} <^s \overline{x}; \\
&(06) && S^{s*}(\overline{x}, \overline{y}) \leftarrow \overline{x} <^s \overline{z}, \overline{z} <^s \overline{y}; \\
&(07) && S^{s*}(\overline{x}, \overline{x}) \leftarrow; \\
&(08) && S^s(\overline{x}, \overline{y}) \leftarrow \neg S^{s*}(\overline{x}, \overline{y}); \\
&(09) && L^{s*}(\overline{x}) \leftarrow \overline{x} <^s \overline{y}; \\
&(10) && L^s(\overline{x}) \leftarrow \neg L^{s*}(\overline{x}); \\
&(11) && I^s(\overline{x}) \leftarrow F^s(\overline{x}), T_m(\overline{x}); \\
&(12) && I^s(\overline{y}) \leftarrow S^s(\overline{x}, \overline{y}), I^s(\overline{x}), T_m(\overline{y}); \\
&(13) && W \leftarrow L^s(\overline{x}), I^s(\overline{x});
\end{aligned}
$$

Notice that in π_ℓ negation occurs only in a stratified manner (cf. [27] for stratification of disjunctive logic programs and databases).

Since $<^s$ occurs only in rule (01) and (02) in the head of a clause, it is not hard to see that in any stable model M of π on D (which is a minimal model) $<^s$ must be interpreted as a linear order of all s-tuples over $U(D)$. Furthermore, it is easy to see that F^{s*}, S^{s*}, and L^{s*} must be interpreted in M as intended.

If W is true in M, then it must be derived by one of the clauses (5) or (6) in π_r and (13) in π_ℓ.

The following property of program π can be shown. The Boolean DDL⌐-query defined from π, $(IO(\pi), \pi)$, computes under BSM-semantics W true on $D \in \mathcal{D}(\overline{R})$ iff $D \models \Psi$.

This proves the theorem. □

Remark: Notice that in the program π of the proof of Theorem 3 negation occurs only in a stratified manner. Thus, the proof basically would work for stratified disjunctive semantics [27] as well.

We obtain a similar result for CSM-semantics.

Theorem 4. *The Boolean DDL⌐-queries under the cautious stable model semantics precisely capture the class of all database properties in Π_2^P.*

Proof. (Sketch) One can easily show that the database mapping defined by a Boolean DDL⌐-query $((\overline{R}, W), \pi)$ under the CSM-semantics is Π_2^P-recognizable (cf. proof of Theorem 3).

We show that every Π_2^P-recognizable database property $\mathbf{P}(\overline{R})$ can be expressed by a Boolean DDL⌐-query under the CSM-semantics as follows. Extend the DDL⌐ program π defined for Ψ in the proof of Theorem 3 by adding the rule

$$W \leftarrow \neg W,$$

and denote with π' the resulting program. Let X be a new propositional letter, and define $IO(\pi') = (\overline{R}, X)$. The following can be shown. The Boolean DDL⁻-query defined from π', $(IO(\pi'), \pi')$, computes under CSM-semantics X true on $D \in \mathcal{D}(\overline{R})$ iff $D \models \neg\Psi$.

   This proves the result. □

4.1 Non-Boolean queries

Having characterized Boolean DDL⁻-queries only is somewhat unsatisfactory. In the next theorem, we precisely characterize the database mappings corresponding to general DDL⁻-queries under the BSM-semantics. Note that several other authors consider only Boolean queries, cf. [15, 29]. We use the following lemma.

Lemma 5. *Let* **C** *be a complexity class closed under* $\leq^P_m$*-transformation and conjunctions. Then, a database property* **P** *is in* **C** *if it is* $\leq^P_m$*-transformable into a conjunction of problems from* **C**.

Theorem 6. *A database mapping is expressible by a DDL⁻-query under the BSM-semantics iff it is* Σ^P_2*-recognizable.*

Proof. (Sketch)   (*only-if*): Easy and omitted here (cf. proof of Theorem 3).
(*if*): Let $q : \mathcal{D}(\overline{R}') \rightarrow \mathcal{D}(\overline{S}')$ be a Σ^P_2-recognizable database mapping. Let **P** be the database property over $\overline{R} = \overline{R}'\overline{S}'$ defined as follows: for every $D \in \mathcal{D}(\overline{R})$,

$$\mathbf{P}(D) = true \quad \text{iff} \quad D[\overline{S}'] \subseteq q(D[\overline{R}']),$$

where $\subseteq$ is applied componentwise. It is readily checked that **P** is in fact a database property. Note that for any instance D of $\overline{R}$, $\mathbf{P}(D)$ is equivalent to a conjunction of QOT-problems for q as follows:

$$\mathbf{P}(D) = \bigwedge_{S'_i \in \overline{S}'} \bigwedge_{\overline{a} \in D[S'_i]} (\overline{a} \in q(D[\overline{R}'])[S'_i]).$$

Since q is Σ^P_2-recognizable, it follows from Lemma 5 that **P** is in Σ^P_2.

   Thus, by Theorem 3, there exists a Boolean DDL⁻-query $(IO(\pi), \pi))$ where $IO(\pi) = (\overline{R}, W)$ for some propositional letter W such that the query computes W true over $D \in \mathcal{D}(\overline{R})$ iff $\mathbf{P}(D) = true$. We may assume that π has exactly the form of the DDL⁻-program in the proof of Theorem 3. Now let π' be the DDL⁻ program with $IO(\pi') = (\overline{R}, \overline{S}')$ obtained by modifying π as follows. Add the rule

$$W \leftarrow \neg W,$$

and for each predicate letter $S'_i \in \overline{S}'$ a rule

$$S'_i(\overline{x}) \vee S'^*_i(\overline{x}) \leftarrow .$$

where S'^*_i is a new relation symbol of the same arity as S'_i. Intuitively, these rules simulate all possible instances for the relations in $\overline{S}'$.

Let $D \in \mathcal{D}(\overline{R})$. It can be shown that the DDL$^{\neg}$-query q' defined by π' has a stable model M on $D[\overline{R}']$ such that $M[\overline{S}'] = D[\overline{S}']$ if and only if $D[\overline{S}'] \subseteq q(D[\overline{R}'])$. Under the BSM-semantics, the query $q'(D')$ yields thus as the result the union of the projections of all stable models of π' on $D' \in \mathcal{D}(\overline{R}')$, i.e.,

$$q'(D') = \bigcup_{D \in \mathcal{D}(\overline{R})} \{ D[\overline{S}'] : D[\overline{R}'] = D', D[\overline{S}'] \subseteq q(D') \} = q(D').$$

This proves the theorem. □

For the cautious stable model semantics, the following result is obtained by similar methods.

Theorem 7. *A database mapping is expressible by a DDL$^{\neg}$-query under the CSM-semantics iff it is Π_2^P-recognizable.*

5 Complexity

In this section we analyze the complexity of DDL$^{\neg}$-queries under stable model semantics. We consider both data and expression complexity under the brave and the cautious stable model semantics, as well as deciding whether a stable model exists measured in the size of the data resp. program.

5.1 Data complexity

The following results on the data complexity are immediate consequences of our results on the expressive power in the previous section. (Constructing for each database property in Σ_2^P a second order sentence as in Theorem 20 is possible by means of a polynomial-time algorithm.)

Theorem 8. *The language of DDL$^{\neg}$-queries under the brave stable model semantics is data-complete for Σ_2^P. The data-complexity is Σ_2^P-hard even for Boolean DDL$^{\neg}$-queries.*

Theorem 9. *The language of DDL$^{\neg}$-queries under the cautious stable model semantics is data-complete for Π_2^P. The data-complexity is Σ_2^P-hard even for Boolean DDL$^{\neg}$-queries.*

The complexity of deciding the existence of a stable model follows from our results on the expressiveness of Boolean DDL$^{\neg}$-queries.

Theorem 10. *Let π be a fixed DDL$^{\neg}$ program, where $IO(\pi) = (\overline{R}, \overline{S})$. Then, given $D \in \mathcal{D}(\overline{R})$, deciding whether π has a stable model on D is Σ_2^P-complete. Hardness holds even if π defines a Boolean query.*

Proof. (Sketch) Membership in Σ_2^P is easy (cf. proof of Theorem 3). For the hardness part, observe that every stable model M of π' on $D[\overline{R}']$ in the proof of Theorem 4 fulfills $M \not\models X$. □

5.2 Expression complexity

In this section we determine the complexity of evaluating DDL$^\neg$ queries under the stable model semantics if the query varies. Intuitively, this causes an exponential increase in complexity, because the size of any model of a DDL$^\neg$-program π over a database D can be exponential in the size of π rather than polynomial. We show that this intuition comes true by establishing expression-completeness (and data/expression-completeness) of DDL$^\neg$ queries under BSM and CSM semantics for the less-known complexity classes NEXPTIME^{NP} and co-NEXPTIME^{NP}. Notice that NP $\subset$ NEXPTIME, hence NP $\subset$ NEXPTIME^{NP}. Since to our best knowledge there are no practical problems (e.g., graph problems) known complete for those classes, we first exhibit such problems and then reduce these problems to DDL$^\neg$-queries. We present for this a technique which combines results from [2, 32].

Complexity and succinct representation

It is well-known that the input representation (e.g., numbers in unary or binary notation) can have a drastic effect on the problem complexity [12]. Such effects were investigated for the "succinct versions" of graph-theoretic problems in [11, 26], where a graph whose vertices are elements of $\{0,1\}^n$ is represented by a Boolean circuit with $2n$ input bits; the circuit outputs 1 if and only if the input represents two vertices which are connected by an edge.

Formally, a Boolean circuit is a finite set of triples (gates) $\{g_i = (a_i, j, l) : 1 \leq i \leq t\}$, where $a_i \in \{in, \ and, \ or, \ not\}$ is the kind of the gate, and $g_j, g_l, j, l < i$ are the inputs of the gate, unless g_i is an in-gate, in which case, say, $j = l = 0$. For not-gates, $j = l$ (cf. [15]). A succinct, ingenious proof in [26] showed that the succinct problem setting often leads to an exponential complexity increase.

The results and techniques of [26] were generalized in [17, 2] to the succinct version of any decisional problem A encoded as a language over $\{0,1\}$. The succinct representation of a binary word w is a Boolean circuit that on input of a number i (in binary), outputs whether $i \leq |w|$ and in that case, the i-th bit of w ($|w|$ denotes the length of w). The succinct version sA of A is as follows: Given a Boolean circuit C_w describing a word w, decide whether $w \in A$.

The following theorem from [2] shows how to obtain hardness results under $\leq_m^p$-transformability for the succinct problem version from hardness of the standard problem under logtime transformability ($\leq_m^{LT}$). Roughly, a $\leq_m^{LT}$-transformation is a problem mapping f such that, given w and an integer i, the i-th bit of $f(w)$ is computable in logarithmic time; note that every such mapping defines a polynomial-time transformation. Let $long(A)$ be defined for problem A as follows: $w \in long(A)$ iff the binary expression of the length of w is in $\{1w : w \in A\}$.

Theorem 11 [2], Th.5. *Let C_1 and C_2 be arbitrary complexity classes such that for every $A \in C_1$, $long(A) \in C_2$. Then, for every B, if B is hard for C_2 under $\leq_m^{LT}$-transformation, then sB is hard for C_1 under $\leq_m^p$-transformation.*

As shown in Appendix B, this result generalizes by replacing $\leq_m^{LT}$-transformation with the more liberal $\leq_m^{PLT}$-transformation, which is obtained by relaxing the logarithmic to a polylogarithmic (i.e., $\log^k(n)$ for any fixed integer k) time bound. Notice that $\leq_m^{PLT}$ is transitive. We use this generalized result to establish a useful co-NEXPTIME^{NP}-complete graph problem below.

5.3   A co-NEXPTIME^{NP}-complete graph problem

The following problem CERT3COL was defined and analyzed by Stewart in [32].

Instance of size n: a graph G on the vertices $\{0, 1, \ldots, n-1\}$ such that every edge is labeled with a disjunction of two literals where each literal is over the Boolean variables $\{X_{i,j} : i, j = 0, \ldots, n-1\}$.

Yes-instance of size n: an instance G of size n such that for every truth value assignment t on the Boolean variables, the graph $t(G)$ obtained from G by including only those edges set true under t can be colored with only three colors.

We encode CERT3COL using a binary relation E and 4-ary relations P and N, such that in any finite structure S, $S \models E(x,y) \vee E(y,x)$ iff "There is an edge between x and y," and $S \models P(x,y,u,v) \vee P(y,x,u,v)$ (resp. $S \models N(x,y,u,v) \vee N(y,x,u,v)$) iff "The edge between x and y is labeled by $X_{u,v}$ (resp. $\neg X_{u,v}$)." (Remark: The formulation in [32] also allows an edge label *True* (which can be simulated by labels $X_{0,0}$ and $\neg X_{0,0}$) and uses a single 5-ary relation R involving constants 0 and *max*; the change of the encoding is not relevant for our purposes.)

This problem is Π_2^P-complete (under $\leq_m^p$-transformation). Stewart shows that completeness holds even under *projection translation*, which is a stricter concept than $\leq_m^p$-transformation. It can be shown that projection translatability implies $\leq_m^{PLT}$-transformability. Thus,

Lemma 12. CERT3COL *is complete for* Π_2^P *under* $\leq_m^{PLT}$-*transformation.*

By Theorem 23, we therefore obtain the following.

Theorem 13. sCERT3COL *is co-NEXPTIME^{NP}-complete (for* $\leq_m^p$-*transformation).*

5.4   Reduction to DDL$^{\neg}$-queries

Armed with the co-NEXPTIME^{NP}-complete problem sCERT3COL, we derive now the expression complexity of DDL$^{\neg}$-queries under the stable semantics.

Our first concern is the issue of transforming an instance of sCERT3COL, which is a Boolean circuit C for a CERT3COL instance, into a DDL$^{\neg}$ query in polynomial time. The key fact is that Boolean circuits can be simulated by DDL$^{\neg}$-programs which are efficiently constructible. (This observation was already used by Kolaitis and Papadimitriou in [15].) Thus, one can efficiently construct from C DDL$^\neg$-programs which compute the relations E, P, and N in the CERT3COL instance of C, and merge these programs with a DDL$^\neg$-program for CERT3COL. The details follow.

Boolean circuit program

We simulate a Boolean circuit $C = \{g_i = (a_i, j, l) : 1 \le i \le t\}$ computing a k-ary relation R over $\{0, 1\}$ by a DDL$^\neg$-program π_C. The program is similar to a DATALOG$^\neg$-program in [15], but uses disjunction instead of negation.

The relation scheme $RS(\pi_C)$ contains the following relation symbols: A propositional letter W, unary relations O and Z to emulate constants 1 and 0, and for each gate g_i a k-ary predicate letter G_i. Informally, $G_i(\overline{x})$ states that on input of tuple $\overline{x}$ to C, the circuit computation sets the output of g_i to 1.

The program π_C consists of the following clauses. For each gate $g_i = (a_i, j, l)$, it contains the clause

(01)　$G_i(\overline{x}) \leftarrow W;$

Depending on the type a_i of gate g_i, there are additional clauses as follows. If $a_i = in$,

(02)　$G_i(\overline{x}) \leftarrow O(x_j)\,.$
(03)　$W \leftarrow G_i(\overline{x}), Z(x_j).$

If $a_i = and$,

(04)　$G_i(\overline{x}) \leftarrow G_j(\overline{x}), G_l(\overline{x}).$
(05)　$G_j(\overline{x}) \leftarrow G_i(\overline{x}).$
(06)　$G_l(\overline{x}) \leftarrow G_i(\overline{x}).$

If $a_i = or$,

(07)　$G_i(\overline{x}) \leftarrow G_j(\overline{x}).$
(08)　$G_i(\overline{x}) \leftarrow G_l(\overline{x}).$
(09)　$G_j(\overline{x}) \vee G_l(\overline{x}) \leftarrow G_i(\overline{x}).$

If $a_i = not$,

(10)　$G_i(\overline{x}) \vee G_j(\overline{x}) \leftarrow\ .$
(11)　$W \leftarrow G_j(\overline{x}), G_i(\overline{x}).$

The input/output scheme of π_C is defined by $IO(\pi_C) = (OZ, G_t)$, where g_t is the output-gate of C. Notice that no negation occurs in π_C; hence, the stable models of π_C coincide with the minimal models of π_C. Let $M_0 \in \mathcal{D}(RS(\pi_C))$ such that $O = \{1\}$, $Z =, \{0\}$, $M_0 \models G_i(\overline{x})$ iff g_i has value 1 in C on input vector $\overline{x}$, for all i and $\overline{x}$, and W is false. It is not hard to check that M_0 is model of π_C, and in fact a minimal model. Moreover, the following can be shown.

Proposition 14. M_0 is the unique minimal (and stable) model of π_C on $D = (\{0, 1\}, \{1\}, \{0\})$.

This can be proved e.g. showing by induction on the levels d of C that each minimal model of π_C on D must coincide with M_0 on all predicates G_i such that g_i occurs in C at level $j \leq d$.

Notice that $M_0 \models (\forall \overline{x})[G_t(\overline{x}) \leftrightarrow R(\overline{x})]$. Consequently, the DDL$^{\neg}$-query defined from π_C computes on D the relation R.

Now proceed as follows. Let C_I be the Boolean circuit for a CERT3COL instance I of size n. We can construct from C_I Boolean circuits C_P and C_N which compute the relations P and N, respectively, where each argument x, y, u, and v is encoded by a string of $\lceil \log n \rceil$ input bits. The circuits output 1 if a tuple is contained in P resp. N and 0 otherwise. In particular, if any argument string represents an illegal number m, i.e., $n \leq m < 2^{\lceil \log n \rceil}$, the output is 0. Semantically, this roughly means that we have added isolated nodes $n, n + 1, \ldots, 2^{\lceil \log n \rceil}$ to the graph which are not labeled and hence never included in the graph $t(G)$. C_P and C_N can be constructed from C_I in polynomial time. Consequently, programs π_{C_P} and π_{C_N} on disjoint gate predicates computing P and N can be constructed in polynomial time (see above). Let $G_{t_P}^P$ and $G_{t_N}^N$ be the predicates describing the output gates.

Labeled graph coloring program

By our results in Section 4 and Theorem 20, we can construct from a $\forall\exists$ second-order formulae Φ expressing CERT3COL a DDL$^{\neg}$-program which defines a DDL$^{\neg}$-query equivalent to Φ under CSM semantics. This program will be quite complex, however. Instead, we present a simpler program π_{C3C}, which is as follows.

We use binary predicates T and T^*, where $T(u, v)$ means that $X_{u,v}$ is set true; T^* is intended to be the complement of T. We further use unary predicates R, B, and G, which encode the color of a node, and a 0-ary predicate (propositional letter) W. The program π_{C3C} consists of the following rules.

(01) $T(x, y) \vee T^*(x, y) \leftarrow$.
(02) $R(x) \vee G(x) \vee B(x) \leftarrow$.
(03) $R(x) \leftarrow W$.
(04) $G(x) \leftarrow W$.
(05) $B(x) \leftarrow W$.
(06) $W \leftarrow R(x), G(x)$.
(07) $W \leftarrow R(x), B(x)$.
(08) $W \leftarrow G(x), B(x)$.
(09) $W \leftarrow P(x, y, u, v), T(u, v), R(x), R(y)$.
(10) $W \leftarrow P(x, y, u, v), T(u, v), G(x), G(y)$.
(11) $W \leftarrow P(x, y, u, v), T(u, v), B(x), B(y)$.
(12) $W \leftarrow N(x, y, u, v), T^*(u, v), R(x), R(y)$.
(13) $W \leftarrow N(x, y, u, v), T^*(u, v), G(x), G(y)$.
(14) $W \leftarrow N(x, y, u, v), T^*(u, v), B(x), B(y)$.

The extensional relations are N and P, and the intensional relation W is the output relation, i.e., $IO(\pi_{C3C}) = (PN, W)$. Notice that no negation occurs in the program, and that therefore the stable models coincide with the minimal models.

Intuitively, the clause (01) requires a choice from $T(a, b)$ and $T^*(a, b)$ which corresponds to assigning a truth value to the Boolean variable $X_{a,b}$; the clauses (06)–(14) check that the graph $t(G)$ from the truth value assignment is *not* colorable with only three colors, i.e., W is derived under all instances of R, G, and B. The following can be shown.

Proposition 15. *Program π_{C3C} has a stable model M on $D \in \mathcal{D}(PN)$ such that $M \models W$ (and thus π_{C3C} computes W true on D) iff the corresponding CERT3COL instance I is not a Yes-instance, i.e., it is a Yes-instance of co-CERT3COL.*

To combine π_{C3C} with the Boolean circuit programs π_P and π_N, we adapt the program to a program π_{C3C}^n over universe $\{0, 1\}$ by replacing each variable by a sequence of $\lceil \log n \rceil$ variables, and by replacing each occurrence of P and N with respectively $G_{i_P}^P$ and $G_{i_N}^N$. Notice that π_{C3C}^n can be constructed in time polynomial in the size of the Boolean circuit C_I.

Now let the DDL$^\neg$-program π_I be the union of the programs π_{C3C}^n, π_{C_P}, and π_{C_N}, and define $IO(\pi_I) = (OZ, W)$. Then, the following can be shown.

Proposition 16. *Program π_I has a stable model M on $D = (\{0, 1\}, \{1\}, \{0\})$ such that $M \models W$ iff the instance I of CERT3COL corresponding to C_I is not a Yes-instance. Moreover, π_I has a stable model M on D such that $M \models W$ iff the DDL$^\neg$-query defined from π_I computes W true under the BSM semantics.*

We thus arrive at the main results of this section.

Theorem 17. *The language of DDL$^\neg$-queries under the brave stable model semantics is expression-complete and data/expression-complete for NEXPTIME^{NP}. Hardness holds even for Boolean DDL$^\neg$-queries.*

Proof. The QOT-problem is certainly in NEXPTIME^{NP}: the size of a stable model M of program π is clearly bounded by n^n, where n is the size of π and D. A guess for M such that $M \models S_i(\bar{a})$ can be verified with an NP oracle in time polynomial in the size of M (cf. Proposition 2); hence, membership in NEXPTIME^{NP} follows.[3] Hardness of the QOT-problem for NEXPTIME^{NP}, even if D is fixed, follows from Proposition 16, Theorem 13, and the fact that π_I can be constructed from the circuit C_I for instance I in polynomial time. $\quad\square$

We again obtain a symmetric result for cautious semantics.

---

[3] Careful analysis shows that for fixed D, the QOT-problem is even in NETIME^{NP}; hence, this query language is expression-complete also for NETIME^{NP}. (Note that by using standard padding arguments (cf. [1]), it can be shown that NETIME^{NP}-complete problems are also NEXPTIME^{NP}-complete.) Analogous results hold for CSM semantics and deciding stable model existence.

Theorem 18. *The language of* DDL⁻*-queries under the cautious stable model semantics is expression-complete and data/expression-complete for co-*NEXP-TIME^NP. *Hardness holds even for Boolean* DDL⁻*-queries.*

Proof. Membership is similar as in case of brave semantics (cf. proof of Theorem 17). Hardness can be easily shown by constructing from π_I a program π_I' by adding the clause

$$W \leftarrow \neg W$$

and defining $IO(\pi_I') = (OZ, X)$, where X is a new 0-ary relation (cf. also proof of Theorem 4). □

From the proof of Theorem 18, the following result for the problem of deciding the existence of a stable model is easily derived.

Theorem 19. *Given a* DDL⁻ *program* π *and* $D \in \mathcal{D}(\overline{R})$, *where* $IO(\pi) = (\overline{R}, \overline{S})$, *deciding whether* π *has a stable model on* D *is* NEXPTIME^NP*-complete. This holds even if* D *is fixed and* π *defines a Boolean query.*

6 Further results

Besides the (disjunctive) stable model semantics, other semantics have been proposed for disjunctive logic programs and databases, cf. [16, 10].

For example, the minimal model semantics [25] (also known as circumscription [24] and Extended Generalized Closed World Assumption (EGCWA) [36]) and the perfect model semantics [27] can be easily adapted to disjunctive datalog. The analysis of expressive power and complexity of disjunctive datalog can be extended to cover other disjunctive semantics as well.

The authors have recently carried out an extensive analysis of all these semantics [8]. The main results are summarized as follows.

- Plain datalog, i.e., datalog without equality atoms $x_i = x_j$, inequality atoms $x_i \neq x_j$, and negation only in front of input relations R_i, augmented with disjunction allows under all three considered semantics (stable model semantics, minimal models, and perfect models) expressing in the brave version some Σ_2^P-hard queries, but not all queries in Σ_2^P. In fact, it does not allow expressing all queries computable in polynomial time. (This is shown by proving a weak form of preservation under supermodels.)

- Disjunctive datalog where negation occurs only in front if input relations captures precisely the Σ_2^P queries under the brave version of all three semantics. Thus, adding $\neq$ (inequality) to plain disjunctive datalog suffices to gain full expressive power. The same holds for adding $\neg$ to plain disjunctive datalog in case of both the stable model semantics and the perfect model semantics; a symmetric result (Π_2^P-expressiveness) holds for cautious reasoning under those two semantics. In particular, the results show that for disjunctive datalog the stable model semantics and the perfect model semantics express precisely the same set of queries; this is probably not true for nondisjunctive datalog programs (cf. the complexity results for perfect model semantics of nondisjunctive propositional logic prgrams in [7]).

- Disjunctive datalog queries are Σ_2^P-complete in the data and NEXPTIME^{NP}-complete in the program size under the brave version of all three semantics. In fact, there are Σ_2^P-hard resp. NEXPTIME^{NP}-hard queries defined by plain disjunctive datalog programs without $\neq$ and $\neg$.

Acknowledgment

We are indebted to Ph. Kolaitis and J.S. Schlipf for several important hints and comments.

A Appendix: Normal form

Theorem 20. *Over finite structures, every existential-universal second order sentence over any finite vocabulary σ is equivalent to an existential-universal second order sentence over σ of the form*

$$(\exists \overline{S})(\forall \overline{T} Z)[(\forall \overline{y})(Z(\overline{y})) \vee (\exists \overline{x})(\vartheta_1(\overline{x}) \vee \cdots \vee \vartheta_k(\overline{x}))] \tag{2}$$

where $\vartheta_1, \ldots, \vartheta_k$ are conjunctions of literals.

Proof. Every existential second order sentence is equivalent to an existential second order sentence of the form

$$(\exists \overline{S})(\forall \overline{x})(\exists \overline{y})\varphi(\overline{x}, \overline{y}), \tag{3}$$

cf. [15]. It is easily checked that this sentence is equivalent to

$$(\exists \overline{S})(\forall T)[(\forall \overline{x})(T(\overline{x})) \vee (\exists \overline{x}\overline{y})(\neg T(\overline{x}) \wedge \varphi(\overline{x}, \overline{y}))], \tag{4}$$

where T is a new predicate variable.

Applying the method in [15] one can easily show that every existential-universal second order sentence is equivalent to a sentence

$$(\exists \overline{S})(\forall \overline{T})(\exists \overline{x})(\forall \overline{y})\varphi(\overline{x}, \overline{y}). \tag{5}$$

Assume that a linear order $\leq$ of the set of all n-tuples is provided, where $\overline{y} = (y_1, \ldots, y_n)$ as well as associated predicates $F(\overline{y}), S(\overline{y}, \overline{y}')$, and $L(\overline{y})$ which describe the first tuple, the successor ($\overline{y}'$ is the successor of $\overline{y}$) and the last tuple in the order. Then, the universal first order quantifier in (5) can be eliminated as follows. Define the formula Ψ as

$$(\forall Z)(\exists \overline{x}\overline{y})[\, F(\overline{y}) \wedge \varphi(\overline{x}, \overline{y}) \wedge \neg Z(\overline{x}, \overline{y})\,]$$
$$\vee (\exists \overline{x}\overline{y})[\, Z(\overline{x}, \overline{y}) \wedge L(\overline{y})\,]$$
$$\vee (\exists \overline{x}\overline{y}\overline{y}')[\, Z(\overline{x}, \overline{y}) \wedge \neg Z(\overline{x}, \overline{y}') \wedge S(\overline{y}, \overline{y}') \wedge \varphi(\overline{x}, \overline{y}')\,],$$

where Z is a new predicate variable. Intuitively, the formula is false if Z consists of the union of $\{(\bar{a}, \bar{b}_1), \ldots, (\bar{a}, \bar{b}_{l_{\bar{a}}})\}$ for all $\bar{a}$, where $\bar{b}_1, \ldots, \bar{b}_{l_{\bar{a}}}$ is the maximum initial segment of the order such that $\varphi(\bar{a}, \bar{b}_i)$ is true, $1, \leq i \leq l_{\bar{a}}$, and each of those segments is strict. We claim that $\Psi \equiv (\exists \bar{x})(\forall \bar{y})\varphi(\bar{x}, \bar{y})$.

Assume that for any finite structure D, $D \not\models (\exists \bar{x})(\forall \bar{y})\varphi(\bar{x}, \bar{y})$, i.e., $D \models (\forall \bar{x})(\exists \bar{y})\neg\varphi(\bar{x}, \bar{y})$. Define $Z_0 = \{(\bar{a}, \bar{b}) : \bar{b}$ is ordered before $min(\bar{a})\}$, where $min(\bar{a})$ is the first $\bar{b}'$ such that $D \not\models \varphi(\bar{a}, \bar{b}')$; notice that $min(\bar{a})$ is well-defined. We check that $(D, Z_0) \not\models A$, where A is the first order part of Ψ. First

$$(D, Z_0) \not\models (\exists \bar{x}\bar{y})[\, F(\bar{y}) \wedge \varphi(\bar{x}, \bar{y}) \wedge \neg Z(\bar{x}, \bar{y})\,],$$

because if $(D, Z_0) \models \varphi(\bar{a}, \bar{b}) \wedge F(\bar{b})$, then by definition $(\bar{a}, \bar{b}) \in Z_0$. Second,

$$(D, Z_0) \not\models (\exists \bar{x}\bar{y})[\, Z(\bar{x}, \bar{y}) \wedge L(\bar{y})\,];$$

for, if $(D, Z_0) \models Z(\bar{a}, \bar{b})$, $\bar{b}$ is ordered by definition of Z_0 before $min(\bar{a})$, hence $(D, Z_0) \not\models L(\bar{b})$. Third,

$$(D, Z_0) \not\models (\exists \bar{x}\bar{y}\bar{y}')[\, Z(\bar{x}, \bar{y}) \wedge \neg Z(\bar{x}\bar{y}') \wedge S(\bar{y}, \bar{y}') \wedge \varphi(\bar{x}, \bar{y}')\,];$$

Assume to the contrary that $(D, Z_0) \models Z(\bar{a}, \bar{b}) \wedge \neg Z(\bar{a}, \bar{b}') \wedge S(\bar{b}, \bar{b}') \wedge \varphi(\bar{a}, \bar{b}')$ for $\bar{a}, \bar{b}$, and $\bar{b}'$. By the definition of Z_0, it follows that $\bar{b}' = min(\bar{a})$. Since $D \models \neg\varphi(\bar{a}, min(\bar{a}))$, a contradiction is reached. It follows that $(D, Z_0) \not\models A$; hence, $D \not\models \Psi$.

Now assume that $D \models (\exists \bar{x})(\forall \bar{y})\varphi(\bar{x}, \bar{y})$, i.e., $D \models (\forall \bar{y})\varphi(\bar{a}, \bar{y})$ for some $\bar{a}$. Consider any Z, and let $\bar{b}_1, \bar{b}_l$ be the first and the last tuple in the order. There are three cases.

Case 1: $(\bar{a}, \bar{b}_1) \notin Z$. Then, $(D, Z) \models F(\bar{b}_1) \wedge \varphi(\bar{a}, \bar{b}_1) \wedge \neg Z(\bar{a}, \bar{b}_1)$; hence, $(D, Z) \models A$.

Case 2: $(\bar{a}, \bar{b}_l) \in Z$. Then, $(D, Z) \models Z(\bar{a}, \bar{b}_l) \wedge L(\bar{b}_l)$; hence, $(D, Z) \models A$.

Case 3: $(\bar{a}, \bar{b}_1) \in Z$ and $(\bar{a}, \bar{b}_l) \notin Z$. Hence, there is a $\bar{b}$ such that $(\bar{a}, \bar{b}) \notin Z$ and $(\bar{a}, \bar{b}') \in Z$ for each $\bar{b}'$ that is ordered before $\bar{b}$. Let $\bar{b}'$ be the predecessor of $\bar{b}$. (Note that $\bar{b}'$ exists.) Then, $(D, Z) \models Z(\bar{a}, \bar{b}') \wedge \neg Z(\bar{a}, \bar{b}) \wedge S(\bar{b}', \bar{b}) \wedge \varphi(\bar{a}, \bar{b})$; hence, $(D, Z) \models A$. $\diamond$

Consequently, $(D, Z) \models A$. It follows that $D \models \Psi$. The claim is proved.

Thus, if F, S, and L are provided, (5) is equivalent to

$$(\exists \bar{S})(\forall \bar{T} Z)(\exists \bar{z})\mu(\bar{z}), \tag{6}$$

where $(\exists \bar{z})\mu(\bar{z})$ is the first order part of Ψ transformed into prenex normal form.

Clearly, $\leq, F, S$, and L can be characterized by a first order sentence, hence, as shown above, by a sentence

$$(\exists \bar{Q})(\forall R)[(\forall \bar{x})(R(\bar{x})) \vee (\exists \bar{u})\beta(\bar{u})], \tag{7}$$

where $\beta(\bar{x}\bar{y}) = \neg R(\bar{x}) \wedge \varphi(\bar{x}, \bar{y})$. The existential closure of the conjunction of (6) and (7) with respect to $\leq, F, S$, and L is equivalent to

$$(\exists \bar{S} \leq FSL\bar{Q})(\forall R\bar{T}) \{\, [(\forall \bar{x})(R(\bar{x})) \vee (\exists \bar{u})\beta(\bar{u})] \wedge (\exists \bar{z})\mu(\bar{z})\, \}, \tag{8}$$

which in turn is equivalent to

$$(\exists \overline{S} \leq FSL\overline{Q})(\forall R\overline{T})\left\{(\forall \overline{x})(R(\overline{x})) \vee [(\exists \overline{u})\beta(\overline{u}) \wedge (\exists \overline{z})\mu(\overline{z})]\right\}. \qquad (9)$$

Here $(\exists \overline{u})\beta(\overline{u}) \wedge (\exists \overline{z})\mu(\overline{z})$ can be rewritten to $(\exists \overline{uz})[\gamma_1(\overline{u},\overline{z}) \vee \cdots \vee \gamma_m(\overline{u},\overline{z})]$, where each γ_i is a conjunction of literals. Hence, for (5) there exists an equivalent sentence of the form of (2). The theorem follows. □

We remark that neither of the disjuncts in (2) can be eliminated; one can show that if the existential (resp. universal) formula is not present, the sentence is preserved under submodels (resp. supermodels; cf. [6] for model preservation properties). This and Theorem 20 generalizes to Σ_k second order sentences for $k \geq 2$, but fails for $k = 1$, i.e., existential second order sentences $(\exists \overline{S})\varphi(\overline{S})$.

B Appendix: Complexity upgrade

We show that Theorem 11 remains valid if $\leq_m^{LT}$-transformation is relaxed to $\leq_m^{PLT}$-transformation. The key observation is that the following lemma, from which Theorem 11 easily follows, remains valid under the same relaxation.

Lemma 21 [2], Conversion Lemma. *If $A \leq_m^{LT} B$ then $sA \leq_m^p sB$.*

Lemma 22. *If $A \leq_m^{PLT} B$ then $sA \leq_m^p sB$.*

Proof. (Sketch) This is easy to see by looking carefully at the proof of the Conversion Lemma in [2].

Assume that A is reducible in time $\log^k(n)$ to B. First note that in the proof of the Conversion Lemma, the equation $|w| \leq 2^{|C_w|}$ is derived because it is needed to establish $\log(|w|) \leq |C_w|$. (Here $|C|$ is the size of Boolean circuit C rather than the cardinality of C as a set.) We derive the following equation from it, which we will use soon:

$$\log^{2k}(|w|) \leq |C_w|^{2k}. \qquad (10)$$

In the second paragraph, a circuit is (virtually) generated. The size of this circuit is now quadratic in $\log^k(|w|)$, i.e., bounded by $c \times \log^{2k}(|w|)$.

In the third paragraph of the proof, it is explained that we need to plug in at several places C_w as sub-circuit into that circuit. Therefore, the total size of the resulting circuit C' satisfies

$$|C'| \leq c \times \log^{2k}(|w|) \times |C_w|,$$

hence by equation (10), $|C'| \leq c \times |C_w|^{2k+1}$.

Thus, the transformation from $sA = C_w$ to $sB = C'$ is still polynomial, and the result follows. □

Theorem 23. *Let C_1 and C_2 be arbitrary complexity classes such that for every $A \in C_1$, $long(A) \in C_2$. Then, for every B, if B is hard for C_2 under $\leq_m^{PLT}$-transformation, then sB is hard for C_1 under $\leq_m^p$-transformation.*

Proof. (Same as the proof of Theorem 5 in [2] using the generalization of the Conversion Lemma.) Assume that B is hard for C_2 under $\leq_m^{PLT}$-transformation, and let $A \in C_1$ be arbitrary. By hypothesis, $long(A) \in C_2$ and therefore $long(A) \leq_m^{PLT} B$. By Lemma 22, $s(long(A)) \leq_m^p sB$. Furthermore, $A \leq_m^p s(long(A))$ ([2, Lemma 4]); by transitivity, $A \leq_m^p sB$, and thus sB is $\leq_m^p$-hard for C_1. □

References

1. J. Balcázar, J. Diaz, and J. Gabarró. *Structural Complexity I.* Springer, 1988.
2. J. Balcázar, A. Lozano, and J. Torán. The Complexity of Algorithmic Problems on Succinct Instances. In R. Baeta-Yates and U. Manber, editors, *Computer Science*, pages 351–377. Plenum Press, New York, 1992.
3. S. Ceri, G. Gottlob, and L. Tanca. *Logical Programming and Databases.* Springer, 1990.
4. A. Chandra and D. Harel. Computable Queries for Relational Databases. *Journal of Computer and System Sciences*, 21:156–178, 1980.
5. A. Chandra and D. Harel. Horn Clause Queries and Generalizations. *Journal of Logic Programming*, 2:1–15, 1985.
6. C. C. Chang and H. J. Keisler. *Model Theory.* North-Holland, 2nd edition, 1973.
7. T. Eiter and G. Gottlob. Complexity Aspects of Various Semantics for Disjunctive Databases. In *Proceedings of the Twelth ACM SIGACT SIGMOD-SIGART Symposium on Principles of Database Systems (PODS-93)*, pages 158–167, 1993.
8. T. Eiter, G. Gottlob, and H. Mannila. Adding Disjunction to Datalog. Manuscript available from the authors, November 1993.
9. R. Fagin. Generalized First-Order Spectra and Polynomial-Time Recognizable Sets. In R. M. Karp, editor, *Complexity of Computation*, pages 43–74. AMS, 1974.
10. J. Fernández and J. Minker. Semantics of Disjunctive Deductive Databases. In *Proceedings of the International Conference on Database Theory (ICDT-92)*, pages 21–50, Berlin, October 1992.
11. H. Galperin and A. Wigderson. Succinct Representations of Graphs. *Information and Computation*, 56:183–198, 1983.
12. M. Garey and D. S. Johnson. *Computers and Intractability – A Guide to the Theory of NP-Completeness.* W. H. Freeman, New York, 1979.
13. Y. Gurevich. Logic and the Challenge of Computer Science. In E. Börger, editor, *Trends in Theoretical Computer Science*, chapter 1. Computer Science Press, 1988.
14. D. S. Johnson. A Catalog of Complexity Classes. volume A of *Handbook of Theoretical Computer Science*, chapter 2. Elsevier Science Publishers B.V. (North-Holland), 1990.
15. P. Kolaitis and C. H. Papadimitriou. Why Not Negation By Fixpoint ? *Journal of Computer and System Sciences*, 43:125–144, 1991.
16. J. Lobo, J. Minker, and A. Rajasekar. *Foundations of Disjunctive Logic Programming.* MIT Press, Cambridge, MA, 1992.
17. A. Lozano and J. Balcázar. The Complexity of Graph Problems for Succinctly Represented Graphs. In *Proceedings of the 15th Intl. Workshop on Graph-Theoretic Concepts in Computer Science*, number 411 in LNCS, pages 277–286, Castle Rolduc, The Netherlands 1989.

18. J. Lynch. Complexity Classes and Theories of Finite Models. *Mathematical Systems Theory*, 15:127–144, 1982.

19. J. Makowsky. Model Theory and Computer Science: An Appetizer. In S. Abramsky, D. Gabbay, and T. Maibaum, editors, *Handbook of Logic in Computer Science*, volume I, chapter 6. Oxford University Press, 1992.

20. W. Marek, A. Nerode, and J. Remmel. A Theory of Nonmonotonic Rule Systems II. *Annals of Mathematics and Artificial Intelligence*, 5:229–264, 1992.

21. W. Marek, A. Nerode, and J. Remmel. How Complicated is the Set of Stable Models of a Recursive Logic Program? *Annals of Pure and Applied Logic*, 56:119, 1992.

22. W. Marek and M. Truszczyński. Autoepistemic Logic. *Journal of the ACM*, 38(3):588–619, 1991.

23. W. Marek and M. Truszczyński. Computing Intersection of Autoepistemic Expansions. In *Proceedings of the 1st Intl. Workshop on Logic Programming and Nonmonotonic Reasoning*, pages 37–50, Washington DC, July 1991. MIT Press.

24. J. McCarthy. Circumscription – A Form of Non-Monotonic Reasoning. *Artificial Intelligence*, 13:27–39, 1980.

25. J. Minker. On Indefinite Data Bases and the Closed World Assumption. In *Proceedings of the 6th Conference on Automated Deduction (CADE)*, pages 292–308, 1982.

26. C. Papadimitriou and M. Yannakakis. A Note on Succinct Representations of Graphs. *Information and Computation*, 71:181–185, 1985.

27. T. Przymusinski. On the Declarative and Procedural Semantics of Stratified Deductive Databases. In J. Minker, editor, *Foundations of Deductive Databases and Logic Programming*, pages 193–216. Morgan Kaufman, Washington DC, 1988.

28. T. Przymusinski. Stable Semantics for Disjunctive Programs. *New Generation Computing*, 9:401–424, 1991.

29. D. Saccà. Multiple Stable Models are Needed to Solve Unique Solution Problems. In *Informal Proceedings of the Second Compulog Net Meeting on Knowledge Bases (CNKBS-93)*, Athens, April 1993.

30. J. Schlipf. The Expressive Powers of Logic Programming Semantics. Technical Report CIS-TR-90-3, Computer Science Department, University of Cincinnati, 1990. Submitted. A preliminary version of this paper appeared in: Proceedings PODS-90, pages 196–204.

31. J. Schlipf. A Survey of Complexity and Undecidability Results in Logic Programming. In H. Blair, W. Marek, A. Nerode, and J. Remmel, editors, *Informal Proceedings of the Workshop on Structural Complexity and Recursion-Theoretic Methods in Logic Programming*, pages 93–102, Washington DC, November 1992. Cornell University, Mathematical Sciences Institute.

32. I. Stewart. Complete Problems Involving Boolean Labelled Structures and Projection Transactions. *Journal of Logic and Computation*, 1(6):861–882, 1991.

33. L. J. Stockmeyer. The Polynomial-Time Hierarchy. *Theoretical Computer Science*, 3:1–22, 1977.

34. J. D. Ullman. *Principles of Database and Knowledge Base Systems*, volume 1. Computer Science Press, 1988.

35. M. Vardi. Complexity of relational query languages. In *Proceedings of the 14th ACM SIGACT Symposium on Theory of Computing (STOC-82)*, pages 137–146, 1982.

36. A. Yahya and L. Henschen. Deduction in Non-Horn Databases. *Journal of Automated Reasoning*, 1(2):141–160, 1985.

Managing Qualitative Temporal Information: Expressiveness vs. Complexity*

Bernhard Nebel[1,2] and Hans-Jürgen Bürckert[2]

[1] University of Ulm, Department of Computer Science
James-Franck-Ring, D-89081 Ulm, Germany
nebel@informatik.uni-ulm.de
[2] German Research Center for Artificial Intelligence (DFKI)
Stuhlsatzenhausweg 3, D-66123 Saarbrücken, Germany
hjb@dfki.uni-sb.de

Abstract. For natural language understanding and generation, plan generation and recognition, and knowledge representation, it is necessary to represent qualitiave temporal information and to reason with it. Allen's interval calculus provides an appropriate framework for such a task. We introduce a new subclass of Allen's interval algebra we call "ORD-Horn subclass," which is a strict superset of the "pointisable subclass." We prove that reasoning in the ORD-Horn subclass is a polynomial-time problem and show that the path-consistency method is sufficient for deciding satisfiability. Further, using an extensive machine-generated case analysis, we show that the ORD-Horn subclass is a maximal tractable subclass of the full algebra (assuming P≠NP). In fact, it is the unique greatest tractable subclass amongst the subclasses that contain all basic relations.

1 Introduction

Temporal information is often conveyed qualitatively by specifying the relative positions of time intervals such as "...point to the figure while explaining the performance of the system ..." Further, for natural language understanding [3, 26], general planning [4, 6], presentation planning in a multi-media context [7], and knowledge representation [33], the representation of qualitative temporal relations and reasoning about them is essential. Allen [2] introduces an algebra of binary relations on intervals for representing qualitative temporal information and addresses the problem of reasoning about such information. Since the reasoning problems are NP-hard for the full algebra [31], it is very unlikely that other polynomial-time algorithms will be found that solve this problem in general. Subsequent research has concentrated on designing more efficient reasoning algorithms, on identifying tractable special cases, and on isolating sources of computational complexity [8, 9, 10, 11, 12, 13, 17, 18, 24, 25, 27, 28, 29, 30, 31, 32].

* This work was supported by the German Ministry for Research and Technology (BMFT) under grant ITW 8901 8 as part of the WIP project and under grant ITW 9201 as part of the TACOS project.

However, it is by no means clear whether the tractable cases that have been identified are maximal and whether the sources of computational complexity found are the only ones.

We extend these previous results in three ways. Firstly, we present a new tractable subclass of Allen's interval algebra, which we call *ORD-Horn subclass*. This subclass is considerably larger than all other known tractable subclasses (it contains 10% of the full algebra) and strictly contains the *pointisable subclass* [17, 28]. Secondly, we show that the *path-consistency method* is sufficient for deciding satisfiability in this subclass. Thirdly, using an extensive machine-generated case analysis, we show that this subclass is a maximal subclass such that satisfiability is tractable (assuming P≠NP).

From a practical point of view, these results imply that the path-consistency method has a much larger range of applicability than previously believed, provided we are mainly interested in satisfiability. Further, our results can be used to design backtracking algorithms for the full algebra that are more efficient than those based on other tractable subclasses.

Some words on methodology may be in order at this point. While proving tractability and the applicability of the path-consistency method is a (more or less) straightforward task, showing *maximality* of a subclass w.r.t. the stated properties requires an extensive case analysis involving a couple of thousand cases, which can only be done by a computer. This case analysis leads to two interesting cases, for which NP-completeness proofs are provided. However, the case analysis itself cannot be reproduced in a research paper or verified manually, either. In order to allow for the verification of our results, we therefore include the abstract form of the programs we used to perform the machine-assisted case analysis.[3]

The paper is structured as follows. Section 2 contains terminology and definitions used in the remainder of the paper. Section 3 introduces the ORD-Horn subclass, which is shown to be tractable. Based on this result, we show in Section 4 that the path-consistency method is sufficient for deciding satisfiability in this subclass. In Section 5, we derive some results on the computational properties of subalgebras. Using these results and an extensive machine-generated case analysis, we show in Section 6 that the ORD-Horn subclass is a maximal tractable subclass of the full algebra and the unique greatest tractable subclass that contains all basic relations.

2 Reasoning about Interval Relations using Allen's Interval Algebra

Allen's [2] approach to reasoning about time is based on the notion of *time intervals* and *binary relations* on them. A **time interval** X is an ordered pair

---

[3] The programs we used and an enumeration of the ORD-Horn subclass can be obtained from the authors or by anonymous ftp from duck.dfki.uni-sb.de as /pub/papers/RR-93-11.programs.tar.Z.

(X^-, X^+) such that $X^- < X^+$, where X^- and X^+ are interpreted as points on the real line.[4] So, if we talk about **interval interpretations** or I-**interpretations** in the following, we mean mappings of time intervals to pairs of distinct real numbers such that the beginning of an interval is strictly before the end of the interval.

Given two interpreted time intervals, their relative positions can be described by *exactly one* of the elements of the set **B** of thirteen **basic interval relations** (denoted by B in the following), where each basic relation can be defined in terms of its **endpoint relations** (see Table 1). An atomic formula of the form XBY, where X and Y are intervals and $B \in$ **B**, is said to be **satisfied** by an I-interpretation iff the interpretation of the intervals satisfies the endpoint relations specified in Table 1.

Basic Interval Relation	Sym-bol	Pictorial Example	Endpoint Relations
X before Y	$\prec$	xxx	$X^- < Y^-, X^- < Y^+,$
Y after X	$\succ$	yyy	$X^+ < Y^-, X^+ < Y^+$
X meets Y	m	xxxx	$X^- < Y^-, X^- < Y^+,$
Y met-by X	$\overset{\smile}{m}$	yyyy	$X^+ = Y^-, X^+ < Y^+$
X overlaps Y	o	xxxx	$X^- < Y^-, X^- < Y^+,$
Y overlapped-by X	$\overset{\smile}{o}$	yyyy	$X^+ > Y^-, X^+ < Y^+$
X during Y	d	xxx	$X^- > Y^-, X^- < Y^+,$
Y includes X	$\overset{\smile}{d}$	yyyyyyy	$X^+ > Y^-, X^+ < Y^+$
X starts Y	s	xxx	$X^- = Y^-, X^- < Y^+,$
Y started-by X	$\overset{\smile}{s}$	yyyyyyy	$X^+ > Y^-, X^+ < Y^+$
X finishes Y	f	xxx	$X^- > Y^-, X^- < Y^+,$
Y finished-by X	$\overset{\smile}{f}$	yyyyyyy	$X^+ > Y^-, X^+ = Y^+$
X equals Y	$\equiv$	xxxx	$X^- = Y^-, X^- < Y^+,$
		yyyy	$X^+ > Y^-, X^+ = Y^+$

Table 1. The set **B** of the thirteen basic relations. The endpoint relations $X^- < X^+$ and $Y^- < Y^+$ that are valid for all relations have been omitted.

In order to express indefinite information, unions of the basic interval relations are used, which are written as sets of basic relations leading to 2^{13} binary **interval relations** (denoted by R, S, T)—including the **null relation** $\emptyset$ (also denoted by $\perp$) and the **universal relation B** (also denoted by $\top$). The set of all binary interval relations $2^{\mathbf{B}}$ is denoted by $\mathcal{A}$.

An atomic formula of the form $X \{B_1, \ldots, B_n\} Y$ (denoted by ϕ) is called **interval formula**. Such a formula is satisfied by an I-interpretation $\mathfrak{S}$ iff $X B_i Y$ is satisfied by $\mathfrak{S}$ for some i, $1 \leq i \leq n$. Finite sets of interval formulas are denoted

---

[4] Other underlying models of the time line are also possible, e.g., the rationals [5, 16]. For our purposes these distinctions are not significant, however.

by Θ. Such a set Θ is called *I*-**satisfiable** iff there exists an *I*-interpretation $\Im$ that satisfies every formula of Θ. Further, such a satisfying *I*-interpretation $\Im$ is called *I*-**model** of Θ. If an interval formula ϕ is satisfied by every *I*-model of a set of interval formulas Θ, we say that ϕ is **logically implied** by Θ, written $\Theta \models_I \phi$.

Fundamental **reasoning problems** in this framework include [12, 17, 18, 29, 31]: Given a set of interval formulas Θ,

1. decide whether there exists an *I*-model of Θ (ISAT),
2. determine for each pair of intervals X, Y the *strongest implied relation* between them (ISI), i.e., the smallest set R such that $\Theta \models_I X R Y$.

In the following, we often consider **restricted reasoning problems** where the relations used in interval formulas in Θ are only from a subclass S of all interval relations. In this case we say that Θ **is a set of formulas over** S, and we use a parameter in the problem description to denote the subclass considered, e.g., ISAT(S). As is well-known, ISAT and ISI are equivalent with respect to polynomial Turing-reductions [31] and this equivalence also extends to the restricted problems ISAT(S) and ISI(S), provided S contains all basic relations.

Proposition 1. *ISAT(S) and ISI(S) are equivalent under polynomial Turing-reductions, provided S contains all basic relations.*[5]

The most prominent method to solve these problems (approximately for all interval relations or exactly for subclasses) is *constraint propagation* [2, 17, 18, 24, 28, 30, 31] using a slightly simplified form of the *path-consistency algorithm* [20, 22]. In the following, we briefly characterize this method without going into details, though. In order to do so, we first have to introduce Allen's interval algebra.

Allen's interval algebra [2] consists of the set $\mathcal{A} = 2^{\mathbf{B}}$ of all binary interval relations and the operations unary **converse** (denoted by $\smile$), binary **intersection** (denoted by $\cap$), and binary **composition** (denoted by $\circ$), which are defined as follows:[6]

$$\forall X, Y: \qquad X R^\smile Y \leftrightarrow Y R X$$
$$\forall X, Y: X (R \cap S) Y \leftrightarrow X R Y \wedge X S Y$$
$$\forall X, Y: X (R \circ S) Y \leftrightarrow \exists Z: (X R Z \wedge Z S Y).$$

Assume an operator Γ that maps finite sets of interval formulas to finite sets

---

[5] Proofs are given in the long paper [23], which can be obtained by anonymous ftp from `duck.dfki.uni-sb.de` as `/pub/papers/RR-93-11.dvi.Z` or `/pub/papers/RR-93-11.ps.Z`.

[6] Note that we obtain a relation algebra if we add *complement* and *union* as operations [17, 18]. For our purposes, this is irrelevant, however.

of interval formulas in the following way:

$$\Gamma(\Theta) = \Theta \cup$$
$$\{X \top Y \mid X, Y \text{ appear in } \Theta\} \cup$$
$$\{X R Y \mid (Y\ R^{\smile}\ X) \in \Theta\} \cup$$
$$\{X\ (R \cap S)\ Y \mid (XRY), (XSY) \in \Theta\} \cup$$
$$\{X\ (R \circ S)\ Y \mid (XRZ), (ZSY) \in \Theta\}.$$

Since there are only finitely many different interval formulas for a finite set of intervals and Γ is monotone, it follows that for each Θ there exists a natural number n such that $\Gamma^n(\Theta) = \Gamma^{n+1}(\Theta)$. $\Gamma^n(\Theta)$ is called the **closure** of Θ, written $\overline{\Theta}$. Considering the formulas of the form $(X\ R_i Y) \in \overline{\Theta}$ for given X, Y, it is evident that the R_i's are closed under intersection, and hence there exists $(XSY) \in \overline{\Theta}$ such that S is the *strongest relation* amongst the R_i's, i.e., $S \subseteq R_i$, for every i. The subset of a closure $\overline{\Theta}$ containing for each pair of intervals only the strongest relations is called the **reduced closure** of Θ and is denoted by $\widehat{\Theta}$.

As can easily be shown, every reduced closure of a set Θ is **path consistent** [20], which means that for every three intervals X, Y, Z and for every interpretation $\Im$ that satisfies $(XRY) \in \widehat{\Theta}$, there exists an interpretation $\Im'$ that agrees with $\Im$ on X and Y and in addition satisfies $(XSZ), (ZS'Y) \in \widehat{\Theta}$. Under the assumption that $(XRY) \in \Theta$ implies $(Y\ R^{\smile}\ X) \in \Theta$, it is also easy to show that path consistency of Θ implies that $\Theta = \widehat{\Theta}$. For this reason, we will use the term **path-consistent set** as a synonym for a set that is the reduced closure of itself. Finally, computing $\widehat{\Theta}$ is polynomial in the size of Θ [21, 22].

3 The ORD-Horn Subclass

Previous results on the tractability of $\mathrm{ISAT}(\mathcal{S})$ (and hence $\mathrm{ISI}(\mathcal{S})$) for some subclass $\mathcal{S} \subseteq \mathcal{A}$ made use of the *expressibility* of interval formulas over $\mathcal{S}$ as certain logical formulas involving endpoint relations.

As usual, by a **clause** we mean a disjunction of literals, where a **literal** in turn is an atomic formula or a negated atomic formula. As **atomic formulas** we allow $a \leq b$ and $a = b$, where a and b denote endpoints of intervals. The negation of $a = b$ is also written as $a \neq b$. Finite sets of such clause will be denoted by Ω. In the following, we consider a slightly restricted form of clauses, which we call **ORD clauses**. These clauses do not contain negations of atoms of the form $(a \leq b)$, i.e., they only contain literals of the form:

$$a = b, \ a \leq b, \ a \neq b.$$

The **ORD-clause form** of an interval formula ϕ, written $\pi(\phi)$, is the set of ORD clauses over endpoint relations that is equivalent to ϕ, i.e., every interval model of ϕ can be transformed into a model of the ORD-clause form over the reals and *vice versa* using the obvious transformation. Consider, for instance,

$\pi(X \{d, o, s\} Y)$:

$$\left\{ \begin{aligned} &(X^- \leq X^+), (X^- \neq X^+), (Y^- \leq Y^+), (Y^- \neq Y^+), \\ &(X^- \leq Y^+), (X^- \neq Y^+), (Y^- \leq X^+), (X^+ \neq Y^-), \\ &(X^+ \leq Y^+), (X^+ \neq Y^+) \right\}. \end{aligned}$$

The function $\pi(\cdot)$ is extended to finite sets of interval formulas in the obvious way, i.e., for identical intervals in Θ, identical endpoints are used in $\pi(\Theta)$. Similarly to the notions of I-satisfiability, we define R-**satisfiability** of Ω to be the satisfiability of Ω over the real numbers.

Proposition 2. Θ *is I-satisfiable iff $\pi(\Theta)$ is R-satisfiable.*

Not all relations permit a ORD-clause form that is as concise as the the one shown above, which contains only *unit clauses*. However, in particular those relations that allow for such a clause form have interesting computational properties. For instance, the **continuous endpoint subclass** (which is denoted by $\mathcal{C}$) can be defined as the subclass of interval relations that (1) permit a clause form that contains only unit clauses, and (2) for each unit clause $a \neq b$, the clause form contains also a unit clause of the form $a \leq b$ or $b \leq a$.

As demonstrated above, the relation $\{d, o, s\}$ is a member of the continuous endpoint subclass. This subclass has the favorable property that the path-consistency method solves ISI($\mathcal{C}$) [28, 30, 32]. A slight generalization of the continuous endpoint subclass is the **pointisable subclass** (denoted by $\mathcal{P}$) that is defined in the same way as $\mathcal{C}$, but without condition (2). Path-consistency is not sufficient for solving ISI($\mathcal{P}$) [28] but still sufficient for deciding satisfiability [17, 31].

We generalize this approach by being more liberal concerning the clause form. We consider the subclass of Allen's interval algebra such that the relations permit an ORD-clause form containing only clauses with *at most one positive literal*, which we call **ORD-Horn clauses**. The subclass defined in this way is called **ORD-Horn subclass**, and we use the symbol $\mathcal{H}$ to refer to it. The relation $\{o, s, f^\smile\}$ is, for instance, an element of $\mathcal{H}$ because $\pi(X \{o, s, f^\smile\} Y)$ can be expressed as follows:

$$\left\{ \begin{aligned} &(X^- \leq X^+), (X^- \neq X^+), (Y^- \leq Y^+), (Y^- \neq Y^+), \\ &(X^- \leq Y^-), (X^- \leq Y^+), (X^- \neq Y^+), \\ &(Y^- \leq X^+), (X^+ \neq Y^-), (X^+ \leq Y^+), \\ &(X^- \neq Y^- \vee X^+ \neq Y^+) \right\}. \end{aligned}$$

By definition, the ORD-Horn subclass contains the pointisable subclass. Further, by the above example, this inclusion is strict.

Consider now the theory ORD that axiomatizes "=" as an equivalence relation and "$\leq$" as a partial ordering over the equivalence classes:

$$\forall x,y: \ x \leq y \wedge y \leq z \rightarrow x \leq z \ \text{(Transitivity)}$$
$$\forall x: \quad x \leq x \qquad\qquad\qquad \text{(Reflexivity)}$$
$$\forall x,y: \ x \leq y \wedge y \leq x \rightarrow x = y \ \text{(Antisymmetry)}$$
$$\forall x,y: \ x = y \qquad\quad \rightarrow x \leq y$$
$$\forall x,y: \ x = y \qquad\quad \rightarrow y \leq x.$$

Although this theory is much weaker, and hence allows for more models than the intended models of ORD clauses, R-satisfiability of a finite set Ω of ORD clauses is nevertheless equivalent to the satisfiability of $\Omega \cup ORD$ over arbitrary interpretations.

Proposition 3. *A finite set of ORD clauses Ω is R-satisfiable iff $\Omega \cup ORD$ is satisfiable.*

Proof Sketch. One direction is trivial. For the other direction note that every partially ordered set can be extended to a linearly ordered set, which in turn can be embedded in the reals. Since in every such linear extension of a partial ordering all formulas of the form $(a = b), (a \neq b)$, and $(a \leq b)$ from Ω are still satisfied, a model of $\Omega \cup ORD$ can be transformed into an R-model of Ω. ■

Note that ORD is a *Horn theory*, i.e., a theory containing only Horn clauses. Since the ORD-clause form of interval formulas over $\mathcal{H}$ is also Horn, tractability of ISAT($\mathcal{H}$) would follow, provided we could replace ORD by a propositional Horn theory. In order to decide satisfiability of a set of ORD clauses Ω in ORD, however, we can restrict ourselves to Herbrand interpretations, i.e, interpretations that have only the endpoints of all intervals mentioned in Ω as objects. In the following, ORD_Ω shall denote the axioms of ORD instantiated to all endpoints mentioned in Ω. As a specialization of the Herbrand theorem, we obtain the next proposition.

Proposition 4. $\Omega \cup ORD$ *is satisfiable iff* $\Omega \cup ORD_\Omega$ *is satisfiable.*

From that, polynomiality of ISAT($\mathcal{H}$) is immediate.

Theorem 5. ISAT($\mathcal{H}$) *is polynomial.*

4 The Applicability of Path-Consistency

Enumerating the ORD-Horn subclass reveals that there are 868 relations (including the null relation $\perp$) in Allen's interval algebra that can be expressed using ORD-Horn clauses. Since the full algebra contains $2^{13} = 8192$ relations, $\mathcal{H}$ covers more than 10% of the full algebra. Comparing this with the continuous endpoint subclass $\mathcal{C}$, which contains 83 relations, and the pointisable subclass

$\mathcal{P}$, which contains 188 relations,[7] having shown tractability for $\mathcal{H}$ is a clear improvement over previous results. However, there remains the question of whether the "traditional" method of reasoning in Allen's interval algebra, i.e., constraint propagation, gives reasonable results. As it turns out, this is indeed the case.

Theorem 6. *Let $\widehat{\Theta}$ be a path-consistent set of interval formulas over $\mathcal{H}$. Then $\widehat{\Theta}$ is I-satisfiable iff $(X\bot Y) \notin \widehat{\Theta}$.*

Proof Sketch. A case analysis over the possible non-unit clauses in $\pi(\widehat{\Theta}) \cup ORD_{\pi(\widehat{\Theta})}$ reveals that no new units can be derived by *positive unit resolution*, if the ORD-clause form of the interval formulas satisfies the requirement that it contains all implied atoms and the clauses are minimal. By refutation completeness of positive unit resolution [14], the claim follows. ∎

The only remaining part we have to show is that transforming Θ over $\mathcal{H}$ into its equivalent path-consistent form $\widehat{\Theta}$ does not result in a set that contains relations not in $\mathcal{H}$. In order to show this we prove that $\mathcal{H}$ is closed under converse, intersection, and composition, i.e., $\mathcal{H}$ (together with these operations) defines a **subalgebra** of Allen's interval algebra.

Theorem 7. *$\mathcal{H}$ is closed under converse, intersection, and composition.*

Proof Sketch. The main problem is to show that the composition of two relations has an ORD-Horn form. We show that by proving that any minimal clause C implied by $\pi(\{XRY, YSZ\})$ is either ORD-Horn or there exists a set of ORD-Horn clauses that are implied by $\pi(\{XRY, YSZ\})$ and imply C. ∎

From that it follows straightforwardly that ISAT($\mathcal{H}$) is decided by the path-consistency method.

Theorem 8. *If Θ is a set over $\mathcal{H}$, then Θ is satisfiable iff $(X\bot Y) \notin \widehat{\Theta}$ for all intervals X, Y.*

5 Subalgebras and Their Computational Properties

While the introduction of the algebraic structure on the set of expressible interval relations may have seemed to be motivated only by the particular approximation algorithm employed, this structure is also useful when we explore the computational properties of restricted problems. For any arbitrary subset $S \subseteq \mathcal{A}$, $\overline{S}$ shall denote the **closure** of S under converse, intersection, and composition. In other words, $\overline{S}$ is the carrier of the **least subalgebra generated by** S.

Theorem 9. *ISAT($\overline{S}$) can be polynomially transformed to ISAT(S).*

---

[7] An enumeration of $\mathcal{C}$ and $\mathcal{P}$ is given by van Beek and Cohen [30].

Proof Sketch. The main things to note are that (1) if $R = S^\smile$ and $S \in \mathcal{S}$ then the interval formula (XRY) in Θ can be replaced by (YSX); (2) if $R = S \cap T$ and $S, T \in \mathcal{S}$, then (XRY) in Θ can be replaced by the two formulas $(XSY), (XTY)$; (3) if $R = S \circ T$ and $S, T \in \mathcal{S}$, then (XRY) in Θ can be replaced by $(XSZ), (ZTY)$, where Z is a fresh interval. Clearly, if Θ is I-satisfiable then the modified set is and *vice versa*. ∎

In other words, once we have proven that satisfiability is polynomial for some set $\mathcal{S} \subseteq \mathcal{A}$, this result extends to the least subalgebra generated by $\mathcal{S}$. Conversely, NP-hardness for a subalgebra is "inherited" by all subsets that generate this subalgebra.

Corollary 10. ISAT$(\mathcal{S})$ *is polynomial iff* ISAT$(\overline{\mathcal{S}})$ *is polynomial and* ISAT$(\mathcal{S})$ *is NP-complete iff* ISAT$(\overline{\mathcal{S}})$ *is NP-complete.*

It should be noted that these results do not hold in their full generality if the interval satisfiability problem is defined somewhat differently. Often, this problem is defined over "binary constraint networks" [12, 13, 24, 30, 32]. Such networks correspond to what we will call **normalized sets** of interval formulas, where for each pair of intervals X, Y we have *exactly one* interval formula. The corresponding decision problem for the satisfiability of normalized sets of interval formulas is denoted by ISAT$_N(\mathcal{S})$. Provided the subclass $\mathcal{S}$ of Allen's interval algebra contains $\top$ and $\{\equiv\}$, which is usually true, then a slight modification of the reduction used in the proof of Theorem 9 leads to identical results.

Theorem 11. ISAT$_N(\overline{\mathcal{S}})$ *can be polynomially transformed to* ISAT$_N(\mathcal{S})$, *provided* $\{\top, \{\equiv\}\} \subseteq \mathcal{S}$.

Proof Sketch. The reduction for converses and composition can be done as in the proof of Theorem 9. Interval formulas XRY that involve a relation R that can only be expressed as an intersection $(S \cap T)$ are transformed into sets of formulas of the following form $\{(XSY), (X\{\equiv\}Z), (ZTY)\}$, where Z is a fresh interval, which leads to a set of interval formulas that is equivalent to the original set with respect to I-satisfiability. ∎

However, if $\top \notin \mathcal{S}$ or $\{\equiv\} \notin \mathcal{S}$, the reduction does not apply any longer. In such a case, polynomiality of a set does not automatically extend to the least subalgebra generated by this set. In fact, Golumbic and Shamir [12, 13] show that for $\mathcal{S}_0 = \left\{ \{\prec\}, \{\succ\}, \{\prec, \succ\}, \mathbf{B} - \{\prec, \succ\} \right\}$ the problem ISAT$_N(\mathcal{S}_0)$ is polynomial, while ISAT$_N(\mathcal{S}_0 \cup \{\top\})$ is NP-complete, despite the fact that $\mathcal{S}_0 \cup \{\top\} \subseteq \overline{\mathcal{S}_0}$.

We believe that for the applications mentioned in the Introduction the definition of the interval satisfiability problem over arbitrary sets of interval formulas is more appropriate than over normalized sets because it allows leaving some relations between intervals unspecified and permits incremental refinements of constraints between intervals (by adding interval formulas to an already existing set). However, the problem definition of ISAT$_N$ is certainly worthwhile in cases where the problem solving process is non-incremental and constraints between all intervals are known.

6   The Borderline between Tractable and NP-complete Subclasses

Having identified the tractable fragment $\mathcal{H}$ that contains the previously identified tractable fragment $\mathcal{P}$ and that is considerably larger than $\mathcal{P}$ is satisfying in itself. However, such a result also raises the question for the the boundary between polynomiality and NP-completeness in Allen's interval algebra.

Although we have narrowed down the space of possible candidates in the previous section from arbitrary subsets of $\mathcal{A}$ to subalgebras, it still takes some effort to prove that a given fragment $\mathcal{S}$ is a *maximal* tractable subclass of Allen's interval algebra. Firstly, one has to show that $\mathcal{S} = \overline{\mathcal{S}}$. For the ORD-Horn subclass, this has been done in Theorem 7. Secondly, one has to show that ISAT$(\mathcal{T})$ is NP-complete for all *minimal* subalgebras $\mathcal{T}$ that strictly contain $\mathcal{S}$. This, however, means that these subalgebras have to be identified. Certainly, such a case analysis cannot be done manually. In fact, we used a program to identify the minimal subalgebras strictly containing $\mathcal{H}$. An analysis of the clause form of the relations appearing in these subalgebras leads us to the formulation of the following machine-verifiable lemma.

Lemma 12. *Let $\mathcal{S} \subseteq \mathcal{A}$ be any set of interval relations that strictly contains $\mathcal{H}$. Then $\{d, d^\smile, o^\smile, s^\smile, f\}$ or $\{d^\smile, o, o^\smile, s^\smile, f^\smile\}$ is an element of $\overline{\mathcal{S}}$.*

For reasons of simplicity, we will not use the ORD clause form in the following, but a clause form that also contains literals over the relations $\geq, <, >$. Then the clause form for the relations mentioned in the lemma can be given as follows:

$$\pi(X \{d, d^\smile, o^\smile, s^\smile, f\} Y) = \left\{ \begin{matrix} (X^- < X^+),\ (Y^- < Y^+), \\ (X^- < Y^+),\ (X^+ > Y^-), \\ \big((X^- > Y^-) \vee (X^+ > Y^+)\big) \end{matrix} \right\},$$

$$\pi(X \{d^\smile, o, o^\smile, s^\smile, f^\smile\} Y) = \left\{ \begin{matrix} (X^- < X^+),\ (Y^- < Y^+), \\ (X^- < Y^+),\ (X^+ > Y^-), \\ \big((X^- < Y^-) \vee (X^+ > Y^+)\big) \end{matrix} \right\}.$$

We will show that each of these relations together with the two relations $\{\prec, d^\smile, o, m, f^\smile\}$ and $\{\prec, d, o, m, s\}$, which are elements of $\mathcal{C}$, are enough for making the interval satisfiability problem NP-complete. The clause form of these relations looks as follows:

$$\pi(X \{\prec, d^\smile, o, m, f^\smile\} Y) = \left\{ \begin{matrix} (X^- < X^+),\ (Y^- < Y^+), \\ (X^- < Y^-),\ (X^- < Y^+) \end{matrix} \right\}$$

$$\pi(X \{\prec, d, o, m, s\} Y) = \left\{ \begin{matrix} (X^- < X^+),\ (Y^- < Y^+), \\ (X^+ < Y^+),\ (X^- < Y^+) \end{matrix} \right\}$$

Lemma 13. ISAT($\mathcal{S}$) *is NP-complete if*

1. $\mathcal{N}_1 = \Big\{ \{\prec, d^\smile, o, m, f^\smile\}, \{\prec, d, o, m, s\}, \{d, d^\smile, o^\smile, s^\smile, f\} \Big\} \subseteq \mathcal{S}$, *or*

2. $\mathcal{N}_2 = \Big\{ \{\prec, d^\smile, o, m, f^\smile\}, \{\prec, d, o, m, s\}, \{d^\smile, o, o^\smile, s^\smile, f^\smile\} \Big\} \subseteq \mathcal{S}$.

Proof Sketch. Since ISAT($\mathcal{A}$) $\in$ NP, membership in NP follows.

For the NP-hardness part we will show that 3SAT can be polynomially transformed to ISAT($\mathcal{N}_k$). We will first prove the claim for $\mathcal{N}_1$. Let $D = \{C_i\}$ be a set of clauses, where $C_i = l_{i,1} \vee l_{i,2} \vee l_{i,3}$ and the $l_{i,j}$'s are literal occurrences. We will construct a set of interval formulas Θ over $\mathcal{N}_1$ such that Θ is I-satisfiable iff D is satisfiable.

For each literal occurrence $l_{i,j}$ a pair of intervals $X_{i,j}$ and $Y_{i,j}$ is introduced, and the following first group of interval formulas is put into Θ:

$$(X_{i,j} \{d, d^\smile, o^\smile, s^\smile, f\} Y_{i,j}).$$

This implies that $\pi(\Theta)$ contains among other things the following clauses $(X_{i,j}^- > Y_{i,j}^- \vee X_{i,j}^+ > Y_{i,j}^+)$.

Additionally, we add a second group of formulas for each clause C_i:

$$(X_{i,2} \{\prec, d^\smile, o, m, f^\smile\} Y_{i,1}),$$
$$(X_{i,3} \{\prec, d^\smile, o, m, f^\smile\} Y_{i,2}),$$
$$(X_{i,1} \{\prec, d^\smile, o, m, f^\smile\} Y_{i,3}),$$

which leads to the inclusion of the clauses $(Y_{i,1}^- > X_{i,2}^-)$, $(Y_{i,2}^- > X_{i,3}^-)$, $(Y_{i,3}^- > X_{i,1}^-)$ in $\pi(\Theta)$.

This construction leads to the situation that there is no model of Θ that satisfies for given i all disjuncts of the form $(X_{i,j}^- > Y_{i,j}^-)$ in the clause form of $\pi(X_{i,j}\{d, d^\smile, o^\smile, s^\smile, f\}Y_{i,j})$. If the jth disjunct $(X_{i,j}^- > Y_{i,j}^-)$ is unsatisfied in an I-model of Θ, we will interpret this as the satisfaction of the literal occurrence $l_{i,j}$ in C_i of D.

In order to guarantee that if a literal occurrence $l_{i,j}$ is interpreted as satisfied, then all complementary literal occurrences in D are interpreted as unsatisfied, the following third group of interval formulas for complementary literal occurrences $l_{i,j}$ and $l_{g,h}$ are added to Θ:

$$(X_{g,h} \{\prec, d, o, m, s\} Y_{i,j}), (X_{i,j} \{\prec, d, o, m, s\} Y_{g,h}),$$

which leads to the inclusion of $(Y_{i,j}^+ > X_{g,h}^+)$, $(Y_{g,h}^+ > X_{i,j}^+)$. This construction guarantees that Θ is I-satisfiable iff D is satisfiable.

The transformation for $\mathcal{N}_2$ is similar. ∎

Based on this result, it follows straightforwardly that $\mathcal{H}$ is indeed a maximal tractable subclass of $\mathcal{A}$.

Theorem 14. *If $\mathcal{S}$ strictly contains $\mathcal{H}$, then* ISAT($\mathcal{S}$) *is NP-complete.*

The next question is whether there are other maximal tractable subclasses that are incomparable with $\mathcal{H}$. One example of an incomparable tractable subclass is $\mathcal{U} = \{\{\prec, \succ\}, \top\}$. Since $\{\prec, \succ\}$ has no ORD-Horn clause form, this subclass is incomparable with $\mathcal{H}$, and since all sets of interval formulas over $\mathcal{U}$ are trivially satisfiable (by making all intervals disjoint), ISAT($\mathcal{U}$) can be decided in constant time. The subclass $\mathcal{U}$ is, of course, not a very *interesting* fragment. Provided we are interested in temporal reasoning in the framework as described by Allen [2], one necessary requirement is that *all basic relations* are contained in the subclass. A machine-assisted exploration of the space of subalgebras leads us to the following machine-verifiable lemma.

Lemma 15. *If S is a subclass that contains the thirteen basic relations, then $\overline{S} \subseteq \mathcal{H}$, or $\{d, d^{\smile}, o^{\smile}, s^{\smile}, f\}$ or $\{d^{\smile}, o, o^{\smile}, s^{\smile}, f^{\smile}\}$ is an element of $\overline{S}$.*

Using the fact that $\{\prec, d^{\smile}, o, m, f^{\smile}\}, \{\prec, d, o, m, s\}$ are elements of the least subalgebra generated by the set of basic relations and employing Lemma 13 again, we obtain the quite satisfying result that $\mathcal{H}$ is in fact the unique greatest tractable subclass amongst the subclasses containing all basic relations.

Theorem 16. *Let S be any subclass of A that contains all basic relations. Then either $S \subseteq \mathcal{H}$ and ISAT(S) is polynomial or ISAT(S) is NP-complete.*

7 Conclusion

We have identified a new tractable subclass of Allen's interval algebra, which we call *ORD-Horn subclass* and which contains the previously identified *continuous endpoint* and *pointisable* subclasses. Enumerating the ORD-Horn subclass reveals that this subclass contains 868 elements out of 8192 elements in the full algebra, i.e., more than 10% of the full algebra. Comparing this with the continuous endpoint subclass that covers approximately 1% and with the pointisable subclass that covers 2%, our result is a clear improvement in quantitative terms.

Furthermore, we showed that the "traditional" method of reasoning in Allen's interval algebra, namely, the *path-consistency method*, is sufficient for deciding satisfiability in the ORD-Horn subclass. In other words, our results indicate that the path-consistency method has a much larger range of applicability for reasoning in Allen's interval algebra than previously believed—if we are mainly interested in satisfiability.

Provided that a restriction to the subclass $\mathcal{H}$ is not possible in an application, our results may be employed in designing faster backtracking algorithms for the full algebra [27, 29]. Since our subclass contains significantly more relations than other tractable subclasses, the branching factor in a backtrack search can be considerably decreased if the ORD-Horn subclass is used.

Finally, we showed that it is impossible to improve on our results. Using a machine-generated case analysis, we showed that the ORD-Horn subclass is the *unique greatest* tractable subclass in the set of subclasses that contain all basic relations. In other words, the ORD-Horn subclass presents an optimal tradeoff between expressiveness and tractability [19] for reasoning in Allen's interval algebra.

Acknowledgements

We would like to thank Henry Kautz, Peter Ladkin, Len Schubert, Ron Shamir, Bart Selman, and Marc Vilain for discussions concerning the topics of this paper. In particular, Ron corrected an overly strong claim we made. In addition, we would like to thank Christer Bäckström for comments on an earlier version of this paper.

References

1. *Proceedings of the 6th National Conference of the American Association for Artificial Intelligence*, Seattle, WA, July 1987.
2. J. F. Allen. Maintaining knowledge about temporal intervals. *Communications of the ACM*, 26(11):832–843, Nov. 1983.
3. J. F. Allen. Towards a general theory of action and time. *Artificial Intelligence*, 23(2):123–154, 1984.
4. J. F. Allen. Temporal reasoning and planning. In J. F. Allen, H. A. Kautz, R. N. Pelavin, and J. D. Tenenberg, editors, *Reasoning about Plans*, chapter 1, pages 1–67. Morgan Kaufmann, San Mateo, CA, 1991.
5. J. F. Allen and P. J. Hayes. A common-sense theory of time. In *Proceedings of the 9th International Joint Conference on Artificial Intelligence*, pages 528–531, Los Angeles, CA, Aug. 1985.
6. J. F. Allen and J. A. Koomen. Planning using a temporal world model. In *Proceedings of the 8th International Joint Conference on Artificial Intelligence*, pages 741–747, Karlsruhe, Germany, Aug. 1983.
7. S. K. Feiner, D. J. Litman, K. R. McKeown, and R. J. Passonneau. Towards coordinated temporal multimedia presentation. In M. Maybury, editor, *Intelligent Multi Media*. AAAI Press, Menlo Park, CA, 1993. Forthcoming.
8. C. Freksa. Temporal reasoning based on semi-intervals. *Artificial Intelligence*, 54(1-2):199–227, 1992.
9. A. Gerevini and L. Schubert. Complexity of temporal reasoning with disjunctions of inequalities. Technical Report 9303-01, IRST, Trento, Italy, Jan. 1993.
10. A. Gerevini and L. Schubert. Efficient temporal reasoning through timegraphs. In *Proceedings of the 13th International Joint Conference on Artificial Intelligence*, pages 648–654, Chambery, France, Aug. 1993.
11. M. Ghallab and A. Mounir Alaoui. Managing efficiently temporal relations through indexed spanning trees. In IJCAI-89 [15], pages 1279–1303.
12. M. C. Golumbic and R. Shamir. Algorithms and complexity for reasoning about time. In *Proceedings of the 10th National Conference of the American Association for Artificial Intelligence*, pages 741–747. MIT Press, San Jose, CA, July 1992.
13. M. C. Golumbic and R. Shamir. Complexity and algorithms for reasoning about time: A graph-theoretic approach. *Journal of the Association for Computing Machinery*, 1993. To appear.
14. L. Henschen and L. Wos. Unit refutations and Horn sets. *Journal of the Association for Computing Machinery*, 21:590–605, 1974.
15. *Proceedings of the 11th International Joint Conference on Artificial Intelligence*, Detroit, MI, Aug. 1989. Morgan Kaufmann.

16. P. B. Ladkin. Models of axioms for time intervals. In AAAI-87 [1], pages 234–239.

17. P. B. Ladkin and R. Maddux. On binary constraint networks. Technical Report KES.U.88.8, Kestrel Institute, Palo Alto, CA, 1988.

18. P. B. Ladkin and R. Maddux. On binary constraint problems. *Journal of the Association for Computing Machinery*, 1993. To appear.

19. H. J. Levesque and R. J. Brachman. Expressiveness and tractability in knowledge representation and reasoning. *Computational Intelligence*, 3:78–93, 1987.

20. A. K. Mackworth. Consistency in networks of relations. *Artificial Intelligence*, 8:99–118, 1977.

21. A. K. Mackworth and E. C. Freuder. The complexity of some polynomial network consistency algorithms for constraint satisfaction problems. *Artificial Intelligence*, 25:65–73, 1985.

22. U. Montanari. Networks of constraints: fundamental properties and applications to picture processing. *Information Science*, 7:95–132, 1974.

23. B. Nebel and H.-J. Bürckert. Reasoning about temporal relations: A maximal tractable subclass of Allen's interval algebra. DFKI Research Report RR-93-11, German Research Center for Artificial Intelligence (DFKI), Saarbrücken, Germany, Mar. 1993.

24. K. Nökel. Convex relations between time intervals. In J. Rettie and K. Leidlmair, editors, *Proceedings der 5. Österreichischen Artificial Intelligence-Tagung*, pages 298–302. Springer-Verlag, Berlin, Heidelberg, New York, 1989.

25. K. Nökel. *Temporally Distributed Symptoms in Technical Diagnosis*, volume 517 of *Lecture Notes in Artificial Intelligence*. Springer-Verlag, Berlin, Heidelberg, New York, 1991.

26. F. Song and R. Cohen. The interpretation of temporal relations in narrative. In *Proceedings of the 7th National Conference of the American Association for Artificial Intelligence*, pages 745–750, Saint Paul, MI, Aug. 1988.

27. R. E. Valdéz-Pérez. The satisfiability of temporal constraint networks. In AAAI-87 [1], pages 256–260.

28. P. van Beek. Approximation algorithms for temporal reasoning. In IJCAI-89 [15], pages 1291–1296.

29. P. van Beek. Reasoning about qualitative temporal information. In *Proceedings of the 8th National Conference of the American Association for Artificial Intelligence*, pages 728–734, Boston, MA, Aug. 1990. MIT Press.

30. P. van Beek and R. Cohen. Exact and approximate reasoning about temporal relations. *Computational Intelligence*, 6:132–144, 1990.

31. M. B. Vilain and H. A. Kautz. Constraint propagation algorithms for temporal reasoning. In *Proceedings of the 5th National Conference of the American Association for Artificial Intelligence*, pages 377–382, Philadelphia, PA, Aug. 1986.

32. M. B. Vilain, H. A. Kautz, and P. G. van Beek. Constraint propagation algorithms for temporal reasoning: A revised report. In D. S. Weld and J. de Kleer, editors, *Readings in Qualitative Reasoning about Physical Systems*, pages 373–381. Morgan Kaufmann, San Mateo, CA, 1989.

33. R. Weida and D. Litman. Terminological reasoning with constraint networks and an application to plan recognition. In B. Nebel, W. Swartout, and C. Rich, editors, *Principles of Knowledge Representation and Reasoning: Proceedings of the 3rd International Conference*, pages 282–293, Cambridge, MA, Oct. 1992. Morgan Kaufmann.

Database Reasoning – A Deductive Framework for Solving Large and Complex Problems by Means of Subsumption

Werner Kießling[1] and Ulrich Güntzer[2]

[1] Lehrstuhl für Informatik 2, Universität Augsburg, D-86135 Augsburg,
kiessling@uni-augsburg.de
[2] Wilhelm-Schickard-Institut, Universität Tübingen, Sand 13, D-72076 Tübingen,
guentzer@informatik.uni-tuebingen.de

Abstract. After two decades of experience with relational databases and almost one decade with deductive databases a substantial amount of knowledge for efficient query processing methods and query optimizer technology is broadly available. So far, however, these research and development efforts have not paid too much attention to optimizations based on semantic or heuristic information as it is often demanded in AI.

This paper coins the notion of *database reasoning* as an approach to open deductive databases for more user-supplied semantic knowledge, both on the object level and meta-control level. We describe how application-specific semantic knowledge in the form of *subsumption* information can be combined with logic programming and fixpoint semantics, proposing the *Datalog-S* language extension. We experiment also with declarative meta-programming, specifying intelligent search procedures known from AI and executing them in a deductive database system. Thus database reasoning has the potential to amalgamate the power of deductive databases and of *heuristic search* , hence it can be applied for solving large and complex problems in a database environment.

1 Introduction

Since the invention of declarative query languages relational database systems have provided deductive capabilities to the user. Today there is a consensus that SQL with its current standard SQL-2 is too limited in terms of deductive capabilities, though. Substantial improvements have been explored in the area of deductive databases over the past decade and have resulted in the declarative *Datalog* query language, extended towards general recursion, function terms, negation and aggregation. Of course, when implementing such a powerful language the biggest challenge is to construct the query optimizer. Recently, as a major milestone for this technology, its viability could be manifested at a Vancouver workshop ([PLD93]), where several implemented systems were demonstrated, and through the project surveys appearing in [VLJ94]. Among the implemented deductive database systems are e.g. Aditi, CORAL, DECLARE, EKS-V1, Glue-NAIL!, LDL, LOLA and Starburst. The advances reached by this community will definitely have their impact on the commercial market place, be it in liaison with the popular object-oriented paradigm or be it grafted on the forthcoming SQL-3 standard, which is supposed to absorb at least some of the powerful *Datalog* features (e.g. concerning recursion). So in a sense deductive database technology has successfully completed its first research and development stage.

If one reviews the achievements attained so far, it becomes conspicuous that deductive databases lack a convenient and general mechanism that allows the user to impart application-specific semantic knowledge to the deductive database system. However, *semantic and heuristic control* knowledge is fundamental for many practical areas involving complex planning processes and combinatorial problems. This paper discusses our approach of *database reasoning* to extend deductive databases towards semantic and heuristic control. The presented material has its origins in early works on this subject ([SKGB89]) and in recent theoretical advances ([KKTG93]).

The rest of this paper is organized as follows. Section 2 is concerned with the theoretical foundations of subsumption as a fundamental paradigm to specify certain semantic knowledge. In section 3 we propose to extend *Datalog* programming by subsumption towards so-called *Datalog-S*, which will be exemplified and matched against comparable CORAL and LDL solutions. Thereafter in section 4 we experiment with *Datalog-S* extented towards semantic and heuristic control in order to combine heuristic search procedures from AI with deductive databases. Section 5 summarizes our approach and outlines the scope of future research.

2 Database Reasoning with Subsumption

The notion of *database reasoning* is understood as an extension of deductive database technology with the ability to define and reason about additional semantic and heuristic knowledge. Database reasoning is supposed to augment database technology by more intelligent deduction capabilities including subsumption and meta-controlled reasoning. In a companion paper in this volume by [Fur94], *theory reasoning* pursues a complementary approach by extending theorem proving to utilize database facilities.

Let us start from logic programming with its conventional fixpoint semantics, which is based on the notion of equality and uses the powerset lattice of the Herbrand base that is partially ordered by set inclusion. Recently, [KKTG93] have introduced a fixpoint iteration not based on equality but on any partial ordering of a basic set (e.g. the Herbrand base of a logic program). This ordering can capture *application semantics* in the sense that one element is preferred over another one, rendering the latter superfluous because of subsumption. A new fixpoint iteration solves the task of computing only the relevant part of the conventional fixpoint of a function, i.e. only those elements that are maximal under the given ordering. In this section we recapture some of the theoretical results from [KKTG93].

2.1 Fixpoints with Subsumption

Our intention is to define a relationship $X \sqsubseteq Y$ which can capture *application semantics* that X *is subsumed by* Y in the sense that Y is preferable over X, or Y is more useful than X, or Y is more intended than X, or Y is better than X, etc.

Lemma 1 Basic notions. *Let* $\langle\, M, \sqsubseteq\, \rangle$ *be a partial ordering, i.e.* $\sqsubseteq$ *is a binary, reflexive, antisymmetrical and transitive relation called* subsumption ordering. *Let* $X, Y \in 2^M$.

1. *The relation* $\sqsubseteq$ *on* 2^M *is defined as* $X \sqsubseteq Y :\iff (\forall x \in X)(\exists y \in Y)\, x \sqsubseteq y$. *It is a pre-order, i.e. reflexive and transitive.*

2. *The relation* $\sim$ *on* 2^M *is defined as* $X \sim Y :\iff X \sqsubseteq Y \wedge Y \sqsubseteq X$. *It is an equivalence relation.*

3. *Let* $[X], [Y] \in 2^M/_\sim$ *denote equivalence classes. We extend* $\sqsubseteq$ *on* 2^M *to* $2^M/_\sim$ *by* $[X] \sqsubseteq [Y] :\iff X \sqsubseteq Y$. *It is a partial ordering and well-defined.*

$\square$

By the definition above the subsumption ordering given on a not necessarily finite set M is extended to a partial ordering on the equivalence classes of the powerset of M induced by $\sim$.

Remark. If the subsumption ordering on the basic set M is given as a not necessarily reflexive but antisymmetrical and transitive partial ordering $\sqsubset$, then we assume $\sqsubseteq$ on M to be the reflexive closure of $\sqsubset$. For specifying subsumption orderings we use $\sqsubset$ or $\sqsubseteq$ depending on what seems more appropriate.

Example 1. Consider the following directed, cyclic graph:

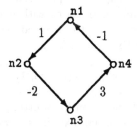

Note that the edges are labeled by positive or negative integers expressing costs. The transitive closure including the costs of all paths is computed by the following non-linearly recursive logic program P (completed by the e-facts given by the graph).

```
p(X, Y, C) ← e(X, Y, C).
p(X, Y, C) ← p(X, Z, CP), p(Z, Y, CE), C = CP + CE.
```

Note that P has an infinite fixpoint. The basic set M in our example is the (typed) Herbrand base B_P:

$$B_P = \{\texttt{p(X, Y, C)} \mid \texttt{X, Y} \in \{\texttt{n1, n2, n3, n4}\}, \texttt{C} \in \mathbb{Z}\} \cup$$
$$\{\texttt{e(X, Y, C)} \mid \texttt{X, Y} \in \{\texttt{n1, n2, n3, n4}\}, \texttt{C} \in \mathbb{Z}\}$$

If we are interested in computing shortest paths, a suitable subsumption ordering on B_P can be given by: $\texttt{p(X, Y, C2)} \sqsubseteq \texttt{p(X, Y, C1)}$, if $\texttt{C1} < \texttt{C2}$. For this irreflexive ordering extended to 2^{B_P} we have e.g.:

$$\{\texttt{p}(\texttt{n1}, \texttt{n3}, 0), \texttt{p}(\texttt{n1}, \texttt{n3}, 1)\} \sqsubseteq \{\texttt{p}(\texttt{n1}, \texttt{n3}, -1)\}$$

$$\{\texttt{p}(\texttt{n1}, \texttt{n3}, 0), \texttt{p}(\texttt{n1}, \texttt{n3}, -1)\} \sim \{\texttt{p}(\texttt{n1}, \texttt{n3}, -1)\} \qquad \square$$

We concentrate on special subsets of M called *reduced sets* and introduce an operation doing this reduction. Important for defining reduced sets is the notion of chains maximal w.r.t. set inclusion. [1]

Definition 2 Reduced sets. Let $X \in 2^M$ and let $\mathcal{C}$ be the set of maximal chains of X w.r.t. set inclusion.

1. The $\sqsubseteq$-*reduced version* of X, denoted by $\mathcal{R}_\sqsubseteq(X)$, is defined as:

$$\mathcal{R}_\sqsubseteq(X) := \bigcup_{C \in \mathcal{C}} R_C \quad \text{where} \quad R_C := \begin{cases} \{m\} & \text{if } m = \max(C) \text{ w.r.t. } \sqsubseteq \text{ exists} \\ C & \text{otherwise} \end{cases}$$

2. The set of reduced subsets of M is denoted by $2^M_\mathcal{R} := \{\mathcal{R}_\sqsubseteq(X) \mid X \in 2^M\}$. $\qquad \square$

Given $X \in 2^M$ the reduction $\mathcal{R}_\sqsubseteq(X)$ has the following effect: maximal chains in X without maximum, as e.g. $C := \{1 - 1/n \mid n \in \mathbb{N}^+\}$ on $\langle \mathbb{R}, \leq \rangle$, are left unchanged. However, maximal chains with maximum are reduced to this maximum. Thus, for a finite set X the reduced version $\mathcal{R}_\sqsubseteq(X)$ consists of the maximal elements of X. In Ex. 1. we get e.g.:

$$\mathcal{R}_\sqsubseteq(\{\texttt{p}(\texttt{n1}, \texttt{n3}, -1), \texttt{p}(\texttt{n1}, \texttt{n3}, 0), \texttt{p}(\texttt{n1}, \texttt{n3}, 1), \dots \}) = \{\texttt{p}(\texttt{n1}, \texttt{n3}, -1)\}$$

In the sequel we simplify notation by omitting the subsumption order $\sqsubseteq$, if it is clear from the context. As usual, fixpoint theory with subsumption is based on a complete lattice, in this case the set of equivalence classes of reduced sets.

Lemma 3. $\langle 2^M_\mathcal{R}/_\sim , \sqsubseteq \rangle$ *is a complete lattice:*

$$\text{lub}\{[X_i]\}_{i \in I} = [\mathcal{R}(\bigcup_{i \in I} X_i)] , \top = [\mathcal{R}(M)] , \bot = [\emptyset] \qquad \square$$

---

[1] The maximal chains of a partially ordered set are the totally ordered subsets that are maximal w.r.t. set inclusion. Let e.g. $M := \{a, b, c, d\}$ be partially ordered by $a \sqsubseteq b \sqsubseteq c$ and $a \sqsubseteq d$. Then the maximal chains are $\{a, b, c\}$ and $\{a, d\}$.

Now let F be a mapping on 2^M, e.g. the immediate consequence operator $T_P(I) := \{A \in B_P \mid A \leftarrow B_1, \ldots, B_n \text{ is ground instance of a rule in P},\ \{B_1, \ldots, B_n\} \subseteq I\}$ of the logic program in Ex. 1. We define the notion of F being monotonic w.r.t. to a subsumption ordering $\sqsubseteq$.

Definition 4 $\sqsubseteq$-monotonic functions.
F is called $\sqsubseteq$-monotonic iff $X \sqsubseteq Y \Rightarrow F(X) \sqsubseteq F(Y)$. $\qquad\qquad\square$

Next we extend a given $\sqsubseteq$-monotonic mapping F on 2^M to a mapping $F^\sim$ on this lattice by introducing the following two associated mappings.

Lemma 5. *Let* $F : 2^M \rightarrow 2^M$ *be a $\sqsubseteq$-monotonic mapping. Then the mappings $F_{\mathcal{R}}$ and $F^\sim$ are well-defined and $\sqsubseteq$-monotonic:*

1. $F_{\mathcal{R}} : 2^M \rightarrow 2^M, \quad X \mapsto \mathcal{R}(F(X))$

2. $F^\sim : 2^M_{\mathcal{R}}/_\sim \ \rightarrow 2^M_{\mathcal{R}}/_\sim\ , \quad [X] \mapsto [F_{\mathcal{R}}(X)]$ $\qquad\qquad\square$

We want to discuss these notions considering the program P in Ex. 1. Choose $M = B_P$ as stated there. The immediate consequence operator $T_P : 2^M \rightarrow 2^M$ computes for a given subset S of M all single-step conclusions which can be drawn from S according to the rules of program P, i.e. in terms of relational algebra:

$$T_P(S) = \pi_{X,Y,CP+CE}(S \underset{=Z}{\bowtie} S) \cup E$$

For $\sqsubseteq$ being the reflexive closure of $\sqsubset$ of Ex. 1, T_P is $\sqsubseteq$-monotonic, namely: If $S_1 \sqsubseteq S_2$, then every atom of S_1 is contained in S_2 or there is a better atom (i.e. connecting the same two vertices, but giving a shorter distance) contained in S_2. Then every conclusion drawn while computing $T_P(S_1)$ can be mimicked for computing $T_P(S_2)$ and yields the same or a better result. Thus indeed T_P is $\sqsubseteq$- monotonic.

The map $(T_P)_{\mathcal{R}} : 2^M \rightarrow 2^M$ computes as a first step the same result as T_P, but then reduces it, i.e. whenever there are two different atoms p(x,y,c1) and p(x,y,c2) in $T_P(S)$, then only the better atom with the shorter distance is retained. Thus $(T_P)_{\mathcal{R}}$ groups the result of T_P by the first two attributes and gives the minimum of the third.

In the situation at hand, two sets S_1 and S_2 can be equivalent only if they are equal, which means that $(T_P)^\sim$ and $(T_P)_{\mathcal{R}}$ coincide. Hence $(T_P)^\sim$ finds all paths which can be constructed by joining two (but not more) distance statements contained in S and among those $(T_P)^\sim$ determines the shortest ones. Obviously by iterating $(T_P)^\sim$ one gets the shortest paths for all pairs of vertices.

Theorem 6 Existence of least fixpoint. *Let* $F : 2^M \rightarrow 2^M$ *be a $\sqsubseteq$-monotonic mapping. Then $F^\sim$ has a least fixpoint.* $\qquad\qquad\square$

Thus $\sqsubseteq$-monotonicity of $F^\sim$ already guarantees the existence of a least fixpoint. The next theorem relates fixpoint iteration of the functions F and $F^\sim$.

Theorem 7 Commutativity of LFP and $\mathcal{R}$. *Let $F: 2^M \to 2^M$ be a $\sqsubseteq$-monotonic and $\subseteq$-continuous mapping, let $\mathrm{LFP}(F^\sim)$ and $\mathrm{LFP}(F)$ be the least fixpoints of $F^\sim$ and F, resp.*

1. *$F^\sim$ is $\sqsubseteq$-continuous.*

2. *$\mathrm{LFP}(F^\sim) = F^\sim \uparrow \omega$*

3. *$[\mathcal{R}(F \uparrow n)] = F^\sim \uparrow n = [F_{\mathcal{R}} \uparrow n]$ for all $n < \omega$*

4. *$[\mathcal{R}(\mathrm{LFP}(F))] = \mathrm{LFP}(F^\sim) = \mathrm{lub}\{[F_{\mathcal{R}} \uparrow n]\}_{n<\omega}$*

5. *If F is finite, i.e. F maps finite sets to finite sets, then equivalence class notation can be omitted: $\mathcal{R}(F \uparrow n) = F_{\mathcal{R}} \uparrow n$ for all $n < \omega$* $\qquad\square$

Note that Thm. 7.5 holds since each finite reduced set is the only representative of its equivalence class. Theorem 7.4 states that *reducing on the fly* is correct. Moreover, if $\mathrm{LFP}(F)$ does not terminate, then reduction on the fly may achieve *safety*.

Since the sample program in Ex. 1 is definite the T_P-operator is $\subseteq$-continuous; additionally T_P is $\sqsubseteq$-monotonic. Reducing the fixpoint of T_P yields exactly the shortest paths. According to Thm. 7.4 the same result can be achieved by discarding subsumed tuples *on the fly*.

Remark. For $\sqsubseteq$ being equality and set inclusion as the corresponding Hoare ordering on 2^M, each set $X \in 2^M$ is already its reduced version and the equivalence classes consist of one element only, i.e. $\mathcal{R}_=(X) = X$. The functions F, $F_{\mathcal{R}}$ and $F^\sim$ coincide and the entire fixpoint of F is computed. Thus conventional fixpoint iteration is just a special case of fixpoint iteration with subsumption.

We want to point out here in particular that usual fixpoint iteration works monotonically under all circumstances, i.e. information generated as an intermediate result can never be withdrawn or overwritten during a later iteration round. But many efficient algorithms simply don't work in this way. Instead of creating *more* information, they create *better* information replacing the old one. This behavior can be modeled by subsumption iteration. Thus it is not only a feature which increases efficiency, it rather opens up a more general and more adequate paradigm to implement algorithms.

Furthermore, *filtering out* information (e.g. by magic-set predicates) can be considered as a special case of subsumption. More precisely, let $F(p(t))$ be a filter predicate with the following meaning: the atom $p(t)$ is to be considered further if and only if $F(p(t))$ holds. Choose some tuple t_0 such that $p(t_0)$ is contained in the desired fixpoint and define the following subsumption ordering:

$$p(t) \sqsubset p(t_0) \; if \; \neg F(p(t)), F(p(t_0))$$

Then all atoms $p(t)$ and only those, which don't pass the filter test, are eventually subsumed by $p(t_0)$ and therefore excluded from further consideration.

2.2 Model Theory with Subsumption

The adaptation of the model-theoretic interpretation of definite logic programs to programs with subsumption can be accomplished in a natural way. To this purpose we define so-called $\sqsubseteq$-models which are closed under application of the T_P-operator w.r.t. the subsumption ordering $\sqsubseteq$.

Let P be a definite program, let $\sqsubseteq$ be a subsumption ordering on the Herbrand base B_P of P, and assume that T_P is $\sqsubseteq$-monotonic.

Definition 8 $\sqsubseteq$-interpretation, $\sqsubseteq$-model. Let $[M] \in 2^{B_P}_{\mathcal{R}}/_\sim$.

1. $[M]$ is called a $\sqsubseteq$-*interpretation*.

2. $[M]$ is called $\sqsubseteq$-*model* of P iff $T_P(M) \sqsubseteq M$. $\qquad\qquad$ □

The intersection of all Herbrand models is known to be a Herbrand model. A similar result holds for $\sqsubseteq$-models.

Lemma 9 Least $\sqsubseteq$-model. *Let $\mathcal{M}$ be the set of all $\sqsubseteq$-models and let $M_{P,\sqsubseteq}$ be a smallest representative of glb($\mathcal{M}$), then:*

$$[M_{P,\sqsubseteq}] := \mathrm{glb}(\mathcal{M}) \ \textit{is a } \sqsubseteq\textit{-model, called} \ \text{least } \sqsubseteq\textit{-model.} \qquad □$$

It is essential to link the least Herbrand model M_P of a program with the least fixpoint of the T_P-operator. We characterize the least $\sqsubseteq$-model as the least fixpoint of the iteration with subsumption and relate it with M_P.

Theorem 10 Fixpoint characterization of least $\sqsubseteq$-model.
Let $\tilde{T_P}$ be the mapping according to Lem. 5, then:

$$[M_{P,\sqsubseteq}] = \mathrm{LFP}(\tilde{T_P}) = [\mathcal{R}_\sqsubseteq(\mathrm{LFP}(T_P))] = [\mathcal{R}_\sqsubseteq(M_P)] \qquad □$$

Corollary 11. *If $[M_{P,\sqsubseteq}]$ has a finite representative $M_{P,\sqsubseteq}$, then equivalence class notation can be omitted:*

$$M_{P,\sqsubseteq} = \mathcal{R}_\sqsubseteq(\mathrm{LFP}(T_P)) = \mathcal{R}_\sqsubseteq(M_P) \qquad □$$

In other words, a least $\sqsubseteq$-model can be gained by $\sqsubseteq$-reduction of its least Herbrand model, i.e. $\sqsubseteq$-maximal atoms are singled out and all other atoms are discarded. Note that many practical cases exist where M_P is infinite, but by $\sqsubseteq$-reduction infinitely many atoms are discarded, leaving only a finite $M_{P,\sqsubseteq}$.

Remark. For $\sqsubseteq$ being equality we have $\mathcal{R}_=(M_P) = M_P$, hence least Herbrand models are just a special case of least $\sqsubseteq$-models.

2.3 Fixpoint Iteration with Subsumption

Fixpoint iteration of $LFP(F^\sim)$, as described in Thm. 7, can be implemented by a naive iteration scheme in a straightforward way. More efficient, however, is a differential iteration scheme.

Differential Fixpoint Iteration. Now we present the new differential iteration scheme for bottom-up fixpoint evaluation, called *delta-iteration with subsumption*. We restrict our attention to the case of finite F. Delta-iteration with subsumption is based on two operations $\oplus_\sqsubseteq$ and $\ominus_\sqsubseteq$ on $2^M_\mathcal{R}$.

Definition 12. Let $X, Y \in 2^M_\mathcal{R}$ be finite, reduced subsets of M.

1. $X \oplus_\sqsubseteq Y := \mathcal{R}_\sqsubseteq(X \cup Y)$

2. $X \ominus_\sqsubseteq Y := \{x \in X \mid (\not\exists y \in Y)\, x \sqsubseteq y\}$ $\qquad\qquad\qquad\square$

Again, we may simplify notation to $\oplus$ and $\ominus$ if no ambiguity can arise. Similar to the usual semi-naive iteration for a fixpoint equation $F(S) = S$, in the presence of subsumption we need a differential expression to efficiently compute the difference $\delta(S, \Delta) := F_\mathcal{R}(S \oplus \Delta) \ominus F_\mathcal{R}(S)$. This is achieved by a so-called *auxiliary function* $\text{Aux}_{F_\mathcal{R}}(S, \Delta)$ with $\delta(S, \Delta) = \text{Aux}_{F_\mathcal{R}}(S, \Delta) \ominus F_\mathcal{R}(S)$. The following lemma establishes a strong connection between auxiliary functions for F and $F_\mathcal{R}$.

Lemma 13 Auxiliary function for subsumption. *Let a mapping Aux_F on 2^M be an auxiliary function for F and let $S, \Delta \in 2^M_\mathcal{R}$ be finite sets such that $S \cap \Delta = \emptyset$. Then:*

$$\delta(S, \Delta) = \mathcal{R}(\text{Aux}_F(S, \Delta)) \ominus F_\mathcal{R}(S) \qquad\qquad\qquad\square$$

In other words, any auxiliary function $\text{Aux}_F(S, \Delta)$ gained from formal differentiation can be used directly for subsumption filtering, i.e.:

$$\text{Aux}_{F_\mathcal{R}}(S, \Delta) = \mathcal{R}(\text{Aux}_F(S, \Delta))$$

The procedural formulation of the differential fixpoint operator with subsumption is as follows:

Theorem 14 Differential fixpoint iteration with subsumption.

```
Delta_iterate_with_subsumption(F, ⊑): S
   begin
      S := ∅;  Δ := R⊑(F(∅));
      while Δ ≠ ∅ do
         AUX := R⊑(Aux_F(S, Δ));
         S := S ⊕⊑ Δ;  Δ := AUX ⊖⊑ S;
      endwhile
   end
```

Subsumption Indexes. An efficient implementation of the subsumptive operators $\mathcal{R}_{\sqsubseteq}$, $\oplus_{\sqsubseteq}$ and $\ominus_{\sqsubseteq}$ requires the maintenance of temporary indexes during the iteration. The following observation suggests the use of tailored index structures:

In many cases for finite sets the reduction operation $\mathcal{R}$ induces a *functional dependency* FD, as can be seen from Ex. 1: Provided that reduction is done on the fly, from "p(X, Y, C2) $\sqsubseteq$ p(X, Y, C1) , if C1 < C2" we get an FD from (X,Y) to the third argument C.

Hence it is attractive to dispose of a *unique index* I on (X,Y), modified towards respection of subsumption in the following sense:

- Insertion of a tuple $t1 = (x, y, c)$:
  - If no entry for a tuple $t2 = (x, y, \_)$ exists in I, then insert t1 into I.
  - If there is an entry for $t2 = (x, y, c)$ in I, then insert $t1$ into I only if $t1$ subsumes $t2$ and then remove $t2$ from I.

- Deletions can be treated analogously.

Unique indexes of this kind are called *subsumption indexes*. They can be employed to efficiently support $\mathcal{R}_{\sqsubseteq}$, $\oplus_{\sqsubseteq}$, and $\ominus_{\sqsubseteq}$, and can be implemented by slight modifications of standard database access paths like e.g. B-trees.

3 Deductive Databases with Subsumption

There have been several proposals to extend deductive databases with second-order constructs, e.g. to cope with aggregation or to express don't-care non-determinism. The theoretical results of the previous section open up a novel way to tackle such problems at two levels:

1. We can extend declarative *Datalog* programming by subsumption knowledge towards *Datalog with Subsumption (Datalog-S)*.
2. We can compile such *Datalog-S* programs efficiently into differential fixpoint iteration with subsumption.

3.1 Datalog-S

For didactical reasons let us develop our ideas in a well-researched area of deductive databases.

Aggregates and Subsumption.

Example 2 (Shortest paths). Reconsider the program P of Ex. 1:

```
p(X, Y, C) ← e(X, Y, C).
p(X, Y, C) ← p(X, Z, CP), p(Z, Y, CE), C = CP + CE.
```

Assume we are interested in computing all shortest paths. This can be achieved in CORAL ([RSS92]) through set grouping followed by minimum selection:

```
shortest_p(X, Y, min(<C>)) ← p(X, Y, C).                    (⋆)
```

In [GSZ93] the following solution using the least-predicate is proposed for LDL :

```
shortest_p(X, Y, C) ← p(X, Y, C), least((X, Y), C).        (⋆⋆)
```

The extreme predicate least(Y, C), given a list of *grouping* variables Y and a *single* cost argument C taken from an ordered domain, computes the minimum value of C per group. The LDL program (⋆⋆) can be rewritten efficiently by the query optimizer as follows:

```
p(X, Y, C) ← e(X, Y, C), least((X, Y), C).
p(X, Y, C) ← p(X, Z, CP), p(Z, Y, CE),
             C = CP + CE, least((X, Y), C).
```

□

These notations treat second-order constructs by first-order syntax to enable "normal" *Datalog* programming. The semantics of least (and similarly of its counterpart most) is expressed by means of rewriting into non-stratified negation with stable model semantics ([GGZ91]). For definite logic programs and a non-decreasing cost argument a unique stable model exists, which can be computed by alternating the computation of the Horn clauses with the set of clauses containing least/most predicates and by selecting from the latter only tuples with least costs.

Datalog-S. The intended semantics of a *Datalog* program P matches the least Herbrand model of P, possessing an equivalent least fixpoint semantics. On the other hand, it is impossible to express notions like subsumption directly in *Datalog* because of its inherent monotonicity: true facts stay true once they have been derived for the first time, and there is no convenient way to get rid of them afterwards.

The model-theoretical results in section 2.2 suggest a promising extension of classical *Datalog* now: Least Herbrand models can be $\sqsubseteq$-reduced to least $\sqsubseteq$-models with an equivalent least fixpoint semantics. This opens the way to extend *Datalog* towards 'Datalog with Subsumption' (*Datalog-S*). Let us convey our ideas by reconsidering Ex. 2. We proceed as follows:

(1) Specify a subsumption ordering *less* on **shortest_p**-atoms by a *subsumption rule*:

```
define subsumption less
    {less(shortest_p(X, Y, C2), shortest_p(X, Y, C1)) ← C1 < C2.}
```

This subsumption rule expresses that a path p_1, considered candidate for being a shortest path between two given nodes X and Y, subsumes another candidate path p_2 iff the costs of p_1 are smaller than those of p_2. It defines an irreflexive partial ordering *less*, hence the results of section 2 apply.

(2) From all paths p(X, Y, C) we extract shortest paths by focusing only on those which are maximal under the subsumption order *less*, i.e. we consider the least *less*-model. This least *less*-model is enacted by a new implication arrow *'less ←'* :

shortest_p(X, Y, C) *less* ← p(X, Y, C).　　　　　　　　　($\star\star\star$)

This is a fully declarative specification of shortest paths. Its intuitive reading is as follows:

"For all X, Y, and C: If p(X, Y, C) holds, then conclude shortest_p(X, Y, C), but only if nothing better w.r.t. *less* can be concluded. In this case, delete also all atoms being worse than shortest_p(X, Y, C) w.r.t. *less*."

Or for short one could say : "Shortest_p is the *less*-reduction of p, i.e. it contains exactly the *less*-maximal (least) elements from p".

Comparing the *Datalog-S* solution ($\star\star\star$) to the LDL solution ($\star\star$), efficiency in ($\star\star$) is achieved through the rewriting as shown in Ex. 2, which pushes least into recursion. According to Thms. 7 and 14 the *Datalog-S* solution ($\star\star\star$) can be compiled by a *Datalog-S* query optimizer into differential fixpoint iteration with subsumption, yielding only those paths in each iteration round that are still potential candidates for being shortest ones. Moreover, a temporary subsumption index on (X, Y) can be maintained for instant and fast *less*-filtering.

For explanatory purposes we can express this on-the-fly optimization of subsumption as a new transformation, called *'push subsumption'*. Application of 'push subsumption' then is equivalent to rewriting ($\star\star\star$) into the following recursive *Datalog-S* program, where *less* acts now on p-atoms:

p(X, Y, C) *less* ← e(X, Y, C).
p(X, Y, C) *less* ← p(X, Z, CP), p(Z, Y, CE), C = CP + CE.

The meta-predicate most((X, Y), C) of LDL can be defined in *Datalog-S* analogously by a subsumption ordering *more*, enabling the use of the implication arrow *'more ←'* :

define subsumption *more*
　{ *more*(p(X, Y, C2), p(X, Y, C1)) ← C1 > C2 . }

From the theoretical results in Sect. 2 it becomes clear that *Datalog-S* has the potential to extend the expressiveness of current deductive databases. Any subsumption order, not just the extrema least and most, can be dealt with in a uniform manner. As a first step we propose *Datalog-S* as the following extension of $Datalog^{fct}$, i.e. including function terms but excluding negation for the time being.

Definition 15 Datalog-S. Let a subsumption ordering $\sqsubseteq$ be defined for the ground instances of a head literal q, and let q appear in a $Datalog^{fct}$ rule $q \leftarrow < body >$. Then the following is an admissable $Datalog\text{-}S$ rule:

- Syntax: $q \sqsubseteq\leftarrow < body >$.

- Intuitive semantics:
  If $< body >$ holds, then conclude q, but only if $q' \sqsubset q$ for all $q' \sqsubseteq q$. Moreover, in this case delete all q' where $q' \sqsubset q$. $\qquad\Box$

Remark. *Datalog*'s standard implication arrow '$\leftarrow$' can be interpreted as just a shorthand for '*equal* $\leftarrow$', where *equal* denotes the trivial subsumption ordering being equality of atoms.

The expressiveness and convenience of *Datalog-S* programming comes at a price: The central Thms. 7, 10 and 14 require $\sqsubseteq$-monotonicity. Since subsumption is a semantical notion, verification of this crucial property cannot be done automatically, instead it is up to the user's responsibility in general.

Example 3. In continuation of Ex. 2 suppose we are interested in all end points and their costs for shortest paths starting from point 7:

```
shortest_from_7(Y, C) ← shortest_p(7, Y, C).
```

How the propagation of constant 7 into the recursive clique for p (e.g. by magic-set transformations) interacts with the on-the-fly reduction capabilities of *Datalog-S* is an open issue. Early results in [SSG*90] for a special subsumption order promise a potential for an additional speedup gain. $\qquad\Box$

3.2 More Complex Subsumptions

From these initial case studies we have seen evidence that it is natural to think in terms of subsumption when it comes to deal with special meta-predicates like **least** or **most**. This shift of paradigm proves beneficial in many more situations.

Example 4 (Safety of probabilistic reasoning). The *DUCK*-system ([GKT91], [KKG93]) for probabilistic reasoning in a deductive database environment requires for safety reasons the following subsumption ordering for probabilistic rules: Given two conditional probability statements, let's say

$$0.7 \leq \text{prob}(B|A) \leq 0.9 \text{ and } 0.75 \leq \text{prob}(B|A) \leq 0.85,$$

the latter clearly subsumes the former one. Denoting conditional probability intervals by $A \xrightarrow{x_1, x_2} B$, one of the inference rules for sound probabilistic reasoning in $DUCK$ is the so-called 'sharpening-rule':

$$\{A \xrightarrow{x_1, x_2} B, A \xrightarrow{y_1, y_2} B\} \vdash A \xrightarrow{z_1, z_2} B, z_1 = max(x_1, y_1), z_2 = min(x_2, y_2)$$

Conditional probability intervals $A \xrightarrow{x_1, x_2} B$ are represented by a predicate `dr(A, B, Z1, Z2)`, yielding the following direct $Datalog$ implementation:

```
dr(A,B,Z1,Z2) ← dr(A,B,X1,X2), dr(A,B,Y1,Y2),
                max(X1,Y1,Z1), min(X2,Y2,Z2).
```

The other inference rules of $DUCK$ can be mapped in a similar straightforward fashion to $Datalog$ rules. However, without reducing subsumed intervals on the fly, the $DUCK$-calculus would be unsafe, i.e. it would not terminate on a standard deductive database system. Now let us define a subsumption ordering *tighter* as follows:

```
define subsumption tighter
  { tighter(dr_safe(A,B,X1,X2), dr_safe(A,B,Y1,Y2))
      ← X1 ≤ Y1 ∧ X2 ≥ Y2. }
```

Since the 'sharpening'-rule and all other inference rules of the $DUCK$-calculus are *tighter*-monotonic, the following $Datalog$-S rule achieves (weak) safety by Thm. 7.4 :

```
dr_safe(A, B, Z1, Z2) tighter ← dr(A, B, Z1, Z2).
```

Applying the 'push subsumption' transformation by the $Datalog$-S query optimizer achieves the desired safety effect by deleting *tighter*-subsumed tuples on the fly. Moreover, whenever the 'sharpening-rule' produces new tuples, they *tighter*-subsume existing ones. A unique subsumption index I on (A, B) can be maintained as follows:
Suppose $((a, b), (0.5, 0.8)) \in I$ and tuple $(a, b, 0.7, 0.9)$ becomes newly generated during the iteration. Then 'sharpening' can be combined efficiently with *tighter*-reduction by the following update: $((a, b), (0.7, 0.8)) \in I$. $\square$

3.3 Annotations

An alternative way to emulate the on-the-fly processing mode of subsumption is by using the low-level *annotation* mechanism of CORAL for controlling bottom-up evaluation. Referring back to Ex. 2, shortest paths can be gained by annotating the two rules as follows:

```
@aggregate_selection p(X,Y,C) (X,Y) min(C).                    (***)
```

This statement causes CORAL to maintain only the minimal C-value for each group of (X, Y)-values and to discard the rest at the end of each iteration step. Note that this works also for cyclic graphs as opposed to the CORAL solution (*).

The simulation of the on-the-fly reduction due to the subsumption ordering *tighter* from Ex. 4 is somewhat trickier in CORAL. Since @aggregate_selection can apply aggregations only on single attributes, we must transform the *tighter*-subsumption, depending on two attributes, into equivalent single-attribute annotations:

```
dr_1(A,B,Z1,Z2,Z3) ← dr(A,B,X1,X2), dr(A,B,Y1,Y2),
                      max(X1,Y1,Z1), min(X2,Y2,Z2),
                      Z3 = Z2 - Z1 .
dr(A,B,Z1,Z2,)     ← dr_1(A, B, Z1, Z2, Z3).

@aggregate_selection dr_1(A,B,Z1,Z2,Z3) (A,B) min(Z3).
```

Since in this solution dr-tuples in the premise of the first rule are not necessarily *tighter*-reduced, a further speedup can be gained by entering the following annotations ahead:

```
@aggregate_selection dr(A,B,Z1,Z2) (A,B,Z1) min(Z2).
@aggregate_selection dr(A,B,Z1,Z2) (A,B,Z2) max(Z1).
```

Thus *Datalog-S* evaluation can be simulated by CORAL in this case, too. Nevertheless, delta_iterate_with_subsumption is potentially more efficient, since the filtering of subsumed tuples can be done instantly by subsumption indexes during iteration. Moreover, *Datalog-S* extends logic programming by integrating subsumption at the logical level, from where it can be compiled automatically into efficient bottom-up evaluation. On the other hand, CORAL's annotations affect bottom-up evaluation without being reflected in the declarative logic language.

4 Heuristic Search and Subsumption

In this section we shall focus on the issue of declarative control for greedy bottom-up deductions. In particular, as a non-trivial case study we investigate how to incorporate bidirectional heuristic search into deductive databases.

4.1 Exploring the Search Space

Answers to a query for a logic program are some subset of the entire Herbrand base, which can be regarded as the *search space* of the logic program given the query. Since in many cases, even after applying sophisticated optimization techniques like magic-sets or subsumption on-the-fly, this search space is prohibitively large, other ways of search space reduction must be taken into consideration.

As reported in [GSZ93], previous research has shown that *Datalog*, enriched with extrema (**least/most**) and **choice** constructs, can express and solve efficiently some optimization problems requiring a greedy search strategy.
Choice(X, Y) is a declarative construct to enforce functional constraints in rules; i.e. it defines a functional dependency $FD : X \longrightarrow Y$.

Example 5 (borrowed from [GSZ93]). A spanning tree for an undirected graph , whose edges are represented as **g(X, Y, C)** and **g(Y, X, C)** for some cost argument **C**, is constructed as follows:

```
st(nil, a, 0) .
st(X, Y, C)   ← st( _ , X, _ ), g(X, Y, C), X ≠ Y,
              choice(Y, (X, C)).
```

$\square$

Similar to **least/most**, the semantics of the meta-level predicate **choice**, supported in LDL ([NT89]) and in CORAL ([RSS92]), can be defined by rewriting into non-stratified negation with stable model semantics ([SZ90, GZG93]). **Choice** supports a don't-care form of non-determinism, hence it may be used to express greedy search strategies. On the other hand, it also carries semantics w.r.t. FDs, which have to hold in the models of a program: Removing **choice(Y, (X, C))** from the program in Ex. 5 would affect its semantics drastically.

In contrast, we aim at a meta-control strategy which does not drastically change the intended models of a program, but should accelerate model computation. For computationally complex programs it should also accept heuristic control information that permits to terminate early with a tolerable approximation of the intended model, as it has been proposed in the past in AI ([Pea84]).

4.2 Declarative Control

We want to demonstrate how semantic control information can be used at the meta-level to declaratively control and accelerate the computation of the desired part of the conventional fixpoint. To this end we discuss how to exploit the subsumption mechanism as presented before. First let us explicate some basic properties of subsumption w.r.t. the problem of search space reduction. Subsumption can be observed in two flavors:

- *Deletion on the fly:* Subsumption orderings can *detect* already generated tuples that can be discarded during the deduction process, once they are recognized as no longer needed due to newly generated tuples or not needed due to old better ones.

– *Pruning:* This is an extreme form of exploitation of subsumption information. In general it requires an additional *declarative control program* that *prevents* subsumed or irrelevant tuples from being generated in the first place.

Bidirectional heuristic search. Let us exemplify our approach by one nontrivial case study taken from the realm of heuristic search in AI.

Problem statement: Let edge(M, N, C) be the edges of a graph labeled by nonnegative costs $c(M, N)$ with two distinguished nodes s and t. The task is to find the cost of an optimal path between s and t. □

We perform bidirectional search on this graph by running two A*-algorithms, one starting at s and heading forward for t and a second one starting at t and heading backward for s as shown in Fig. 1. Those nodes of the search trees already covered by the opposite direction — like p in Fig. 1 — are pruned. The heuristic functions h_1 and h_2 are used to estimate the cost h_1^* and h_2^* of the optimal path from a node to the corresponding goal nodes t and s, resp., yielding an algorithm similar to BS* ([Kwa89]).

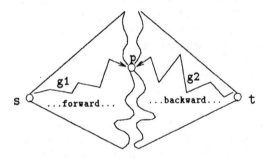

Fig. 1. Forward and backward search tree

Two predicates f_reached(N, G, F) and b_reached(N, G, F) are introduced for the forward and backward search tree, resp., where N is a node, G are the costs of the currently optimal path from the corresponding start node to N and F are the heuristic estimates h_i(N) plus G. A predicate optimal(Q) is to represent the cheapest cost of a path found between s and t.

Figure 2 specifies a *Datalog-S* program BS with interpreted heuristic functions h_1 and h_2. The stated subsumptions *cheaper_f* and *cheaper_b* allow us to get rid of f_reached and b_reached tuples, resp., with worse G-values. The cost of an optimal path between s and t is singled out by employing the subsumption ordering *cheaper_c*.

Note that program BS does not yet exploit its heuristic parameter F for purposes of greedy search. Hence evaluation of BS by delta-iteration with subsump-

```
define program BS {

    subsumptions {
        cheaper_f(f_reached(M,G2, _ ), f_reached(M,G1, _ )) ← G1 < G2.
        cheaper_b(b_reached(N,G2, _ ), b_reached(N,G1, _ )) ← G1 < G2.
        cheaper_c(optimal(Q2), optimal(Q1)) ← Q1 < Q2. }

    rules {
        f_reached(s, 0, h₁(s)).
        f_reached(M, G, F) cheaper_f ← f_reached(N, G1, _ ), edge(N, M, C),
                                       G = G1 + C, F = G + h₁(M).
        b_reached(t, 0, h₂(t)).
        b_reached(N, G, F) cheaper_b ← b_reached(M, G2, _ ), edge(N, M, C),
                                       G = G2 + C, F = G + h₂(N).
        optimal(Q)          cheaper_c ← f_reached(N, G1, _ ),
                                        b_reached(N, G2, _ ), Q = G1 + G2.}}
```

Fig. 2. *Datalog-S* program for bidirectional search

tion would correspond to an uninformed breadth-first search. (For instance, one could run BS on CORAL by a proper choice of annotations as discussed before.) However, in this problem domain we can reduce the search space enormously due to the following heuristic and semantic control knowledge.

Lemma 16 Search space reduction. *(cf. [Kwa89])*

1. *Nodes with minimal F-value are preferred to be expanded during the search.*

2. *A node can be pruned during the search,*
   - *as soon as its parent node (seen in search direction) is already reached by the opposite search, or*
   - *whose F-value is not better than the currently optimal cost.*

3. *If there are still nodes to be expanded in forward and in backward direction, then continue the search, otherwise terminate early.* □

For instance, all successors of node p of Fig. 1 can be pruned in the forward search tree, because p is already reached in the backward direction.

4.3 Sloppy-delta iteration with subsumption

The challenge now is to find to a way to express this semantic and heuristic control knowledge in a declarative fashion and, secondly, to automatically compile it into some efficient greedy iteration scheme.

In [KKTG93] it has been reported how this BS*-like search procedure can be implemented by sloppy-delta fixpoint iteration with subsumption and pruning.

But this was mainly achieved by manual compilation, lacking a general methodology. The *sloppy-delta iteration scheme* ([GKB87, SKGB87]) is a very powerful operator to control bottom-up evaluation. In its general form it has various degrees of freedom to control the deduction process in a greedy or goal-directed manner. In addition to continuation conditions (to control early termination) it maintains four sets during the iteration:

- S accumulates the result set representing the already *expanded* tuples.
- Σ contains the set of tuples yet *unexpanded* but potentially relevant.
- Δ contains the tuples *to be expanded* in the next iteration round.
- AUX contains the set of *newly generated* tuples, determined by a differential expression dependent on Δ and S in general.

Moreover, sloppy-delta iteration possesses two function parameters called *Nice* and *Rest*, which can control the *choice* of tuples from Σ into Δ and the *pruning* of tuples from Σ or AUX, resp. These parameters give an enormous flexibility in controlling the deduction process. Extremes are:

- $\Delta := \Sigma; \Sigma := \emptyset$: this corresponds to a breadth-first search.
- Organize Σ as a stack; $\Delta := pop(\Sigma)$: this simulates a depth-first search.

Depending on the goal pursued anything between these two extreme expansion modes is feasible, e.g. simulation of `choice(X, Y)` can be done in a straightforward manner. Nonwithstanding, the gap between concepts used in heuristic search and these rather technical sets and parameters prohibits an automatic compilation so far. We take a first step to narrow down this gap by identifying related concepts in heuristic search and sloppy-delta iteration, which have been developed independently.

In terms of deductive database terminology, Σ implements *memoization* to enable intelligent backtracking or resumption of work at a different point in the search space. But in terms of AI terminology, at a closer look it turns out that the set Σ closely relates with the notion of an *open list* in heuristic search. Concerning the result set S, it has its correspondence in the notion of a *closed list*. To carry on this analogy we informally introduce the following meta-predicates to control the semantic and heuristic pruning of the search space:

- *CLOSED:* Set of nodes already *expanded* during the search.
- *OPEN:* Set of *unexpanded* nodes, potentially becoming expanded during the further search.
- *NEXT:* Set of nodes actually chosen from *OPEN to be expanded* immediately for continuing the search.
- *NEW:* Set of *newly generated* nodes to be included into *OPEN*.
- *CONTINUE:* Condition to be satisfied by the *OPEN* nodes for search continuation.

We can record the following correspondences of (abstract) heuristic search and sloppy-delta iteration:

$$
\begin{array}{lll}
CLOSED \Longleftrightarrow & \text{expanded set} & \Longleftrightarrow S \\
OPEN \Longleftrightarrow & \text{unexpanded set} & \Longleftrightarrow \Sigma \\
NEXT \Longleftrightarrow & \text{to-be-expanded set} \Longleftrightarrow \Delta \\
NEW \Longleftrightarrow & \text{newly generated set} \Longleftrightarrow \text{AUX}
\end{array}
$$

Now we can transform Lem. 16 into these more high-level constructs instead of lower-level sloppy-delta parameters. By means of reification and assuming w.l.o.g. that all heuristic estimates are different, the transformation into a declarative meta-control specification for greedy search can then be thought as follows:

1. Meta-subsumptions for heuristic control of expansion:

```
define meta_subsumptions {
    prefer_f(NEXT(f_reached( _ , _ , F2)),
            NEXT(f_reached( _ , _ , F1))) ← F1 < F2.
    prefer_b(NEXT(b_reached( _ , _ , F2)),
            NEXT(b_reached( _ , _ , F1))) ← F1 < F2. }
```

```
NEXT(f_reached(M, G, F)) prefer_f ← OPEN(f_reached(M, G, F)).
NEXT(b_reached(N, G, F)) prefer_b ← OPEN(b_reached(N, G, F)).
```

2. Meta-rules for semantic control of pruning:

```
define meta_rules {
    PRUNE(f_reached(M, G, F))
      ← NEW(f_reached(M, G, F)),
        (CLOSED(f_reached(N, _ , _)), edge(N, M, _),
        CLOSED(b_reached(N, _ , _)) or optimal(Q), F ≥ Q).
    PRUNE(b_reached(N, G, F))
      ← NEW(b_reached(N, G, F)),
        (CLOSED(b_reached(M, _ , _)), (edge(N, M, _),
        CLOSED(f_reached(M, _ , _)) or optimal(Q), F ≥ Q). }
```

3. Meta-condition for early termination:

```
define meta_conditions {
    CONTINUE ← OPEN(f_reached( _ , _ , _ )),
              OPEN(b_reached( _ , _ , _ )). }
```

This declarative specification on the meta-level (though informal for the time being) facilitates an automatic compilation into sloppy-delta iteration with subsumption and pruning. For instance, the *Nice*-function can be determined by the given meta-subsumptions which express a (deterministic) choice. The *Rest*-function, responsible for prunings from Σ or AUX, can be synthesized from the auxiliary meta-predicate **PRUNE**. Note that prunings can be interpreted as extreme cases of subsumption (filtering out). Ideally, atoms identified for pruning should be eliminated before being materialized into AUX or Σ. But a complete compilation procedure, building on the established correspondence between abstract heuristic search and the variety of sloppy-delta parameters, must be left for future research.

5 Summary and Outlook

Based on theoretical foundations for differential fixpoint iteration with subsumption we have proposed to extend deductive databases by logic programming with subsumption. The introduced *Datalog-S* language extension is considered only as a first step towards more powerful database reasoning, supporting semantic and heuristic control for large and complex applications. Naturally, there exist several open problems on the route the this goal. To name some of them, extensions of the theory to handle negation, issues of query optimization in the presence of subsumption (e.g. improving magic-sets by exploitation of subsumption) or language issues for declarative heuristic control beyond *choice* demand solutions. Last but not least, the effectiveness of database reasoning has to be verified by really complex applications, like e.g. the *DUCK*-system for probabilistic reasoning.

Acknowledgment: We would like to thank Gerhard Köstler for many constructive discussions and suggestions during the preparation of this article.

References

[Fur94] U. Furbach. Theory Reasoning - Extending First Order Calculi to Handle Theories. In *this volume*.

[GGZ91] Sumit Ganguly, Sergio Greco, and Carlo Zaniolo. Minimum and maximum predicates in logic programming. In *Proc. ACM SIGACT-SIGMOD Symp. on Principles of Database Systems*, pages 154–163, Denver, CO, May 1991. ACM Press.

[GKB87] Ulrich Güntzer, Werner Kießling, and Rudolf Bayer. On the evaluation of recursion in (deductive) database systems by efficient differential fixpoint iteration. In *Int'l. Proc. IEEE Conf. on Data Engineering*, pages 120–129, Los Angeles, CA, Feb. 1987.

[GKT91] Ulrich Güntzer, Werner Kießling, and Helmut Thöne. New directions for uncertainty reasoning in deductive databases. In *Proc. ACM SIGMOD Conf. on Management of Data*, pages 178–187, Denver, CO, May 1991.

[GSZ93] Sergio Greco, Domenico Sacca, Carlo Zaniolo. Dynamic Programming Optimization for Logic Queries with Aggregates. In *Int'l. Conference on Logic Programming*, Vancouver, Nov. 1993, pp. 575 - 589.

[GZG93] S. Greco, C. Zaniolo, S. Ganguly: Greedy by Choice. In *Proc. of the 11th ACM Symposium on Principles of Database Systems*, 1992, pp. 105 - 113.

[KKG93] Werner Kießling, Gerhard Köstler, and Ulrich Güntzer. Fixpoint evaluation with subsumption for probabilistic uncertainty. In *GI-Conference Datenbanksysteme in Büro, Technik und Wissenschaft (BTW'93)*, pages 316–333, Braunschweig, Germany, Mar. 1993. Springer-Verlag.

[KKTG93] Gerhard Köstler, Werner Kießling, Helmut Thöne, and Ulrich Güntzer. The differential fixpoint operator with subsumption. In *Proc. of the 3rd Int'l. Conf. on Deductive and Object-Oriented Databases*, Scottsdale, AR, Dec. 1993, pp. 35 - 48.

[Kwa89] James B. H. Kwa. BS*: An admissible bidirectional staged heuristic search algorithm. *Artificial Intelligence*, 38:95–109, 1989.

[NT89] S. Naqvi, S. Tsur. *A Logic Language for Data and Knowledge Bases.* Computer Science Press, 1989.

[Pea84] Judea Pearl. *Heuristics*, Addison Wesley, 1984.

[RSS92] Raghu Ramakrishnan, Divesh Srivastava, and S. Sudarshan. CORAL— Control, Relations and Logic. In *Proc. Int'l. Conf. on Very Large Data Bases*, pages 238–250, Vancouver, BC, Canada, 1992.

[PLD93] *International Workshop on Programming with Logic Databases*, R. Ramakrishnan (ed), Vanvouver, Nov. 1993.

[SKGB87] Helmut Schmidt, Werner Kießling, Ulrich Güntzer, and Rudolf Bayer. Compiling exploratory and goal-directed deduction into sloppy delta-iteration. In *Proceedings of the Symposium on Logic Programming*, pages 233–243, San Francisco, CA, Sep. 1987.

[SKGB89] Helmut Schmidt, Werner Kießling, Ulrich Güntzer, and Rudolf Bayer. DBA*: Solving combinatorial problems with deductive databases. In *Proc. GI/SI-Conference on Datenbanksysteme in Büro, Technik und Wissenschaft (BTW'89)*, pages 196–215, Zürich, Switzerland, 1989.

[SZ90] D. Sacca, C. Zaniolo. Stable Models and Non-Determinism in Logic Programs with Negation. In *Proc. of the 9th ACM Symposium on Principles of Database Systems*, 1990, pp. 205 - 217.

[SSG*90] H. Schmidt, N. Steger, U. Güntzer, W. Kießling, R. Azone, R. Bayer. Combining Deduction by Certainty with the Power of Magic. In *Deductive and Object-Oriented Databases*, Kim, Nicolas and Nishio (eds.), Elsevier Science Publishers, North-Holland, 1990, pp. 103 - 122.

[VLJ94] *Special Issue on Prototypes of Deductive Databases*, VLDB Journal, K. Ramamohanarao (ed), to appear 1994.

Theory Reasoning in First Order Calculi

Ulrich Furbach

Universität Koblenz
Institut für Informatik
Rheinau 1
56075 Koblenz, Germany

Tel.: +49–261–9119–433
E-mail: uli@informatik.uni-koblenz.de

Abstract. Building in special theories into first order calculi is used in various applications of deduction to increase efficiency of proof procedures. We give a brief review of methods for the combination of theories with deduction or logic programming. We show how a whole family of first order calculi can be extended for theory handling; these calculi are related to each other by a simulability relation. One of these calculi is tableau model elimination which can be implemented very efficiently by Prolog Technology Theorem Proving (PTTP). A PPTP-prover which is able to handle universal theories is presented and some examples are given to show that the use of built-in theories can increase efficiency drastically.

1 Deduction with Theories

Automated reasoning is a discipline of AI research which has been lively since the early days of this science. During the last 40 years of AI research there have been numerous shifts of paradigms. One of those significant changes was rejecting the general problem-solving approach towards special domain-dependent, knowledge-based systems. Of course, this development can be observed in automated reasoning and theorem proving as well. Theorem provers nowadays aim at incorporating specialized and efficient modules for the incorporation of special domains of knowledge.

To a certain extent that has been minded even from the very beginning in theorem proving. *Equality handling* in predicate logic, i.e. the task of considering the special theory given by the axioms of equality is such an early theory handling approach. There are numerous proposals to build in this theory, reaching from paramodulation to completion based techniques.

Another very well-investigated example for theory handling is the design of calculi and proof procedures, which use *many-* or *order-sorted* logics. Here, the aim is to take care of a sort hierarchy in a direct way, e.g. by using a special unification procedure. This is in contrast to relativation approaches which transform the sort information into formulas of the unsorted logics.

A stream of research, which combines so-called *constraints* with first order deduction stems from logic programming. These constraints can be understood as a means to encapsulate efficient deduction techniques for special domains (e.g. finite domains or rationals) and to combine it with the main calculus used within the system.

For *knowledge representation purposes* there are approaches which aim at the combination of taxonomical and assertional knowledge: taxonomical knowledge is used as a special theory, which has to be handled outside the deduction mechanism which processes the assertional knowledge. One of the most prominent examples of those approaches is KRYPTON [BFL83], where the semantic net language KL-ONE is used as a theory-defining language, which is combined with a theorem prover for predicate logic. This system is based on the theory resolution calculus [Sti85], which will be discussed later on. Nowadays numerous works on defining *concept* languages with well-understood semantics for the definition of taxonomical knowledge exist [Hol90].

Another promising approach towards more intelligent systems is *hybrid reasoning*. The aim is to combine different paradigms of reasoning into a unique system; this could include symbolic with sub-symbolic reasoning methods.

A Classification. Theory reasoning always deals with two kinds of reasoning: background reasoning for the theory, and foreground reasoning for the actual problem specification. We are mostly interested in studying the interface between foreground and background reasoning. We give a formal description of this interface which applies to a wide class of theories. We will not focus on the question of how to build dedicated background reasoners for *special* theories, even though we give some examples in section 4.

It has to be said what kinds of theories we are interested in. The "upper boundary" is given by the *universal theories*, i.e. theories that can be axiomatized by a set of formulas that does not contain $\exists$-quantifiers. Universal theories are expressive enough to formulate e.g. equality or interesting taxonomic theories. Moreover, the restriction to universal theories is not essential. A theory which contains existential quantifiers may be transformed by Skolemization into a universal theory by preserving satisfiability. Universal theories also mark the limit of what can be built into a calculus preserving the completeness of calculus (cf. [Pet91]).

Due to the great variety of approaches for theory reasoning, we prefer to bring in structure by classifying the various approaches. Of course there are plenty of ways of doing this. The classification we use is by *level of connection*. In order to explain this term it is necessary to recall the nature of theory reasoning as interfacing background reasoning and foreground reasoning. Now, by "level of connection" we mean the common subpart of the foreground and the background language, that is used for their interfacing. To be concrete, we will distinguish the three levels *literal level, term level* and *variable level*. Figure 1 is a classification of the approaches to be described with respect to level of connection. The *literal level* is the most general of all; it allows for theory reasoning with literals with *different* predicate symbols (general theory reasoning approaches and equality). This is different from *term level* theory reasoning, where unification on terms is replaced by some unification modulo a theory (typing, dedicated unification, universal unification). A further specialization is the *variable level* theory reasoning which is bounded to variables (typing of variables, constraints).

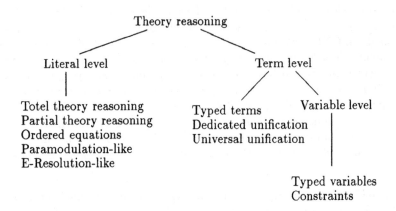

Fig. 1. Classification wrt. level of connection

The methods subsumed by "theory reasoning" in figure 1 are subject to enormous research activities and results. Thus it would be too a big task to give a deep overview of all of them. Since there are excellent overviews of *term level* (usually known as "unification theory") (e.g. [Sie89]) and *constraints* (see e.g. [Mes89], or [Van89] for a textbook on constraints in logic programming), we will concentrate on the *literal level*.

Plan of this Paper. In the next section we fix a class of calculi for which we demonstrate how theory handling on literal level can be defined; this will be done for the model elimination calculus. In section 3 we present our theorem proving system PROTEIN which is a *Prolog Technology Theorem Prover* with an interface for the combination of universal theories. In section 4 we give applications of theory theorem proving using PROTEIN: We depict a completion technique, which aims at using a subset of the set of clauses as a theory, in order to increase efficiency of the prover. We discuss the combination of a theorem prover with taxonomical reasoning and we demonstrate how spatial reasoning can be understood as a special kind of theory.

2 Extending a Class of Calculi

In this section we will combine a certain class of first order calculi with universal theories. This class is depicted in the diagram in Figure 2. This set of calculi is relevant for the field of automated deduction in so far as most high speed theorem provers are based on one of them. The relation indicated by arrows compares the calculi with respect to stepwise simulability; this is done in detail in [BF92] by using the consolution calculus as a framework, which is used to formulate and to compare the other calculi. For the most of these calculi there are theory-handling variants in the literature. All these developments are more or less based on the seminal work of Mark Stickel on theory resolution ([Sti85]): Baumgartner defined the combination of universal theories with tableau model elimination ([Bau92]) and Petermann did the same for Bibel's connection method ([Pet93]). In [BFP] an approach very similar to the one in Figure 2 is proposed. Theory handling is defined for consolution and completeness of all other theory handling variants of the calculi is proven by using the consolution framework.

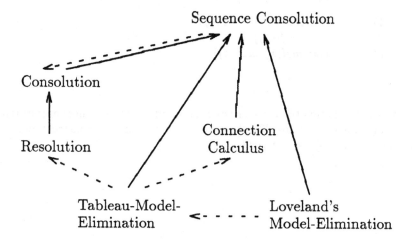

Fig. 2. Relations between calculi

For this paper only two aspects of the diagram are of interest: firstly it is obvious that tableau model elimination plays a distinguished role. It is the weakest of the calculi we related together; a proof within the tableau model elimination calculus can be simulated stepwisely either by resolution, by the connection calculus or by consolution. Hence, whenever we study refinements of tableau model elimination we can be sure that, in principle, it is possible to use the improvement in the other calculi as well. This class of calculi of which tableau model elimination is the weakest is the second aspect we want to point out. For the rest of this paper we can focus on theories in model elimination, bearing in mind that everything holds for the whole class of calculi.

In the following subsection we will introduce theory model elimination by an example before we give a formal definition.

Theory Model Elimination — An Example. We will follow the lines of [LSBB92] and understand the inference rules of the calculus as tree-transforming operators. Then the calculus is much in the spirit of semantic tableau with unification for clauses (see [Fit90]), but with an important restriction. This restriction will be explained below and justifies using the new name "tableau model elimination" instead of qualifying it as "analytical tableaux for clauses with unification".

As an example take the following theory T together with the "foreground" axioms from C.

$T:$ (T-1) $\forall x((mammal(x) \land thinker(x)) \rightarrow person(x))$
        (T-3) $\forall x(man(x) \rightarrow person(x))$

$C:$ (1) $\{\neg person(fred), \neg man(y)\}$
      (2) $\{thinker(fred)\}$
      (3) $\{mammal(x), man(z)\}$

Model elimination tries to construct a semantic tableau, where every branch is T-complementary ("closed"). We have to pick a clause and construct an *initial tableau*; selecting clause (1) yields:

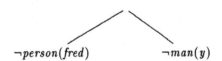

We will show a *theory extension step*, using from the left branch $\neg person(fred)$ and from clauses (2) and (3) the literals $thinker(fred)$ and $mammal(x)$ (respectively) as a T-unsatisfiable literal set. It can easily be seen that $\{X \leftarrow fred\}$ is a substitution, such that the set is T-unsatisfiable (join the clause form of (T-1) to this set and find a resolution refutation). Hence the tableau can be extended at the left branch with clauses (2) and (3) in such a way that a branch labelled with the T-unsatisfiable literal set comes up:

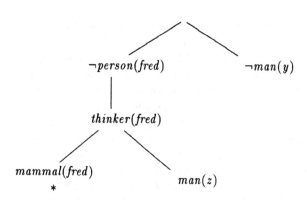

The path containing the set of T-unsatisfiable literals is closed, i.e. it is marked with an asterix and the corresponding substitution is applied to the whole tree.

Such a closing of a path can also be done by the second inference rule, the *reduction step*: if a path contains a set of literals that are theory complementary by some σ, it can be closed and the σ is applied to the entire tree. The branch ending in $man(z)$ can be closed in a reduction step, because by (T-3) the literals $man(z)$ and $\neg person(fred)$ are T-complementary by $\{z \leftarrow fred\}$.

This process has to be repeated until a tree is derived where all branches are marked with a star. Then a refutation is found.

Theory Model Elimination – Formal Definition. A *clause* is a multiset $\{L_1, \ldots, L_n\}$ of literals, usually written as the disjunction $L_1 \vee \cdots \vee L_n$. As usual, clauses are considered implicitly as being universally quantified, and a clause set is considered logically as a conjunction of clauses.

Instead of the *chains* of the original model elimination calculus we follow [BF92] and work in a branch-set setting as in the consolation calculus ([Ede91]). A *branch* is a finite sequence of literals, written by juxtaposing its constituents $L_1 L_2 \cdots L_n$. A *branch set* is a finite multiset of branches.

The primary data structures of model elimination are branches, i.e. *sequences* of literals, rather than sets or multisets. Occasionally, however, the ordering of literals along a branch plays no role, and a branch occurs in a place where a set or a multiset is required. In this case the type conversion is done as expected; e.g. we will write $L \in p$ to indicate that the literal L occurs in the branch p, or in $p \cup M$ p is to be read as a set. Substitutions are applied to branches, path sets and sets of these as expected.

Next, the necessary semantic preliminaries are introduced. Concerning basic notions such as substitutions, atoms, literals, junctors and quantifiers and associated definitions of interpretation, model, satisfiability, validity etc. we refer to the standard literature (e.g. [Llo87, CL73]). Rather than dealing with general interpretations we restrict ourselves to *Herbrand-Interpretations* over a (mostly implicitly) given finite signature Σ. Furthermore we suppose every Σ to contain the 0-ary predicate symbol F (meaning "false"), and we suppose Σ to contain at least one constant symbol (which can always be added if none is there).

We assume a *theory* to be given by a satisfiable set of universally quantified formulas, e.g. as a clause set. In the sequel T always denotes such a theory.

The restriction to universally quantified theories is necessary because precisely for those theories a Herbrand theorem holds (see [Pet91]).

A *Herbrand T-interpretation* I for a formula F is a Herbrand interpretation over $\Sigma_T \cup \Sigma_F$ satisfying the theory T, i.e. $I \models T$. Since we deal with Herbrand T-interpretations only, the prefix "Herbrand" can be omitted from here on. We write $I \models_T F$ to indicate that I is a T-interpretation and I satisfies F. Furthermore, F is called T-valid, $\models_T F$ iff every T-interpretation satisfies F, and F is T-(un-)satisfiable iff some (none) T-interpretation satisfies F.

As a consequence of these definitions it holds $\models_T F$ iff $\neg F$ is T-unsatisfiable iff $T \cup \{\neg F\}$ is unsatisfiable.

As usual, clause sets are, semantically, conjunctions of disjunctions of literals. Branches are semantically considered as conjunctions of literals. With these conventions, T-satisfiability and T-validity of branches, clauses and clause sets is thus well-defined. For example $I \models_T M$ for a clause set M iff $I \models_T C$ for every $C \in M$.

We quite often make use of minimality properties: A T-unsatisfiable clause set M is called *minimal T-unsatisfiable wrt. a clause* $C \in M$ iff $M \setminus \{C\}$ is T-satisfiable.

Below we will consider implications of the form $\forall(L_1 \wedge \cdots \wedge L_n \rightarrow L_{n+1})$ where $n \geq 1$, $L_1, \ldots, L_n$ are literals different from F and L_{n+1} is a literal. An implication of this form is called *background justification* iff it is T-valid, i.e. iff

$$\models_T \forall(L_1 \wedge \cdots \wedge L_n \rightarrow L_{n+1})$$

The motivation for this name is to become clear soon. In *ground background justifications* no variables occur. Hence the $\forall$-sign can be dropped and the resulting formula will still be called this way.

A background justification is called *minimal T-valid wrt. L_j*, where $1 \leq j \leq n$, iff

$$\not\models_T \forall(L_1 \wedge \cdots \wedge L_{j-1} \wedge L_{j+1} \wedge \cdots \wedge L_n \rightarrow L_{n+1})$$

A background justification is called *minimal T-valid wrt. L_{n+1}* iff it either $L_{n+1} \equiv$ F or

$$\not\models_T \forall(L_1 \wedge \cdots \wedge L_n \rightarrow \text{F})$$

A background justification is called *minimal T-valid*[1] iff it is minimal T-valid wrt. every L_j and also wrt. L_{n+1}.

---

[1] Minimal T-validity is related to the concept of *prime implicates*, a familiar concept in logic. The only difference is that prime implicates may not be tautologies. However this demand is too strong for our purposes.

Definition 1. ($\mathcal{T}$-extension step) the inference rule $\mathcal{T}$-*extension step* is defined as follows (cf. Figure 3):

$$\frac{\{K_1 \cdots K_m\} \cup \mathcal{Q} \quad L_1 \vee R_1 \quad \cdots \quad L_n \vee R_n}{(\{K_1 \cdots K_m K \mid K \in Res \vee R_1 \vee \cdots \vee R_n\} \cup \mathcal{Q})\sigma} \quad \textbf{Ext}$$

iff

1. $\{K_1 \cdots K_m\} \cup \mathcal{Q}$ is a branch set ($m \geq 1$, $K_1 \cdots K_m$ is called the *selected branch*, and K_m is called the *extended literal K_m*), and
2. $n \geq 0$ and $L_i \vee R_i$ are clauses ($i = 1 \ldots n$; the L_is are called *extending literals*) where R_i denotes the rest of the *extending clause* $L_i \vee R_i$, and
3. there exist indices $1 \leq j_1, \ldots, j_k \leq m-1$ and there exists a substitution σ such that

$$\forall(K_{j_1} \wedge \cdots \wedge K_{j_k} \wedge K_m \wedge L_1 \wedge \cdots \wedge L_n \rightarrow Res)\sigma$$

is a minimal $\mathcal{T}$-valid background justification. Here Res is a literal[2], which is also called *residue* in this context. Following [Sti86], the set $\{K_{j_1}, \ldots, K_{j_k}, K_m, L_1, \ldots, L_n\}$ is called the *key set* of the inference.

An extension step with $Res \equiv F$ is called *total*, otherwise it is called *partial*.

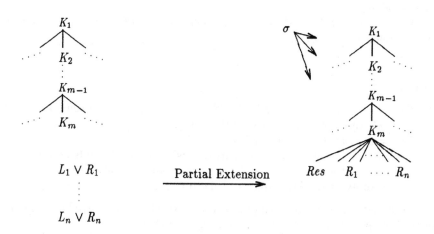

Fig. 3. Partial $\mathcal{T}$-extension step. The branch sets are indicated in tableaux-style as a tree (cf. [LSBB92]).

Thus, "extension step" derives from a branch set and some clauses a new branch set. The minimality requirement for the background justification in 3

---

[2] Residues can be generalized to clauses as in [Sti86], if it is of interest.

states that when joined with some literals from the branch, the leaf as well as all the extending literals must be essential for the extension step in the sense that without any of these literals the implication would not hold. This restriction is important for practical implementations since it allows the search for the extending literals to be centered around the leaf literal K_m.

Note that the extending literals are not contained anywhere in the new branches. This is a difference and improvement on the works in [Bau92] and [Pet93]. This difference may be significant for implementations, since it reduces search in the ancestor lists of leaves.

This formulation of the extension rule includes reduction steps as well. In the case that no extending clauses are needed (i.e. $n = 0$ in 3) of the above definition) we have a reduction of a branch. Note, however, that this "reduction" may introduce a residue.

Definition 2. (Deletion step, T-model elimination) As a second inference rule we define T-*deletion step*:

$$\frac{\{K_1 \cdots K_m \mathsf{F}\} \cup \mathcal{Q}}{\mathcal{Q}} \ \mathbf{Del}$$

Thus the deletion step allows branches ending in F to be removed. The calculus of *total* T-model elimination consists of the inference rules *total* T-*extension step* and *deletion step*, and *partial* T-model additionally consists of *partial* T-*extension step*.

A *(total, partial)* T-*model elimination derivation of* $\mathcal{Q}_n$ *from a clause set* M then is defined as a sequence $(n \geq 1)$

$$\mathcal{Q}_1, \ldots, \mathcal{Q}_n$$

such that

1. $\mathcal{Q}_1 = \{L_1, \ldots, L_n\}$, i.e. a multiset of branches of length 1, for some $L_1 \vee \cdots \vee L_n \in M$; this clause is also called the *query*, andg
2. for $i = 2 \ldots n$, $\mathcal{Q}_i$ is obtained either
   - by applying the total, resp. partial version of the **Ext** inference rule to $\mathcal{Q}_{i-1}$ and some new variants of clauses from M, or else
   - by applying the **Del** inference rule to $\mathcal{Q}_{i-1}$.

For brevity prefixes are often dropped. E.g. we will write "partial derivation" instead of "partial T-model elimination derivation" etc.

A *refutation of* M is a derivation of the empty branch set $\{\}$ from M.

Completeness and correctness of the calculus is proven elsewhere ([Bau93b]). For the completeness result it must be assumed that the background reasoner, i.e. the inference mechanism from the theory, is able to enumerate for a set of literals all substitutions, which make it T-unsatisfiable.

With respect to implementation there is another serious problem: the explosion of search space. Particularly when partial theory reasoning is to be implemented a tremendous search tree comes from the choices, which extending clauses and which residues are used for an extension step.

In the next section we depict an implementation of a prover with a theory interface and in section 4 we discuss various applications.

3 PROTEIN — A PTTP-Implementation

In the previous section, we argued that model elimination is a good candidate to act as a representative of the whole class of calculi from Figure 2. Concerning implementation there is another good argument; model elimination can be implemented by using Sickels' PTTP-technique ([Sti88]). The idea of this "Prolog Technology Theorem Prover" is to view Prolog as an "almost complete" theorem prover, which has to be extended by only a few ingredients in order to handle the non-Horn case. By this technique the WAM-technology and other benefits of optimizing Prolog compilers are accessible to theorem proving.

Model elimination turns out to be particularly useful for this, since it is, like Prolog, an input proof procedure. So Prolog has to be extended only by the following features (see [Sti88] again for details):

- Prolog's unsound unification has to be replaced by a sound unification algorithm. This can either be done by directly building in sound unification into the Prolog implementation, or by reprogramming sound unification in Prolog and calling this code instead of Prolog's unsound unification. Our practical experiments consider both cases.
- A complete search strategy is needed. Usually depth-bounded iterative deepening is used. The strategy can be compiled into the Prolog program by additional parameters, being used as "current depth" and "limit depth". The cost of an extension step can be uniformly 1 (depth-bounded search), or can be proportional to the length of the input clause (inference-bounded search).
- The model elimination reduction operation has to be implemented. This can be realized by memoizing the subgoals solved so far as a list in an additional argument, and by Prolog code that checks a goal for a complementary member of that list. Of course, this check has to be carried out with sound unification.

All this can be done by preprocessing, which gives a PROLOG program that can be processed by any Prolog-system.

Our system PROTEIN (*PRO*ver with a *T*heory *E*xtension *IN*terface) is a PTTP-based first order theorem prover over built-in theories.

PROTEIN is characterized by the following features:

- PROTEIN is based on the *PTTP implementation technique*
- PROTEIN offers alternate inference rules for *case analysis* [Lov91, BF93]. In this setting no contrapositives are needed, and hence the system is well suited as an interpreter for disjunctive logic programming.
- PROTEIN includes *theory reasoning* as introduced in the previous section. An auxiliary program, called the *theory completer*, can be used to derive a suitable background reasoner from a given Horn theory in a fully automatic way. This will be discussed further in the following section.

– PROTEIN includes several *calculus refinements and flags*.

PROTEIN compares very well with other high speed theorem provers like OTTER and SETHEO. Exact figures will be given in the next section where we discuss applications of theory reasoning.

4 Applications

In this section we will discuss various applications of theory handling in model elimination. These applications have different status with respect to their realisation: for *linear completion* there exists a worked out theory and it is fully implemented; for *spatial reasoning* there is an interface for a spatial reasoner implemented for PROTEIN and for *knowledge representation* there are only ideas and plans.

Linear Completion

This approach is proposed by Baumgartner and is described in detail in [Bau93a]; we just want to demonstrate that theory reasoning can very well be used to increase efficiency of a theorem prover.

Assume we have a Horn theory and an arbitrary set of clauses as foreground. Recalling the definition of the total extension step from theory model elimination we convince ourselves that there is a very elementary and all the same very costly task:

(*)   Is a set of literals inconsistent under the given Horn theory?[3]

Baumgartners *linear completion technique* transform the Horn theory at compile time, such that this special Horn theory can be combined more efficiently with the foreground reasoner.

Let us discuss this with an example from Figure 4. The left side of the picture depicts one total theory extension step. The right side shows that this step can be broken down in a sequence of two partial theory extension steps. A first extension step yields the residue $a < c$ and in the second step we get $a < a$ as a residue, which can finally be marked as unsatisfiable within the theory. Both residues, per definition, are logical consequences of the theory. However, in this special example we did not choose an arbitrary logical consequence, moreover we used *one* Horn clause from our theory to generate a consequence. This was done by using the transitivity clause from the theory and by extending the current path with the help of those input clauses, that the extending literals can be unified with the entire body of the Horn clause. I.e. the Horn clause is used as an inference rule in a bottom up manner.

Obviously we have broken down the big total inference step with proof task (*) into smaller partial steps. For the computation of the residues we used the

---

[3] The set of literals are the literals on the path, which have to be closed.

Input Clauses: $(a < b) \vee P$ *Theory:* $\forall x: \neg(x < x)$

               $(b < c) \vee Q$ $\forall x, y, z: (x < y) \wedge (y < z) \rightarrow (x < z)$

               $(c < a) \vee R$

               ...

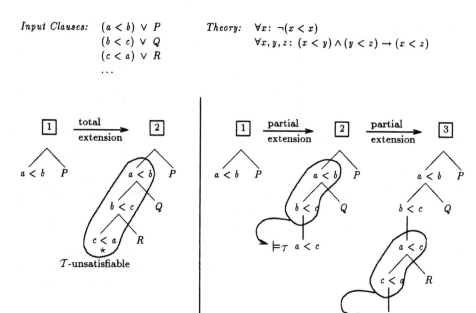

Fig. 4. A *total* theory model elimination derivation (left side) and a *partial* theory model elimination derivation (right side).

Horn clauses from the theory as inference rules. It is easy to see that this indeed yields logical consequences, but unfortunately this strategy is not complete. Baumgartner proved in [Bau93a], that it is possible to transform the Horn clause theory, such that the above depicted startegy is complete. This transformation is similar to Knuth-Bendix completion and hence is called *linear completion*. Figure 5 shows again our simple example with the completed theory, called *background inference system* therein. We will not give the technical details of the completion procedure (see [Bau93a]), moreover we show that this method yields a dramatic speed-up of our PROTEIN theorem prover.

The table from figure 6 contains the runtime results (in seconds) for various problems, obtained on a Sparc Station 2 running ECLiPSe Prolog:

Column 1 contains the data for a non-theory reasoning version of PROTEIN (i.e. the theory was supplied as axioms to the input set), while Column 2 is the linear completion based prover. Column 3 contains data for Setheo [LSBB92] in its latest version (Version 3.0). It was run in the default mode. Like Setheo, the

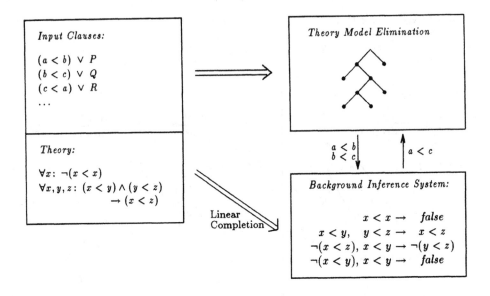

Fig. 5. Application of *Linear Completion* within *partial theory model elimination*.

Example	∅-PROTEIN	T-PROTEIN	SETHEO	METEOR
Non-Obvious	3.7	2.4	0.5	657
				1.4[2]
Graph	11.6	0.25	6.12	
Wos4	29	0.7	28	
Pelletier 48	1.2	0.1	0.4	
Pelletier 55	7.2	1.7	1.3	
IVT	∞	3319[2]	6787	∞
			14[3]	915[2]
Bledsoe3	∞	1637	∞	23324[1]

Remarks: 1 – with caching, 2 – with lemmas,
   3 – SETHEO with factorisation and anti-lemmas

Fig. 6. Runtime Results for various provers (in seconds). Obtained on a SPARC station 2 running ECLiPSe Prolog.

METEOR prover [AS92] is also based on model elimination and makes heavy use of caching and lemmaizing. The data in column 5 for METEOR are taken from [AS92].

Spatial Reasoning

In this section we will focus on a special kind of hybrid reasoning, namely the combination of spatial with propositional reasoning. With spatial reasoning we refer to a mechanism which represents and processes spatial knowledge. Examples of those representational formats and its application are e.g. within the LILOG-system ([HR91]); there is a modul within this natural language understanding system, which combines depictional components with a propositional, rule-based reasoner. The depictional reasoner uses for the analogical representation so-called cell-matrices together with a set of inspection processes ([Khe90]). Another application for spatial reasoning is demonstrated in [MM92], where a robot's view of a natural environment is represented and processed by means of geometrical methods.

For our purposes we want to abstract from the concrete spatial reasoner. We simply assume a device for representing spatial knowledge together with an interface which allows this representation to be queried. The spatial part plays the role of the theory, which will be combined with predicate logic.

The *theory* we are using consists of a map depicting the public transportation system of a city. Together with inspection processes we assume that this system is able to answer typical questions a traveler has. In Figure 7 a very small portion of such a map is given.

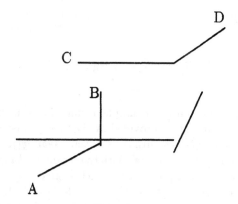

Fig. 7. Map of a public transportation system.

The *propositional part* contains information about a travelers' possibilities of changing lines, i.e. clauses 1,2,3 and a special context, i.e. clauses 4 and 5, and the query in clause 6, which asks whether *joe* is able to travel from A to D.

$$change(x, p1, p2, taxi) \leftarrow has\_luggage(x) \wedge distance(p1, p2, d) \wedge d > 200 \quad (1)$$
$$change(x, p1, p2, foot) \leftarrow has\_luggage(x) \wedge distance(p1, p2, d) \wedge d \leq 200 \quad (2)$$
$$change(x, p1, p2, foot) \leftarrow \neg has\_luggage(x) \quad (3)$$
$$travel(x, p1, p2) \leftarrow subway(x, p1, p2) \quad (4)$$
$$has\_luggage(joe) \quad (5)$$
$$\neg travel(joe, A, D) \quad (6)$$

The following is a theory model elimination proof of the set of clauses (1) – (6) with respect to the theory from Figure 7.

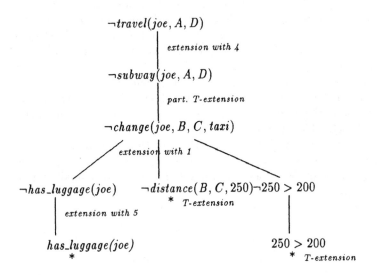

Fig. 8. A theory refutation for spatial reasoning

We want to point out that this example demonstrates the bidirectional interface between the two paradigms, provided by the theory reasoning. In the second inference step the map is queried with the subgoal $\neg subway(joe, A, D)$; instead of answering yes or no the "map answers" with the residue $\neg change(joe, B, C, taxi)$. This can be understood as a proof task, which is given back to the foreground reasoner. And indeed, the rest of the deduction deals with the refutation of this goal. The total extension steps performed therein can be interpreted as queries to the map, which are answered with "yes" without yielding an additional proof task.

Our implementation of PROTEIN provides an interface for combining theories given e.g. by Prolog-code with model elimination. At the moment we are searching for *fully implemented* spatial reasoners to run experiments.

Knowledge Representation

There exists significant research in cognitive science, which proves that mental representation of knowledge makes use of multiple representational formats. These different formalisms have to be combined for problem solving tasks. In the previous section we demonstrated such a combination for analogical with propositional knowledge. However, those multiple representation are useful even within one single knowledge representation paradigm.

One of the best known proposals to this end, is perhaps the KRYPTON system ([BGL85]. KRYPTON is the combination of a semantic net language with predicate logic. As net language the system contains KL-ONE for the definition of taxonomies; these can be used as theories in the predicate logic part. In KL-ONE jargon: The T-box for defining taxonomical knowledge is build with KL-ONE, while assertional knowledge is defined with full first order logic within the A-box. One outstanding success of KRYPTON is the formal definition of the interface between the two reasoners. The implementation of the system is based on Stickels theory resolution, which was built into a connection graph theorem prover developed by Stickel in the early eighties. With respect to KRYPTON's performance the opinion within the knowledge representation community is not too enthusiastic.

We see two developments which give raise to the hope, that it is possible to build hybrid systems a la KRYPTON with acceptable performance. On the assertional knowledge part we see, that there is substantial success in theorem proving. Nowadays provers are much more efficient and, moreover, as discussed in this paper, we have mechanisms to improve the interface for theory reasoning. On the taxonomical part there is a lot of work with respect to formalisation and implementation of terminological knowledge representation systems. There are various concept language proposed in the literature, which can be seen as decidable sublanguages of predicate logic with specialized deduction services (see e.g. [BDS93]).

There is work described in [FH93], which combines a concept language with Prolog, by implementing the combination via Prologs constraint mechanism. We are currently developing a similar system, based on our PTTP prover PROTEIN, which is built on top of a Prolog system with constraints.

5   Conclusion

We have presented a general viewpoint of theory handling in first order calculi. For a class of calculi, for which model elimination is a representative we defined a theory handling variant.

We described PROTEIN, an implementation of this theory model elimination calculus on the base of PTTP and we discussed, that this approach can be used in various application fields. All this applications show, that we can profit from the framework given by the theory model elimination, in so far that the interface to the background reasoner is defined within this framework.

A further application we could think of, is the combination of a database with a theorem prover. The database would define the theory, and a total extension step would be a query to the database system. In [KG93] the authors propose a somewhat different approach: they start with a deductive database and extend it towards database reasoning. For this they enhance the database inference methods with declarative meta-programming and intelligent search procedures from AI. This is inverse to our approach, where we propose to take automated reasoning systems from AI and interface it with a database system.

References

[AS92]   Owen L. Astrachan and Mark E. Stickel. Caching and Lemmaizing in Model Elimination Theorem Provers. In D. Kapur, editor, *Proceedings of the 11th International Conference on Automated Deduction (CADE-11)*, pages 224–238. Springer-Verlag, June 1992. LNAI 607.

[Bau92] P. Baumgartner. A Model Elimination Calculus with Built-in Theories. In H.-J. Ohlbach, editor, *Proceedings of the 16-th German AI-Conference (GWAI-92)*, pages 30–42. Springer, 1992. LNAI 671.

[Bau93a] P. Baumgartner. Linear Completion: Combining the Linear and the Unit-Resulting Restrictions. Research Report 9/93, University of Koblenz, 1993. (submitted).

[Bau93b] P. Baumgartner. Refinements of Theory Model Elimination and a Variant without Contrapositives. Research Report 8/93, University of Koblenz, 1993.

[BDS93] M. Buchheit, F.M. Donini, and A. Schaerf. Decidable reasoning in terminological knowledge representation systems. *Journal of Artificial Intelligence Research*, 1:109 – 138, 1993.

[BF92]   P. Baumgartner and U. Furbach. Consolution as a Framework for Comparing Calculi. Forschungsbericht 11/92, University of Koblenz, 1992. (to appear in *Journal of Symbolic Computation*).

[BF93]   P. Baumgartner and U. Furbach. Model Elimination without Contrapositives and its Application to PTTP. Fachbericht Informatik 12/93, Universität Koblenz, 1993. (submitted).

[BFL83] R. Brachmann, R. Fikes, and H. Levesque. KRYPTON: a functional approach to knowledge representation. *IEEE Computer*, 16(10):67–73, October 1983.

[BFP]   Peter Baumgartner, Ulrich Furbach, and Uwe Petermann. A unified approach to theory reasoning. To appear.

[BGL85] R. Brachman, V. Gilbert, and H. Levesque. An Essential Hybrid Reasoning System: Knowledge and Symbol Level Accounts of Krypton. In *Proc. IJCAI*, 1985.

[CL73]   C. Chang and R. Lee. *Symbolic Logic and Mechanical Theorem Proving*. Academic Press, 1973.

[Ede91] E. Eder. Consolution and its Relation with Resolution. In *Proc. IJCAI '91*, 1991.

[FH93] T. Frühwirt and P. Hanschke. Terminological reasoning with constraint handling rules. Manuscript ECRC Munich, 1993.

[Fit90] M. Fitting. *First Order Logic and Automated Theorem Proving.* Texts and Monographs in Computer Science. Springer, 1990.

[Hol90] B. Hollunder. Hybrid Inferences in KL-ONE-based Knowledge Representation Systems. Research Report RR-90-6, DFKI, May 1990.

[HR91] Otthein Herzog and Claus-Rainer Rollinger. *Text Understanding in LILOG - Integrating Computational Linguistics and Artificial Intelligence, Final Report on the IBM Germany LILOG-Project.* Springer-Verlag, 1991. LNAI 546.

[KG93] W. Kießling and U. Günzer. Database reasoning - a deductive framework for solving large and complex problems by means of subsumption. This volume, 1993.

[Khe90] Mohammed Nadjib Khenkhar. Eine objektorientierte Darstellung von Depiktionen auf der Grundlage von Zellmatrizen. In C. Freksa and C. Habel, editors, *Repräsentation und Verarbeitung räumlichen Wissens*, pages 99–112. Springer-Verlag, 1990. Informatik-Fachberichte 245.

[Llo87] J. Lloyd. *Foundations of Logic Programming.* Symbolic Computation. Springer, second, extended edition, 1987.

[Lov91] D. Loveland. Near-Horn Prolog and Beyond. *Journal of Automated Reasoning*, 7:1–26, 1991.

[LSBB92] R. Letz, J. Schumann, S. Bayerl, and W. Bibel. SETHEO: A High-Performace Theorem Prover. *Journal of Automated Reasoning*, 8(2), 1992.

[Mes89] P. Meseguer. Constraint Satisfaction Problems: An Overview. *AICOM*, 2(1), March 1989.

[MM92] Jörg-Peter Mohren and Jürgen Müller. A geometrical approach to depicitonal representation of spatial relations. In *Proc. of ECAI*, 1992.

[Pet91] U. Petermann. How to build in an open theory into connection calculi. *submitted to J. on Computers and Artificial Intelligence*, 1991.

[Pet93] U. Petermann. Completeness of the pool calculus with an open built in theory. In Georg Gottlob, Alexander Leitsch, and Daniele Mundici, editors, *3rd Kurt Gödel Colloquium '93*, number 713 in Lecture Notes in Computer Science, pages 264–277. Springer-Verlag, 1993.

[Sie89] Jörg H. Siekmann. Unification Theory. *Journal of Symbolic Computation*, 7(1):207–274, January 1989.

[Sti85] M.E. Stickel. Automated Deduction by Theory Resolution. *Journal of Automated Reasoning*, 1:333–355, 1985.

[Sti86] M. Stickel. Schubert's Steamroller Problem: Formulations and Solutions. *Journal of Automated Reasoning*, 2:89 – 101, 1986.

[Sti88] M. Stickel. A Prolog Technology Theorem Prover: Implementation by an Extended Prolog Compiler. *Journal of Automated Reasoning*, 4:353–380, 1988.

[Van89] Pascal Van Hentenryck. *Constraint Satisfaction in Logic Programming.* Logic Programming. The MIT Press, Cambridge, Massachusetts, USA / London, England, UK, 1989.

Modelling Information Systems as Object Societies[*]

Gunter Saake
Thorsten Hartmann

Abt. Datenbanken, Techn. Universität Braunschweig
POBox 3329, D–38023 Braunschweig
E-mail {saake|hartmann}@idb.cs.tu-bs.de

Abstract

Conceptual modelling of complex information systems requires the use of a formal design approach covering both static and dynamic aspects of the system and the modelled Universe of Discourse. Viewing an information system as a collection of communicating objects is close to the intuitive perception of such systems on a conceptual level. Objects have a local state, show a specific behaviour, communicate with other objects and may be itself composed from smaller objects. This article presents an abstract concept of such dynamic objects and discusses language features of a specification language for describing object systems. The presented language TROLL2 supports structuring mechanisms of semantic data models together with process specification constructs to cover object dynamics. Extensions of the presented framework are discussed covering the step from communicating objects to cooperating agents allowing more flexible system structures.

1 Introduction

Conceptual modelling of information systems requires the description of the application domain, the so-called *Universe of Discourse* (UoD), on a high abstraction level. This description should be independent from any implementation details and should be build on an exact formal description technique. Such a *conceptual model* should cover both the structural aspects, i.e. the information entities and their relationships, as well as the dynamics aspects, i.e. application specific functions and processes.

Many current description approaches agree in conceptually modelling the UoD as a *collection of interacting objects*. Objects encapsulate structure *and*

---

[*]This work was partially supported by the CEC under ESPRIT-III BRA WG 6071 IS-CORE (Information Systems – COrrectness and REusability). The research work of Thorsten Hartmann is supported by Deutsche Forschungsgemeinschaft under Sa 465/1-3.

behaviour, and the commonly used inter-object relations (like aggregation, communication, specialization with inheritance etc.) offer the basic abstraction mechanisms known from semantic data modelling [Saa93]. Moreover, the object paradigm may be used for describing not only the UoD but also the information system itself allowing to integrate existing subsystems into the conceptual model [SJH93].

Looking at an information system (and its environment) as a collection of interacting objects seems to be a very natural way for conceptualizing information structures and processes. This observation is confirmed by the current success of object-oriented analysis and design frameworks [Boo91, CY91, RBP+90]. Several conceptual modelling approaches follow this idea by offering a framework based on a formal concept of dynamic objects. Languages supporting this object paradigm are for example Albert [DDP93], CMSL [Wie90], Oblog [SSE87], Object Behaviour Diagrams [KS91], TROLL [JSHS91] and TROLL *light* [CGH92]. These languages combine language features known from semantic data models [HK87] with formal techniques for describing object behaviour.

In this paper we will discuss some features common to these object-oriented conceptual modelling approaches. The formal foundations of TROLL-like languages have stabilized during the last years and will be sketched only. The language TROLL2 [HSJ+93], a revised version of the TROLL language [JSHS91], will be presented using small examples. Shortcomings of the underlying object model will be discussed afterwards and a possible extended framework is sketched.

The rest of the paper is organized as follows. Section 2 gives a short overview of the underlying semantic structures and related logics. The two following sections present the basic language features of the TROLL2 language: first we discuss the basic abstraction principles to relate objects used in information systems and their realization in TROLL2, and afterwards we present the concrete logic-based specification of object structure and behaviour. Section 5 discusses extensions of the presented object concept to capture more flexible and adaptable object behaviour.

2   Basic Concepts and Formal Background

An object is constructed from a possible behaviour and observations over that behaviour associated with local states. In this section, we are concentrating on the model level rather than on the specification of such models in terms of a language. Some language features will be used for presentation purposes.

2.1   Objects as Observable Processes

Each object has a set of *events EVT*. An event can be regarded as an abstraction of a *possible atomic state transition* and is strictly *local to an object*. The declaration `debit(Amount:money)` declares a set of events, one for each possible value in the carrier set of the data sort `money`. A particular event is described by an *event term*, e.g., debit(m) where m is a variable instantiated by a value of sort **money**. Some events may be marked as being *active*, i.e. in a closed world of a specification they may occur without request.

Over a set of events EVT we define *snapshots s* as sets of simultaneous events $s \in 2^{EVT}$, i.e. each s is a set of simultaneous occurrences of local events.

Definition 2.1 (*Object Life Cycle*) Let EVT be a set of events. A sequence $\hat{s} = s_0 s_1 s_2 ...$ such that all s_i ($i \in \mathbb{N}$) are snapshots over EVT, is called an *object life cycle*. A finite prefix of length i $\sigma = s_0 s_1 ... s_i$ for $i \in \mathbb{N}$ is called the *i-th state*. The last snapshot s_i in a state σ is denoted by $last(\sigma)$.

Thus, the evolution of an object over time is described by a sequence of snapshots, i.e. the sequence of sets of local events. Many occurrences of the same event can occur in several snapshots in an object life cycle. We do not exclude the presence of empty snapshots in object life cycles. Empty snapshots represent states where no event can be observed. This way, we may "stretch" life cycles by inserting empty snapshots and we may restrict ourselves to infinite life cycles since finite ones can be expanded by appending empty snapshots.

Definition 2.2 (*Object Behaviour*) Let EVT be a set of local events. A set B of object life cycles over EVT is called *possible object behaviour*.

Events may not occur in arbitrary states within an object life cycle. In each state, we have a set of *enabled events*. An event a may occur in a snapshot s_i only if it is enabled in state σ where $last(\sigma) = s_i$. This is written as enabled$_\sigma(a)$. In this paper, we will not enter into conditions telling us whether an event is enabled in a certain state or not – the reader is referred to [EDS93, Jun93].

A set of *attributes* as usual denotes the state-dependent observable properties of objects. We assume a fixed universe of data types and sorts S to be given. Each attribute $att \in ATT$ is *typed*, i.e. it has an associated sort $sort(att) \in S$. The interpretation of a sort is a suitable set of values and is denoted by $\mathcal{U}(s)$ for a sort $s \in S$.

The declaration IncomeInYear(Year:nat):money declares an attribute set, one attribute for each possible value in the carrier set of the data sort **nat**. Particular attributes are described by *attribute terms*, e.g. IncomeInYear(y) where y is a variable instantiated by a value of sort **nat**. With each state σ of an object life cycle we associate a *current observation* giving us the current *values* of the attributes.

Definition 2.3 (*Observations*) Let B be an object behaviour, $\mathcal{S}(B)$ be the set of states over B, and ATT a set of attributes. The set $O(ATT) = \{(att, d) \mid att \in ATT, d \in \mathcal{U}(sort(att))\}$ denotes the possible observations over ATT. A mapping

$$obs : \mathcal{S}(B) \to 2^{O(ATT)}$$

is called an *observation structure over B* iff for each state σ of an object life cycle $\hat{s}$ the observation $obs(\sigma)$ fulfills the following condition:

$$[(att, d) \in obs(\sigma) \wedge (att, d') \in obs(\sigma)] \Rightarrow d = d'$$

That is, attributes cannot have more than one value in each state, but they are allowed to be undefined in a state.

An object now is composed from an object behaviour and suitable observations over the possible object life cycles.

Definition 2.4 (*Object Model*) An *object model* ob = (EVT, B, ATT, obs) consists of a set of events EVT, an object behaviour B over EVT, a set of attributes ATT, and an observation structure obs such that for each pair of subsequent states $\sigma, \sigma' \in \mathcal{S}(B)$ where $\sigma' = \sigma s$ the following condition holds:

$$(s = \emptyset) \Rightarrow [obs(\sigma') = obs(\sigma)]$$

s is the current snapshot in state σ'.

Only the occurrence of events may alter an observation, i.e. empty snapshots do not have any effect on observations over an object life cycle.

When we put objects together to form composite objects, we are interested in the behaviour of the composite object as a whole. Now, the events local to all components are local to the composite object, i.e. the components are *embedded* into the composite object. Each snapshot in the object life cycle of the composite object may include events of components. A composition is admissible if the restriction of each snapshot of each object life cycle of the composite object to the events local to a component yields an object life cycle equivalent to an object life cycle of the component.

Composition of objects thus means the following:

- Snapshots over components are merged, i.e. we are constructing unions of component snapshots (please recall that snapshots may be empty, i.e. we may have stretched life cycles);

- observations over components are merged according to the merging of life cycles.

The composition of snapshots and observations includes the *synchronization of events* since all events in a snapshot are occurring simultaneously. Synchronization along with parameter passing models *communication*.

In our model, communication is only possible *inside composite objects*. Certain composite objects, however, can be regarded as being virtual, i.e. a system of communicating objects may be regarded and modeled as a composite object.

2.2 Object Interaction

As mentioned in the previous section, communication is achieved by synchronization. We have, however, to introduce a notation that allows us to describe communication. Furthermore, communication almost always involves control flow, i.e. there are objects that initiate communications and there are objects that are requested to communicate by others.

The basic primitive in our approach to describe communication is *event calling*. Specificationwise, it is defined as a *state dependent relation* over events.

Definition 2.5 (*Calling Relation*) Let EVT be a set of events. The *calling relation* $\gg_\sigma \subseteq EVT \times EVT$ relates events wrt. a state σ of an object life cycle $\hat{s}$.

The calling relation is *transitive*, i.e. the following condition always holds:

$$(e_1 \gg_\sigma e_2) \wedge (e_2 \gg_\sigma e_3) \Rightarrow (e_1 \gg_\sigma e_3)$$

Intuitively, calling should be understood as *asymmetric, synchronous communication*. Calling is written as

```
{ condition } event_term1 >> event_term2 ;
```

This means that the calling relation only holds between events denoted by the event terms if the condition holds in the current state. This notation can also be interpreted as some kind of *ECA-rule* [DBM88]: an event denoted by **event_term1** causes other *Events* (or *Actions*) denoted by **event_term2** depending on certain *Conditions*.

Definition 2.6 (*Closure of Calling*) Let a be an event occurring in state σ. The *closure of a wrt. calling in state σ* is defined as

$$\mathtt{cl}_\sigma(a) = \{a' \mid a \gg_\sigma a'\}$$

As mentioned earlier we distinguish between active and passive events, the former defining the events that can occur by own initiative. For calling closures we require that for all passive events a there exists an active event a' such that $a \in \mathtt{cl}_\sigma(a')$.

2.3 Temporal Logic View on Objects

The basic semantic concept of the presented object model is the characterization of object behaviour by a set of life cycles, i.e. *observable linear process runs*. Another view on life cycles is to see them as a *sequence of states*, where state transitions are labelled with event snapshots. These state transitions can even be encoded into the states using an **occurs** predicate [SSC92, Jun93] or — equivalently — an **after** predicate [JSHS91, Saa93].

State sequences are the interpretation structures for *linear temporal logic* [MP92]. Therefore, a logic-based specification of object behaviour can be done in temporal logic. The concrete syntax of the TROLL languages allows at some places direct formulation of temporal axioms (for example, as temporal integrity constraints); other language features can be translated to temporal logic (see [Jun93, Saa93] for concrete translations). Instead of introducing a complete temporal logic and the translation of TROLL language features into it we will present some typical specification patterns and show how they can be expressed in temporal logic.

- The temporal constraint "The **Counter** attribute always increases." can be expressed by the formula

$$\forall x(\mathbf{always}((\mathtt{Counter} = x) \Rightarrow (\mathbf{next}(\mathtt{Counter} \geq x))))$$

- The effect of the `Increase(n)` event to increase the `Counter` attribute by the value n can be expressed as

$\forall x \forall n(\textbf{always}(((\texttt{Counter} = x) \land \textbf{occurs}(\texttt{Increase}(n)))) \Rightarrow$
$(\textbf{next}(\texttt{Counter} = x + n))))$

The variable x stores the 'old' value of the `Counter` attribute to be used in the **next** state.

- We can restrict the permission of the `Decrease(n)` event to those states where the `Counter` attribute has a value larger than n.

$\forall n(\textbf{always}(\textbf{occurs}(\texttt{Decrease}(n)) \Rightarrow (\texttt{Counter} \geq n)))$

- The effect of a calling declaration $a_1 >> a_2$ is simply expressed by

$\textbf{always}(\textbf{occurs}(a_1) \Rightarrow \textbf{occurs}(a_2))$

TROLL object specifications are equivalent to a set of temporal axioms describing the possible behaviour of an object. Observable processes are equivalent to state sequences serving as interpretation structures for this temporal logics, and therefore the usual satisfaction relation holds between object descriptions and object models. We will come back to this point in Section 5.

3 Abstraction Principles in TROLL2

In this section we will introduce the basic abstraction mechanisms of TROLL2 [HSJ+93] that are used to model the relevant parts of real world objects in terms of a formal language. These principles are classes, roles, composite objects, views on objects and synchronization between objects.

To talk about objects in some formal language we firstly have to introduce a suitable vocabulary. As for algebraic specification of data types [EM85], we adopt the notion of a signature to define a *set of symbols* that are used to describe various properties of objects later on. For a formal language to specify objects in the context of information systems we have to describe different kinds of abstractions, thus we need different kinds of symbols.

First of all objects in information systems have properties that can be *observed* from other objects. Symbols to describe this part of objects are usually called instance variables or state variables. In TROLL2 such symbols are *attributes*. To describe not only the observable part of objects, we have to specify the *state changes* an object can show during its life time. In TROLL2 *event symbols* denote such state changes. Last but not least objects can be composed of other objects. For this case we introduce *component symbols*. In Section 4 we will introduce the detailed specification of attributes, events and components and their use in the *template specification* of an object.

3.1 Classes

Usually if we model objects in some formal language we abstract away differences
between objects in the real world and group objects together that are related
by a similar structure and behaviour. Object oriented languages introduce the
notion of *classes* for this purpose. An object class in TROLL2 is described as a
set of objects that behaves like modelled in a common *template*.

To distinguish between objects of a class we introduce a *naming mechanism*
that is based on observable object properties, i.e. attributes (see Section 4).
Tuples of attribute values (an *identification*) are thus defined as *keys* to objects
of a class. Apart from such attribute values, each object of a given class has a
unique *identity*. An injective mapping from identifications to identities ensures
that we can non-ambiguously refer to a *formal object* if we know a class and
an identification of the corresponding real world object. As an example we may
specify a class **Person** as follows:

object class Person
  identification
    ByName:(Name,BirthDate) ;
    BySocSecNo:(SocialSecNo) ;
    ...
end object class Person ;

where the symbols **Name**, **BirthDate**, and **SocialSecNo**, denote attributes defined in the template of **Person** (not shown here), and the tuple **ByName** defining
a (named) key for persons.

3.2 Object Roles and Specialization

The notion of classes is not sufficient if we want to model real world entities.
Usually an abstraction in terms of similar structure and behaviour yields object
descriptions that are untractable with respect to size and complexity. Object
oriented programming languages introduce the notion of *inheritance* for structuring code and to support code reuse. TROLL2 introduces the notion of *roles* to
factor out structure and behaviour of objects according to different viewpoints
or aspects [ESS92] and in different phases of their life (see also [WJ91]).

As in programming languages, role classes in TROLL2 *inherit* the specification
of their base classes. Moreover role class objects in TROLL2 *contain* their base
objects leading to an inheritance mechanism based on *delegation* [Ste87]. Objects
of role classes are born sometime during the lifetime of their base objects due
to occurrence of *events*. Similarly they leave a role with occurrence of events.
In contrast to syntactical inheritance also the objects themselves are *inherited*.
The concept of roles resembles the *is-a* hierarchies known from semantic data
models [HK87]. In TROLL2 the behaviour of objects is integrated in that a role
object *is-a* base object for a specific time span. As an example we may specify
a class **Employee** as a role of **Person** as follows:

```
object class Employee role of Person
  events
    becomeEmployee birth .
end object class Employee ;
```

where an *event* `becomeEmployee` is introduced as the *creation event* for `Employee` objects. For a more detailed description of events see the next section.

A role class *inherits* also the naming mechanism, that is, we can refer to `Employees` via their `SocialSecNo` for example. A special case of roles is a role that is 'played' for the *whole life of the base class* – a *derived* role class like `Woman`:

```
object class Woman role of Person P derived as P.Sex = 'female'
  ...
end object class Woman ;
```

Here a creation event must not be specified since it is also *derived* for a role class as `Woman`.

3.3   Composite Objects

The use of classes and roles as abstractions still is not sufficient to map real world entities to objects. Nearly all objects we observe are *composed of parts*. Basically we can distinguish two kinds of part objects, *dependent* and *sharable* parts. The former are local to an object in that they cannot be parts in other objects. They are also dependent with respect to the life of the surrounding object. The latter are independent and may be part of *different* objects.

TROLL2 supports both views by means of components drawn from *local* or *global* classes. A local class is specified the same way as a global class, i.e. it has a template and a naming mechanism. The uniqueness of identifications is supported in the context of *one* object only. For example a company class can contain a local department class with objects identified by department names where different companies have departments with the same name.

Orthogonally to dependent and sharable components TROLL2 supports the component constructors *set* and *list* that can be used to describe sets respectively lists of component objects taken from a given class. The composition of a composite object can be altered by events that are *generated* with a component specification. Such events are for example insert respectively remove events for a given component. As an example we specify a `Company` class containing a local class `Department` as sketched above:

```
object class Company
  identification ByName:(Name) ;
  local classes
    object class Department
      identification ByDepName:(CompName)
      ...
    end object class Department
```

components
  Deps:Department set .

  ...
end object class Company ;

The **Deps** component is specified as a *set component*. Insert and delete events for such a component are implicitly available, for example an event **Deps.Insert(x)** where **x** denotes an identifier for **Department** objects. For details how objects can be referenced the interested reader may refer to [HSJ+93]. Note that the component symbols are part of the signature of objects and are used in constructing *path expressions* referencing objects chained together in *part hierarchies*.

3.4 Views on Objects

The mechanisms sketched so far are used to introduce the core of an object society. When it comes to describing the relationships between objects we first have to introduce suitable *views* on objects. Views are used to clarify which parts of an object society are relevant for communication relationships between objects, in other words which parts are visible and necessary to describe the communication between objects.

TROLL2 introduces the view concept similar to views known from relational databases, that is, we can specify selection, projection, and join views. Optionally views can contain *derived attributes* and also *derived events* describing information that can be calculated from existing information, and operations (events) that are defined in terms of existing events. Objects 'contained' in views can be referred to with keys defined in the view specification or directly via their identities (identities cannot be encapsulated). In case of join views such an identification mechanism via keys must be constructed from existing keys.

The view definition resembles the role specification in that the keyword **role of** is substituted by **view of**. A derived classification is used for views that describes a *selection condition* much like a condition for a derived role specifies the objects that are members of a role class. In contrast to roles, a view specifies no new attributes, events, and components. It is only possible to specify *derived* attributes, events and components in terms of already existing properties. As an example we provide a view of **Company** containing only companies with more than 5000 employees:

object class BigCompany
  view of Company C derived C.NoOfEmps ¿= 5000 ;
  identification ByName:(Name) ;
  ...
end object class BigCompany ;

assuming that the **Company** specification defined an attribute **NoOfEmps**. The attributes, events, and components parts of a view specification introduced in the next section list the symbols visible for other objects and possibly describes derivation rules for attributes and events (see below). In a more realistic example big companies may as well be specified as roles because usually there have to be specified additional rules for big companies in a society.

3.5 Communication Relationships

After having specified objects and suitable views on objects we may *relate* objects by means of communication. Although relationships in TROLL2 can be used to describe constraints between objects, i.e. integrity rules referring to the observable part of objects, their main purpose is relating events i.e. communication. The concept of event calling introduced in Section 2.1 is extended to objects not related by inheritance or components using *relationships* leading to a system description where relationships between loosely connected objects is not buried in the object descriptions themselves [JHS93]. As an example we may specify parts of a `User-ATM` interaction by relating the relevant objects and synchronizing on their events:

```
relationship User_ATM between User U, ATM ;
  interaction
    variables atm:|ATM| ;
    U.insertMyCardInto(atm) ¿¿ ATM(atm).readUserCard ;
    ...
end relationship User_ATM ;
```

where `insertMyCardInto` and `readUserCard` are events of the communicating objects.

After having sketched the basic abstraction principles in TROLL2 we will now have a look at the template specification for TROLL2 objects.

4 Specifying Objects in TROLL 2

Specifications in the language TROLL2 are based on a number of sublanguages, that are the basic formalisms underlying the language TROLL2. These sublanguages are *data terms* for data values and expressions (involving signatures of constant symbols and operation symbols as well as terms over such signatures), *first order logic* for a variety of assertions that can be formulated for objects, *future directed temporal logic* for dynamic constraints on attribute evolutions, *past directed temporal logic* for enabling conditions for event occurrences referring to the history of objects, and a language for *process specification* to specify fragments of life cycles explicitly.

Typed data terms are used throughout a specification in many different places as for describing the change of attribute values, values of event parameters used for communication etc. For TROLL2 there exist several predefined data types like *integer*, *nat*, *string*, etc. as well as the type constructors *set*, *list*, *tuple* that can be used to define arbitrary nested data structures. TROLL2 provides no sublanguage for the *definition* of user defined data types. Such user defined types can be specified in some suitable framework for the specification of data types and then be *included* into the society specification.

The sublanguages are used for specifying features of the concepts *attributes*, *events*, and *components* that we will describe in the next sections.

4.1 Features of Attributes

Attributes in TROLL2 are specified with a name and type. Optionally attributes may have parameters, thus introducing *sets of attributes*. Attribute parameters are specified with a name, which is considered as a formal parameter declaration.

Each attribute has associated a set of *features* further specifying properties of objects. The possible features are restricted, constant, initialized, and derived. A restricted attribute may have only values defined by a constraint formulated in first order logic. A constant attribute is an attribute that can never change its value after creation of an object. With an initialization we can define the initial value of attributes using data terms. Derived attributes are defined via a data term referencing other attributes.

As an example see the following attribute specifications taken from an artificial person object specification:

```
attributes
    PersonalID:nat constant .
    Age:nat
      restricted Age >= 0 and Age <= 150 ;
      initialised 0 .
    IncomeInYear(Year:nat):money
      restricted Year ¿ 1870  and Year ¡= 2030 .
    HasBooks:set(tuple(Author:list(string),Title:string))
      initialised emptyset .
    NoOfBooks:nat derived card(HasBooks) .
    ...
```

The attribute **PersonalID** is classified as constant and must be set with creation of the object. For the attribute **Age** we specified a restriction and an initial value. **IncomeInYear** is an attribute generator defining attributes for all values of the parameter **Year**, the restriction rule stating that only particular attributes can have a value different from **undefined**. The **HasBooks** attribute has a complex structured codomain describing a set of books. This attribute is provided for presentation purpose only. In a more realistic example we would specify books separately. The last attribute specified here is derived from the **HasBooks** attribute, the derivation rule calculates the cardinality of the set **HasBooks**. Card is predefined for the set constructor.

4.2 Features of Events

Events in TROLL2 are specified in the same manner as attributes. Events define the state changing operations for objects. Event parameters are considered to be formal parameters specified with a name. A parameterized event thus describes a set of events one for each possible tuple of parameter values.

Each event has associated a set of features that specify its properties. Event features are **birth**, **death**, **active**, **enabled**, **changing**, **calling**, and **binding**. Birth and death events create respectively destroy objects. Thus a birth event can only occur at the beginning of a life cycle whereas a death event can only occur at the end of a life cycle. Birth events are required for an object specification, death events are optional since we may want to model objects that are never destroyed.

The notion of *active* events comes in due to the requirement to abstract from causality. Usually an event must be triggered, i.e. caused by some other event. In modelling real world entities, we sometimes do not want to or cannot specify such a causality. Examples are representations of user objects that have their own *initiative*. The cause for their events is often not in the scope of such a specification.

Events can be enabled or be forbidden in a given state of an object. Depending on current attribute values or the current history of an object we describe such conditions by the use of past directed temporal logic formulae as *enabling* conditions.

Another event feature is used to describe the change of attribute values triggered by an event. With a *changing rule* specification we describe the assignments of new attribute values denoted by data terms referring to the current state and possible event parameters. An imperative style of specifying attribute updates is chosen.

Similar to attribute updates we can specify *locally bounded parameters* for events using *binding rules*. Such parameter values are determined by data terms referring to attributes of the object and parameters of the event. The name of such a parameter is marked with a preceding !.

To describe more complex state changes we may *call for* or *trigger* other events of the object when an event occurs. The underlying execution model is a *synchronous* execution of all events called transitively [HS93].

As an example for most of the features for attributes and events introduced briefly we specify the attributes and events for a stack object that stores natural numbers:

```
attributes
  Top:nat derived if Empty then undefined else Array(Pointer-1) fi .
  Empty:bool  derived (Pointer = 0) .
  Array(No:nat):nat initialised Array(No) = undefined .
  Pointer:nat initialised 0 .
events
  Create birth .
  Destroy death .
  Push(Elem:nat)
    changing  Array(Pointer) := Elem;  Pointer := Pointer + 1 .
  Pop
    enabled not Empty ;
    changing Pointer := Pointer - 1 .
```

In this example the event `Push` has a parameter `Elem` that denotes the element to be pushed on the stack. The changing rules define the new observable object state, here the value is stored in the `Array` attribute with index `Pointer` and the `Pointer` attribute is incremented. The `Pop` event is only enabled if the stack is not empty.

A more liberal specification of stacks can be described in the following way without a precondition for `Pop` events but an additional parameter delivering a status. The `Pop` event is no more disabled for a stack that is empty, but it has *no effect* on the observable state of the stack and returns false if the stack is empty:

```
events
  pop( ! Status:bool )
    changing  { not Empty } Pointer := Pointer - 1 ;
    binding  Status = not Empty .
```

The condition in the changing rule states that a decrement of the `Pointer` variable is only performed if the stack is not empty. The value of the parameter `Status` must not be set by the caller of the event but is determined locally.

4.3   Features of Components

Component specification are a means to describe the *part-of* relationship between objects. Parts may be *local* to an object or *shared* between objects. The former can only be accessed in the context of the enclosing object and are thus closely related to the composite object, the latter can be components in different objects in a society. Here we will only describe shared components.

In TROLL2 we may describe *single* and *set valued* components. Both concepts are closely related to the concept of object classes and single objects. We provide also a construct to specify *list valued* components that are handled similar to set valued components plus additional access to objects at the head or tail of the list and indexed accesses.

The component specification has a similar notation as the attribute and event specification. But there is an important difference to attributes. Components do not describe *object valued attributes* that are often called *references* in popular object oriented (programming) languages. Attributes of an object describe *data values* whereas components describe *part objects* which define a stronger relationship than object references. The component objects being part of a composition can be restricted in their behaviour by the embedding object. For example we can specify conditions that inhibit event occurrences in components.

Components were already introduced briefly in the last section. The *features* of components resemble attribute features with the difference that we have to handle *objects* and *object populations* in contrast to *data values*. For components we provide the features set, list, restricted, initialized, and derived. The features set and list define multiobject components (object sets) and optionally ordered components (lists).

Restriction for components are described with first order formulae stating properties that objects must have to be incorporated and to remain parts in a composition. The formulae may refer to attributes of the component objects and to attributes of the embedding object. In contrast to attributes where initializations and derivations are specified with data terms, for components also formulae are used. An initialization formula describes properties that objects of the domain class of a component symbol must have to be initially in the composition (a very simple query against the population of a class). Similarly a derivation is formulated as a formula selecting the subset of objects from a component class that qualify for a given condition.

To alter the composition of a composite object dynamically TROLL2 provides special events to insert and delete objects from components. For observing the current contents special attributes are generated. The interested reader may refer to [HSJ+93] for more details. As an example for components see the following component specifications taken from a bank example:

```
components
  Manager:Person .
  Acct:Accounts A
    set; derived A.No¿100000 and A.No¡999999 .
  ServiceQueue:Person list
    initialised false; restricted ServiceQueue.Length ¡ 10 .
events
  Arrival(P:|Person|)
    calling ServiceQueue.InsertLast(P) .
  Serviced(P:|Person|)
    calling ServiceQueue.RemoveFirst .
```

The **Manager** component is a single object component describing the person that is currently the manager of the bank. It can be changed using the events **Manager.Insert** and **Manager.Remove** where we have to supply identifiers for person instances. The component **Acct** is set valued and derived as all accounts (specified elsewhere) with numbers in the given range. The component **ServiceQueue** denotes a list of objects initialised to the empty list by means of a condition qualifying for no objects and restricted to have at most the length 10.

The events **Arrival** and **Serviced** denote events that occur if persons are arriving or if they are being served at a bank desk. Both events *call for* the insert and remove events generated for the list valued component **ServiceQueue**. The notation |**Person**| denotes the data type of *identifiers* for objects of class **Person**.

4.4 Object Behaviour

The specification of life cycles of an object is the main part of the overall behaviour specification and describes the possible *evolution* of objects. *Constraints* formulated in future directed temporal logic are used to describe the evolution of attribute values. For example we can specify account objects with attributes like **Balance**, denoting the balance of an account or **Red** that is true if the account is overdrawn. Constraints may look like the following examples:

constraints
    initially (Balance ¿ 100 before Red) ;
    Red =¿ sometime(not Red) ;
    not (Red and Balance ¿ 10000) ;

stating that the Balance of an account must be at least 100 before it can be overdrawn (first rule), and that an account in 'red condition' must be filled up in the future (second rule), and that an account cannot be overdrawn more than 10000$. The keyword initially states that the constraint is relative to the creation of the object whereas the second and third rules are invariant.

For the behaviour in terms of allowed operations we have to formulate event sequencing patterns. An event description merely describes the conditions and effects local to event occurrences. To describe entire life cycles we have to talk about *event sequences* and *dependencies* among events that occur sequentially.

Like for attributes, events and components we specify named processes that are further depicted with process features. The features are active, interleaving, start, and completeness. The process sequence is written down in a process language that mainly provides *sequencing* and *alternatives* described by a set of *guarded processes*. Recursion is introduced using process identifiers in the sequence.

As an example we provide a process defining the sequence of a user interacting with an automatic teller machine (ATM). We assume attributes **MyPIN** and **MyCard** be defined in the surrounding object specification:

process declaration
    variables A:money; Valid:bool;
    UserATMInteraction =
        arrival -¿ enterCard(MyCard) -¿
        enterPINCode(MyPIN) -¿ checkPinCode(?Valid) -¿
        ({Valid}
            enterAmount(?A) -¿ throwOutCard -¿
            removeCard -¿ throwOutMoney -¿ getMoney(A)

            —

            {not Valid} throwOutCard -¿ removeCard
) -¿ leave .
process
    UserATMInteraction
        interleaving normal ;
        start after(decisionToGetMoneyAtATM) ;
        completeness strict .

After arrival at the machine a card (attribute **MyCard**) has to be inserted and after entering the PIN-code (attribute **MyPIN**) the code is checked. The parameter **Valid** is set somewhere else and is henceforth bound to a value of type

bool. Depending on the value of **Valid** the usual process of interacting with the machine has to be executed or the card is removed and the user leaves the machine (a *choice* between different *alternatives*). Event parameters preceded with a **?** are bound to values during execution of the process and can be used in the sequel.

After declaring the process, the process **UserATMInteraction** is *defined* and further specified with features to be a *pattern of possible behaviour* for the object specified. Interleaving normal means that all events used in the definition must respect the sequencing conditions, e.g. a **throwOutMoney** event must be preceded by a **removeCard** event etc. The process starts in the state after the event **decisionToGetMoneyAtATM**, and the sequence *cannot* be exited without violating the specification (completeness strict). For details on process features see [HSJ+93].

Behaviour involving several objects of a compound object is modelled via event calling as introduced in Section 2.1 and also sketched in Section 3.5. After having introduced the main features of TROLL2, we will now continue to sketch a possible future evolution of TROLL2.

5 Extending the Object Model

The semantic foundations and corresponding language proposals for object oriented conceptual modelling were investigated for several years now and have come to a state where the basic concepts seem to be stabilizing. In the following section, we will discuss some directions for future work extending this framework allowing more flexible object concepts. This work is in its early stages and the following subsections should be read as proposals for future research rather than as a presentation of stabilized results.

5.1 Limits of the Object Model

In section 2.1 we have characterized objects as linear processes observable by attributes. Each object state is completely characterized by a snapshot trace which determines the current attribute values. Therefore, the values of object attributes may change during object life time. The *current object behaviour* may depend on the attribute values, of course, but *the behaviour specification* remains fixed during the object life.

However, information system objects (like account objects) are persistent in the sense that they 'live' considerably longer than program runs or application sessions. Accounts (identified by an account number), for example, have a typical life span of several years. Bank rules, financial laws, computation of yearly interests etc may change several time during the life span of an account object — even without changing its attribute values.

To capture these effects we have to find a semantic model for objects where the behaviour specification of an object may be modified *during its existence*, which is not expressible in the framework underlying TROLL until now. In the following subsections, we will sketch a semantic structure enabling such behaviour evolution and give an outlook on applications of this extension.

5.2 Theories as Object States

A logical view on TROLL2 objects regards an object as an process connected with a temporal logic specification which is *satisfied* by the object behaviour. At the birth of an object, we have an initial set of temporal axioms restricting the future state evolution. Each event occurrence adds a new next time point to the object history, and at each of these transitions the set of temporal axioms is checked and the next set of axioms to be satisfied in the future is derived — a liveness requirement may be satisfied by this transition and therefore removed from the current temporal axioms. This complies to the known operational stepwise valuation of temporal formulae for a given state sequence [MP92, Saa91].

The idea to extend the object model to allow changing object behaviour is to keep the temporal valuation but to add the possibility to *modify the current set of temporal axioms depending on the transition*.

More formally, we keep the notion of object life cycle as a sequence of event snapshots as the formalization of the temporal object behaviour. For states, we use a *two-level* approach: the base level defines object states σ_i as before using a mapping to attribute-value-pairs extended by the **occurs** predicate. The second level characterizes states as sets of temporal logic axioms. Both together constitute a dynamic structure D, if for each tail sequence starting at time i the i-th state axiom set Ax_i is entailed by the base level. With other words, the state axioms of the second level restrict the future evolution of the base level using usual temporal logic entailment, i.e., we require

$$\langle \sigma_i, \sigma_{i+1}, \sigma_{i+2}, \ldots \rangle \models Ax_i$$

The axiom sets Ax_i are modified by events and may change from state to state. This formalization guarantees that temporal constraints are never overwritten by changing the state axioms. Therefore it offers a restricted way of modifying the temporal specification in contrast to completely override temporal obligations. A formalization of these ideas can be found in [SSSJ93].

An intuitive view on this extended object model is to think of an additional attribute **Axioms** with domain *set of temporal axioms*. An object specification has to fix the ways this attribute is modified during object life. The simpler object model described in Section 2 is a special case, where this attribute is initialized in the first state with the complete temporal logic specification. To handle temporal logic axioms as attribute *values* enables to transfer specification parts between objects using event parameters, too (see the alarm clock example below).

5.3 Applications of the Extended Model

In the following subsections we will sketch some application areas of the extended object model to show its expressive power.

5.3.1 Behaviour Evolution versus Object Migration

Typical information systems objects may have a longer life span than their functional aspects or restrictions on their behaviour. This effect partly results from having objects representing real world entities (like employees and accounts) in artificial systems realizing for example company policies — the way to compute current interests for an account or the maximal withdraw per month may change each year. With other words, existing objects have to be adapted to new behaviour patterns that cannot be anticipated in the original system specification.

A common solution for example in object-oriented database systems is to offer the possibility to change the class membership of existing objects. This concept of *class migration* [Su91] allows to handle this situation but does not fit very well to the conceptual role of classes — conceptually, the objects do not move to another class but the class description is adapted to new requirements.

The extended object model discussed above gives an intuitive semantic framework for adapting behaviour specifications to new requirements. Besides a stable immutable description of the invariant object properties we can add the possibility of an additional behaviour description modifiable during system runtime.

Another aspect of class migration is *signature modification*. In our framework, this should be handled by defining appropriate views or new role classes for objects rather than introducing object migration. In fact, many other needs for class migration only arise in data models which do not support a dynamic role concept.

5.3.2 Programmable Objects

As mentioned before, handling temporal axioms as attribute and attribute values allows to modify (or even 'program') objects via event calling. The expressive power of this approach is shown by the following example realizing an alarm clock which can be programmed to arbitrary behaviour. The syntax of the following examples should be understood as an ad hoc notation for presentation purposes, not as a language proposal.

The example is written in a syntactical style which is close to the original TROLL language features [JSHS91]. The reason is that these language features are closer to a temporal logic representation. Attribute modifications are written in the 'positional style' where for example the notation

[Tic] Minutes = Minutes + 1 mod 60;

defines the new value of the Minutes attribute after the Tic event.

The following specification models a *programmable alarm clock* as an object. The clock has a basic specification part being invariant during the life of the clock. It can be programmed to arbitrary alarm behaviour by sending a temporal theory to it using an event parameter of type SpecAxioms.

object alarm_clock
template

```
    attributes Minutes, Hour : nat;
            Alarm: bool;
    events birth CreateClock;
        Tic;
        AlarmOn; AlarmOff;
        Pause; Reset;
        SetAlarmMode(AlarmProgram: TempAxioms);
specification
   BaseAxioms =
        begin axioms
            valuation
              [ CreateClock ] Minutes = 0, Hour = 0, Alarm = false;
              [ Tic ] Minutes = Minutes + 1 mod 60;
              { Minutes = 59 } ==¿
                  [ Tic ] Hour = Hour + 1 mod 24;
              [ AlarmOn ] Alarm = true;
              [ AlarmOff ] Alarm = false;
            end axioms;
    behavior valuation
       [ CreateClock ] Axioms = BaseAxioms;
       [ Reset ] Axioms = BaseAxioms;
       [ SetAlarmMode(x) ] Axioms = Axioms union x;
            /* changing the temporal theory by adding axioms */
end object alarm_clock;
```

The value of the attribute `Axioms` defines the current axiom set Ax_i at time i. This clock can be 'programmed' to an arbitrary alarm behaviour by sending a specification of the interplay of the `Tic` event with the other events. Additionally, we can even send a specification to the clock such that it triggers some object outside in case of alarm. To show the possibilities, we give two examples for the first case.

As a first example, we set the parameter `x` of the `SetAlarmMode` event to following behaviour specification:

```
begin axioms
   interaction
      { Minutes = 59 } ==¿ Tic ¿¿ AlarmOn;
      { Minutes = 0 } ==¿ Tic ¿¿ AlarmOff;
end axioms;
```

The resulting behaviour after the occurrence of `SetAlarmMode` is a one minute alarm each hour. The second example programs the clock to give alarm at noon for 10 minutes. The value of `x` is the following set of axioms. Additionally, we allow to interrupt the alarm using the `Pause` event.

```
begin axioms
   interaction
      { Minutes = 59 and Hour = 11 } ==¿ Tic ¿¿ AlarmOn;
      { Minutes = 9 and Hour = 12 } ==¿ Tic ¿¿ AlarmOff;
```

valuation
   [Pause] Alarm = false;
end axioms;

These examples show modifications of the current axioms directly via the
`SetAlarmMode` event. A more flexible approach is even to allow **behavior valuation** rules as part of the modifying axioms, which allows complete restructuring
of behaviour specifications during runtime (and should therefore be used with
care).

5.3.3   From Objects to Agents

A possible generalization of the object concept is the notion of *agent*. The
concept of agent is used as an important concept in many fields of information
technology, among them requirements engineering, software design, distributed
databases, distributed artificial intelligence as well as organization technology.
The key facets of agents can be characterized by the following properties:

- Agents may be active (in contrast to passive objects). Agents have *goals*
  which they try to achieve through cooperation under given constraints.

  Goals may be represented as temporal obligations to be satisfied by the
  agent.

- Agents have an internal *state* which includes an internal, imperfect representation of the world (including knowledge about the state of other
  agents).

  This concept of state goes far beyond the state concepts of objects where
  state information is coded in attribute values only. It requires disjunctive
  knowledge as well as handling of default knowledge [BLR93].

- Agents act, communicate and perceive, thus showing an external *behaviour*
  that obeys the given constraints [DDP93].

Following this characterization of agents, semantic models for agents should
be similar to those discussed for objects: agents show behaviour resulting in
life cycles like for objects, and they have a state determined by their history.
But states are represented by theories rather than by attribute values, and state
changes are therefore theory revisions.

We think that the presented extended object concept can serve as the first
step towards an appropriate semantic model for agents. It offers temporal logic
for describing goals, and (restricted) state changes are part of the model. However, we are aware of the fact that pure temporal logic is not adequate for
handling all aspects of agents as mentioned above. Moreover, the two level
formalization does not allow disjunctive information for attribute values. This
restrictions avoids on the other hand some problems arising with arbitrary theory
revision.

We are aware of the fact that the ideas presented in this section are in a preliminary state. The presentation aims at showing current research efforts rather than stabilized results.

6 Conclusions

In this paper we have introduced a framework for specifying information systems on a high level of abstraction. After describing the basics of the underlying object model, we sketched the language TROLL2 based on these formal ideas. We introduced the basic abstraction mechanisms of TROLL2 used for relating objects and continued with the specification of templates defining the structure and behaviour of objects. Then we discussed the limits of the object model described so far in terms of necessary adaptions of object behaviour during lifetime of objects. A possible integration of a theory based approach into the TROLL2 framework was sketched.

As mentioned already in the discussion of possible application areas, the approach can be extended to handle more application specific logics for example based on deontic logics [MW93]. An interesting extension is to combine the extended object model with non-monotonic logics for revising temporal logic goals. A related approach is reported in [BLR93].

A necessary extension to handle problems of schema evolution is to extend the state modification to allow changes of the object signature, too. To avoid problems with changes of the external object interface this may be restricted to internal 'hidden' attributes. Currently, schema evolution is handled by creating new views for existing object classes which allows to modify the external signature.

For the more practical areas of research in the direction of modelling of information systems we are currently working on an environment for TROLL2 specification integrating the modelling process, prototyping and documentation of specifications and on a graphical representation of TROLL2 object societies [WJH+93] that draws on concepts known from *OMT* [RBP+90].

Acknowledgements

We are grateful to Peter Hartel, Ralf Jungclaus, Jan Kusch, and Cristina Sernadas who developed the basic features of TROLL2 with us. The topics discussed in Section 5 are part of a current joint research effort with Amílcar and Cristina Sernadas. The concept of agents and the search for a common formal model for agents is topic of the ESPRIT BRA WG 8319 ModelAge (*A Common Formal Model of Cooperating Intelligent Agents -a multidisciplinary approach-*, coordinator: P.-Y. Schobbens, Namur) which will start in early 1994. For many fruitful discussions on the TROLL2 language we are grateful to all our colleagues in Braunschweig, and to the members of IS-CORE, especially to Hans-Dieter Ehrich, Amílcar Sernadas, José Fiadeiro, Udo Lipeck and Roel Wieringa.

References

[BLR93]   S. Brass, U. W. Lipeck, and P. Resende. Specification of Object Be-
           haviour with Defaults. In U.W. Lipeck and G. Koschorreck, editors,
           *Proc. Intern. Workshop on Information Systems – Correctness and
           Reusability IS-CORE '93, Technical Report, University of Hannover
           No. 01/93*, pages 155–177, 1993.

[Boo91]   G. Booch. *Object Oriented Design with Applications.* Benjamin /
           Cummings, Redwood City, 1991.

[CGH92]   S. Conrad, M. Gogolla, and R. Herzig. TROLL *light*: A Core Lan-
           guage for Specifying Objects. Informatik-Bericht 92–02, TU Braun-
           schweig, 1992.

[CY91]   P. Coad and E. Yourdon. *Object-Oriented Design.* Prentice Hall,
           Englewood Cliffs, New Jersey, 1991.

[DBM88]   U. Dayal, A.P. Buchmann, and D.R. McCarthy. Rules are Objects
           Too: A Knowledge Model for an Object-Oriented Database System.
           In K.R. Dittrich, editor, *Advances in Object-Oriented Database Sys-
           tems*, pages 129–143. Springer, Berlin, LNCS 341, 1988.

[DDP93]   E. Dubois, P. Du Bois, and M. Petit. O-O Requirements Analysis:
           An Agent Perspective. In O. Nierstrasz, editor, *ECOOP'93—Object-
           Oriented Programming (Proc. 7th European Conference)*, pages 458–
           481, Kaiserslautern, 1993. LNCS 707, Springer-Verlag, Berlin, 1993.

[EDS93]   H.-D. Ehrich, G. Denker, and A. Sernadas. Constructing Systems as
           Object Communities. In M.-C. Gaudel and J.-P. Jouannaud, editors,
           Proc. TAPSOFT'93: Theory and Practice of Software Development,
           pages 453–467. LNCS 668, Springer, Berlin, 1993.

[EM85]   H. Ehrig and B. Mahr. *Fundamentals of Algebraic Specification 1.
           Equations and Initial Semantics.* Springer-Verlag, Berlin, 1985.

[ESS92]   H.-D. Ehrich, G. Saake, and A. Sernadas. Concepts of Object-
           Orientation. In *Proc. of the 2nd Workshop of "Informationssysteme
           und Künstliche Intelligenz: Modellierung", Ulm (Germany)*, pages
           1–19. Springer IFB 303, 1992.

[HK87]   R. Hull and R. King. Semantic Database Modeling: Survey, Applica-
           tions, and Research Issues. *ACM Computing Surveys*, 19(3):201–260,
           1987.

[HS93]   T. Hartmann and G. Saake. Abstract Specification of Object In-
           teraction. Informatik-Bericht 93–08, Technische Universität Braun-
           schweig, 1993.

[HSJ+93] T. Hartmann, G. Saake, R. Jungclaus, P. Hartel, and J. Kusch. Revised Version of the Modelling Language TROLL. "Informatik-Bericht", TU Braunschweig, 1993. *In preparation.*

[JHS93] R. Jungclaus, T. Hartmann, and G. Saake. Relationships between Dynamic Objects. In H. Kangassalo, H. Jaakkola, K. Hori, and T. Kitahashi, editors, *Information Modelling and Knowledge Bases IV: Concepts, Methods and Systems (Proc. 2nd European-Japanese Seminar, Hotel Ellivuori (SF))*, pages 425–438. IOS Press, Amsterdam, 1993.

[JSHS91] R. Jungclaus, G. Saake, T. Hartmann, and C. Sernadas. Object-Oriented Specification of Information Systems: The TROLL Language. Informatik-Bericht 91-04, TU Braunschweig, 1991.

[Jun93] R. Jungclaus. *Modeling of Dynamic Object Systems—A Logic-Based Approach.* Advanced Studies in Computer Science. Vieweg Verlag, Braunschweig/Wiesbaden, 1993.

[KS91] G. Kappel and M. Schrefl. Object / Behavior Diagrams. In *Proc. 7th Int. Conf. on Data Engineering*, pages 530–539, Kobe, Japan, 1991. IEEE Computer Society Press, Los Alamitos.

[MP92] Z. Manna and A. Pnueli. *The Temporal Logic of Reactive and Concurrent Systems. Vol. 1: Specification.* Springer-Verlag, New York, 1992.

[MW93] J.-J. Ch. Meyer and R. J. Wieringa, editors. *Deontic Logic in Computer Science. Normative System Specification.* Wiley, Chichester, 1993.

[RBP+90] J. Rumbaugh, M. Blaha, W. Premerlani, F. Eddy, and W. Lorensen. *Object-Oriented Modeling and Design.* Prentice-Hall, Englewood Cliffs, NJ, 1990.

[Saa91] G. Saake. Descriptive Specification of Database Object Behaviour. *Data & Knowledge Engineering*, 6(1):47–74, 1991. North-Holland.

[Saa93] G. Saake. *Objektorientierte Spezifikation von Informationssystemen.* Teubner, Stuttgart/Leipzig, 1993. Habilitationsschrift.

[SJH93] G. Saake, R. Jungclaus, and T. Hartmann. Application Modelling in Heterogeneous Environments using an Object Specification Language. In M. Huhns, M.P. Papazoglou, and G. Schlageter, editors, *Int. Conf. on Intelligent & Cooperative Information Systems (ICICIS'93)*, pages 309–318. IEEE Computer Society Press, 1993.

[SSC92] A. Sernadas, C. Sernadas, and J. F. Costa. Object Specification Logic. Research report, INESC/DMIST, Lisbon (P), 1992. *To appear in Journal of Logic and Computation.*

[SSE87]   A. Sernadas, C. Sernadas, and H.-D. Ehrich. Object-Oriented Speci-
           fication of Databases: An Algebraic Approach. In P.M. Stoecker and
           W. Kent, editors, *Proc. 13th Int. Conf. on Very Large Databases
           VLDB'87*, pages 107–116. VLDB Endowment Press, Saratoga (CA),
           1987.

[SSSJ93]   Gunter Saake, Amílcar Sernadas, Cristina Sernadas, and Ralf Jung-
           claus. Evolving Object Specifications. Technical report, INESC Lis-
           bon & TU Braunschweig, Draft Version, 1993.

[Ste87]   L.A. Stein. Delegation is Inheritance. *SIGPLAN Notices, Special
           Issue OOPSLA87*, 22(12):138–146, 1987.

[Su91]   J. Su. Dynamic Constraints and Object Migration. In G. M.
           Lohmann, A. Sernadas, and R. Camps, editors, *Proc. Intern. Conf.
           on Very Large Databases VLDB'91, Barcelona*, pages 233–242, 1991.

[WJ91]   R. Wieringa and W. de Jonge. The Identification of Objects and
           Roles – Object Identifiers Revisited. Technical Report IR–267, Vrije
           Universiteit, Amsterdam, 1991.

[Wie90]   R. J. Wieringa. *Algebraic Foundations for Dynamic Conceptual Mod-
           els*. PhD thesis, Vrije Universiteit, Amsterdam, 1990.

[WJH+93]   R. Wieringa, R. Jungclaus, P. Hartel, T. Hartmann, and G. Saake.
           OMTROLL – Object Modeling in TROLL. In U.W. Lipeck and
           G. Koschorreck, editors, *Proc. Intern. Workshop on Information Sys-
           tems – Correctness and Reusability IS-CORE '93, Technical Report,
           University of Hannover No. 01/93*, pages 267–283, 1993.

Conceptual Modelling of Large Reusable Knowledge Bases *

B.J. Wielinga   A.Th. Schreiber

University of Amsterdam, Social Science Informatics
Roetersstraat 15, NL-1018 WB Amsterdam, The Netherlands
E-mail: {wielinga,schreiber}@swi.psy.uva.nl

Abstract

Large amounts of knowledge are available in many knowledge bases for a variety of applications. This knowledge is however usually application specific, and thus not reusable. This paper discusses the problem of making knowledge shareable over applications and reusing it. Three principles are formulated that can form a basis for a methodology for designing sharable knowledge bases. The separation of domain and control knowledge, the explication of meta-models of the domain knowledge (ontologies), and the distinction between ontologies that submit to different classes of assumptions commitments are described as ways of achieving shareable and reusable knowledge bases.

1   Introduction

Knowledge technology is becoming of age: operational knowledge-based systems are used routinely in many companies and organisations, methods for developing knowledge-based systems are being consolidated [Schreiber *et al.*, 1993b] and many small and large knowledge bases have been built for a variety of applications. A major problem with current knowledge technology is however that these knowledge bases -however valuable their content may be- are usually idiosyncratic, i.e. they are designed to serve a specific application task and have little or no generality. It is a major challenge to investigate the question how this growing body of formalised

---

*The research reported here was carried out in the course of the KADS-II project. This project is partially funded by the ESPRIT Programme of the Commission of the European Communities as project number 5248. The partners in this project are: Cap Gemini Innovation (F), Cap Programator (S), Netherlands Energy Research Foundation ECN (NL), Eritel SA (ESP), IBM France (F), Lloyd's Register (UK), Swedish Institute of Computer Science (S), Siemens AG (D), Touche Ross MC (UK), University of Amsterdam (NL) and Free University of Brussels (B).

This article expresses the opinions of the authors and not necessarily those of the consortium.

knowledge can be reformulated in such a way that it can be (re)used on a broader scale.

In a similar vein, there exist scientific disciplines where an enormous amount of knowledge is being gathered, but where the accessibility of that knowledge is becoming more and more of a problem. For example, researchers in molecular biology are gathering large amounts of information about DNA sequences in the genetic material of many organisms. Although this information is currently stored in large databases that are world-wide accessible, the actual knowledge in these databases is often difficult to obtain in a form that is readily usable. In other scientific fields similar problems exist.

There are a number of problems that hamper the (re-)usability of large amounts of information in data and knowledge bases. The first problem is that of application dependency. While current data-base technology allows a clear separation between data represented in a data base and the application program, and thus ensures independence of data and its use, this is not the case with most knowledge bases. Knowledge is represented in a way that is application specific and contains a mixture of factual knowledge that is general in nature and heuristic knowledge that is specific for the application task. A second problem concerns the terminology and representational structures that are used to represent information. Few standards exist and more importantly, no agreed methods are available to define standard ways of representing data and knowledge in a particular domain. A third problem is that of navigation. In particular in large knowledge bases that contain heterogeneous information it is difficult to find the appropriate elements that answer a certain query or solve a particular problem. A fourth problem concerns the representation of hypothetical or contextually determined information. The latter two problems relate to the fact that no high-level query languages exist for complex knowledge bases. A final problem -or rather a set of interrelated problems- relates to the semantics of the information represented in a data or knowledge base. How can we know that a certain knowledge element can be used in solving a problem? How do we assess the quality of a knowledge base? How can we integrate knowledge from different sources? What are the assumptions that underlie a particular piece of knowledge?

In this paper we will analyse some of these problems and seek ways for solving them.First we will discuss how structuring of knowledge systems leads to modularisation as a first step towards reusability. We then proceed to develop the concepts of meta-model and ontology, as means of explicating terminology and structure of large knowledge bases. Finally, we investigate the sources of ontological assumptions and commitments and how explication of such assumptions can shed light on issues of knowledge reuse and knowledge sharing. For purpose of illustration we will provide examples from two domains: the configuration of elevators [Schreiber et al., 1994] and analysis of DNA sequences.

2 Structuring Knowledge Systems

A central issue related to the (re)usability of knowledge is how a large knowledge base can be structured such that modularity can be achieved. A principle that underlies much recent work in knowledge engineering, is that of distinguishing different types of knowledge according to their function. Where first generation expert systems represented factual knowledge about the application domain and knowledge about how to organise the reasoning process in a mixed representation, i.e. rules, current knowledge modelling approaches distinguish between two basic types of knowledge: knowledge about the application domain and knowledge about the task that needs to be performed. The *application domain knowledge* (or domain knowledge for short) is static in nature, it consists of the concepts, relations and facts that are needed to reason about a certain application domain. The *control knowledge* describes *how* reasoning with the application domain knowledge is done in terms of reasoning operations on the domain knowledge and in terms of control structures and decompositions of the task as a whole. Figure 1 schematically represents this view on knowledge systems.

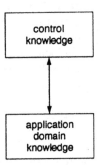

FIGURE 1: Two types of knowledge in a KBS

The KADS approach to knowledge-based system development [Wielinga & Breuker, 1986; Wielinga *et al.*, 1992; Schreiber *et al.*, 1993b] has refined the two-tier model that was among others proposed by Clancey [Clancey, 1983] and Steels [Steels, 1990]. CommonKADS distinguishes between *inference knowledge*, knowledge about how to use the application domain knowledge in elementary reasoning steps, and *task knowledge* describing how to decompose the top-level reasoning task and how to impose control on the elementary operations. Inference knowledge is modelled in CommonKADS in terms of the operations on domain knowledge (*inferences*) and in terms of *roles*, descriptions of classes of domain knowledge elements that are used in a particular inference operation. Figure 2 shows an example inference performing a match operation between data and a pattern, producing information on the match as output. Inferences represent the functional view on knowledge, but do not describe when and why a particular reasoning step is performed.

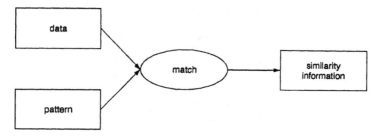

FIGURE 2: An example inference

Task knowledge in CommonKADS is modelled as a hierarchy of goals and corresponding goal-satisfaction procedures.

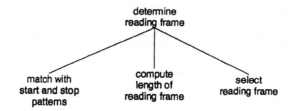

FIGURE 3: A simple task decomposition

Figure1 3 shows a simple task decomposition for determining a reading frame (a sequence of DNA nucleotide codes beginning with a *start code* and ending with a *stop code*) in a sequence of DNA codes. The leaf nodes in the task decomposition correspond to applications of inference operations such as *match, compute* and *select*.

Knowledge about how to control the reasoning process of a problem solver can come in one of two forms: a fully instantiated model of how to perform a reasoning process for a specific application, or in the form of knowledge that describes how to decompose a problem into subproblems and how to achieve primitive subproblems [Benjamins, 1993]. We will call the former a *task model* and the latter a set of *problem solving methods*. Thus, a problem solving method can be viewed as a prescription of how to construct part of a task model, and a task model as a fully instantiated set of problem solving methods. Whether or not a knowledge system will have to contain explicitly represented knowledge about problem solving methods depends on the flexibility required. In some applications a fixed task structure, derived by "compiling out" the problem solving methods, will suffice. If the problem solving behaviour of the system has to be adapted to specific problem situations, an explicit strategic reasoning component can be needed. In any case, it is important to make the problem solving methods explicit in the knowledge analysis stage. As we shall see in section 6, a problem solving method employed in an application introduces assumptions and commitments that have an impact on the required application domain knowledge.

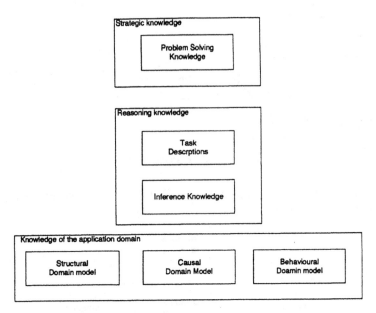

FIGURE 4: A differentiated structure of knowledge systems

The application domain knowledge can often be partitioned into a number of separate modules, each representing a particular view on the world. In CommonKADS such partitions are called *domain models*. In figure 4 the different sub-structures of a CommonKADS model are shown schematically, together with three example domain models representing a structural, causal and behavioural viewpoint on the domain.

The differentiated structure of a CommonKADS knowledge model has several advantages. First, it provides a way of modularising the system. A second advantage is the reusability of the various components. The library of reusable task and inference models that was produced in KADS-I [Breuker *et al.*, 1987] has proved to be a powerful tool in knowledge engineering. A third advantage of the approach is that operations on the application domain knowledge (inferences) are made explicit, thus providing a first handle on the problem of designing a high-level access or query language for large and complex knowledge bases.

In summary, the separation of application domain knowledge is a first step towards the solution of some of the problems mentioned above. However, several problems remain. First there is the problem of how to link the knowledge elements in different layers. Second there is the problem of dependency between layers. These problems will be discussed below.

3 Meta-Models of Domain Knowledge

When the KADS research hit the problem of interfacing the domain knowledge to the inference knowledge -a link that initially was left obscure- the solution was found [Schreiber, 1992] in building a meta-model, called domain view, of the structure of the domain knowledge and use this meta-model as a means of interfacing classes of domain knowledge statements to the inference operators. The *domain view* specifies how particular parts of the domain theory can be used as a "body of knowledge" by an inference (see figure 5 for an example).

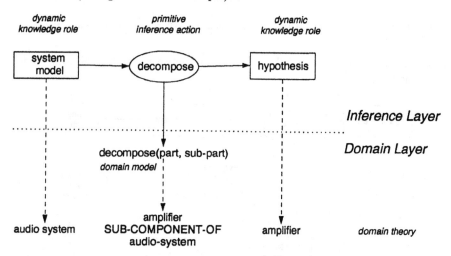

FIGURE 5: A primitive inference performing a decomposition action on a model of a faulty system. *System model* and *hypothesis* are examples of knowledge roles. They describe the role that domain objects like `audio-system` and `amplifier` can play in the problem-solving process. The domain view of the *decompose* inference specifies that tuples of the `SUB-COMPONENT-OF` relation in the domain theory can be used as decomposition knowledge.

In more recent work in the KADS-II project [Wielinga *et al.*, 1993] a full language was developed for meta-modelling the application domain knowledge: Conceptual Modelling Language (CML). Although parts of the CML definitions are specified in natural language, it has a very expressive syntax and has proved to be a powerful tool for meta-modelling.

Figure 6 shows the basic modelling constructs of the CML. These constructs can be used both for typing the application domain knowledge as well as for meta modelling. The basic constructs in the CML are similar to those in object oriented analysis approaches such as OMT [Rumbaugh *et al.*, 1991], with the exception of the notion of *constructed objects*. This construct is needed to describe complex expressions. Such expressions can be reified and can be assigned names. The CML contains the usual constructs such as sub-type relations and part-of relations, as well as the notion of set. When CML is used both for representing the domain

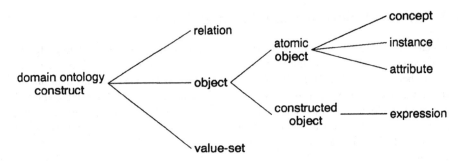

FIGURE 6: Hierarchy of object types in the CommonKADS conceptual modelling language

knowledge and for meta-modelling, a mapping between elements of both models can be indicated.

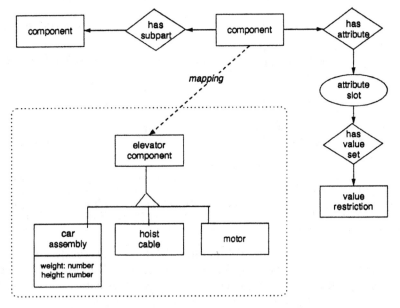

FIGURE 7: CML meta-model for elevator domain

Figure 7 shows a meta-model of a small part of the domain knowledge base for elevator configuration. The boxes represent (meta-)concepts, the diamonds represent relations and the ellips represents a reified function. The model defines the meta-concept *component*, the fact that it has attributes with value restrictions and the *has-subpart* relation between components. The bold arrow indicates a mapping between the meta-concept component and the actual concepts in the elevator domain. An important advantage of the explicit mapping between meta-model elements and the domain knowledge elements, rather than making component a super concept of the elevator-component concept, is that a meta-model can represent a particular *viewpoint* on the domain knowledge. If for example, one would want to construct a model of the elevator for qualitative reasoning the elevator components could be viewed as physical objects. In addition the meta-model can contain knowledge (e.g. axioms) about the domain knowledge. Apart from the mapping construct, the model of concepts and relations is similar to modern object-oriented models such as OMT. This similarity falls short if one would need to represent knowledge of more complex relations, such as the following:

```
if platform-depth <60 then hitchcar-offset = 2.
```

In this case, we need to model complex expressions and relations between them.

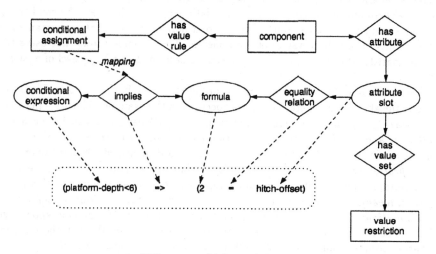

FIGURE 8: CML meta-model for conditional assignments

Figure 8 shows the meta-model for complex expressions representing conditional value assignments to an attribute of a component. The ovals *conditional expression* and *formula* represent reified functions of logical and arithmetic expressions over attribute values of components. An example of a tuple representing an actual element of the domain knowledge corresponding to conditional assignments is given in the lower part of the figure. Note that the relation between the attribute slot and the formula is an equality relation and not an assignment. The relation can also be interpreted as a constraint that must hold. However, through the mapping process we have reified the conditional expression as a meta-concept *conditional assigment* that has a *has value rule* relation with *component*, indicating how this knowledge can be used to compute values for attributes of components.

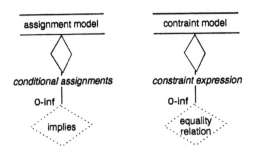

FIGURE 9: CML meta-model of two domain models

Figure 9 shows the meta-model in the CML of two domain knowledge base partitions (domain models). The small diamond represents the part-of relation. The conditional assignment model is build from relational tuples that describe conditional assignements as discussed above. The second domain model contains instances of constraints on attribute values of components. The example shows that using the CML, partitions of the knowledge base can be described at a high level of abstraction.

Several knowledge abstraction operations are involved in the example. Figure 10 shows the abstraction operations as they occured in the example. The first operation is *knowledge typing*: knowledge elements are assigned basic types such as *concept*, *attribute* and *relation*. A second operation consists of *basic schema definition*: the argument structure of relations and expressions are identified. A third operation is *reification* or *mapping into a meaningful name space*: relations and expressions of a certain type are reified as meta-concepts and get names assigned to them that have a meaning in the context of the domain and the task. A fourth operation is *instantiation*: reified schemata get instantiated as elements of a domain knowledge base. The final form of knowledge abstraction is *aggregation*: through the *has-part* relation groups of knowledge elements are aggregated to *domain models*.

Although these knowledge abstraction mechanisms are complex, they provide ways of solving some of the problems that we have outlined in the introduction. Modularisation and navigation are clearly easier when use is made of the abstraction mechanisms. The mapping mechanism provides ways of separating the application domain knowledge from the inference knowledge. The terminology introduced in the reified schemata can provide a basis for defining high level query and access languages. For example, one can see how the following query could be processed using the schemata:

```
What constraints involving platform-depth are violated
when model MC23 is used for car-assembly?
```

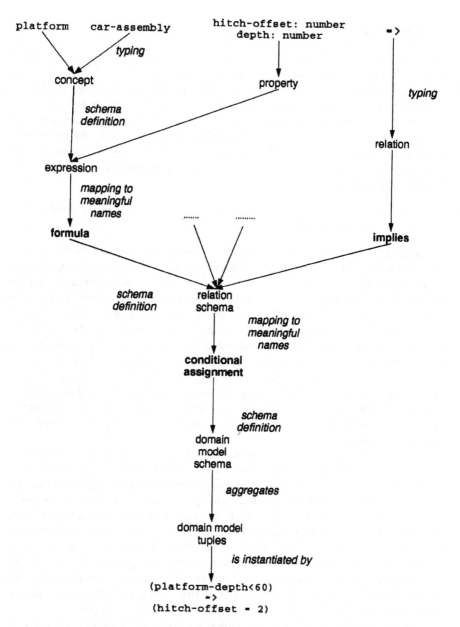

FIGURE 10: Knowledge Abstraction in the example

4 Ontologies as Meta-Models

The commonly used term for meta-models describing the structure of a knowledge base is *Ontology*. In some ways this term is unfortunate, since it has a well defined meaning in philosophy that differs from the sense in which the knowledge engineering community uses it. In the philosophical tradition an Ontology is a theory about that what can exist. In the context of knowledge-based system research not many people claim to say anything about what exists in the real world. We do however, make claims about what knowledge entities are manipulated by our programs when they perform a task. So, we could rephrase the traditional definition of the term "ontology" as follows:

> *An (AI-) Ontology is a theory of what entities can exist in the mind of a knowledgeable agent.*

What kind of theory is an ontology? A knowledge base can be viewed as a model of some part of the world, that allows us - given some inference mechanism- to reason about that world. The model is described in some language, that has a vocabulary and a syntax. An ontology defines constraints about what can be expressed in the model, in addition to the constraints imposed by the syntax. In KADS the ontology defines the vocabulary and the structure of the statements that express elements of the model. It does not define the full semantics of the domain model. Ontolingua takes similar decisions: in Ontolingua the structure of the terms that can occur in a knowledge base are defined, as well as some useful properties of those structures, but not the full range of possible uses that can be made of such a term. In KADS the use of the domain knowledge model is defined in the inference specification, while Ontolingua leaves the inference mechanisms to be specified in the target environment.

How does this help in knowledge sharing? The terminology that the ontology introduces are in essence representations of ontological commitments. So, by explicating the ontology, we also make the ontological commitments explicit and as such enable the definition of procedures that relate, compare or translate the knowledge from one set of commitments to another. Similarly a task model can be applied to an application domain knowledge base, as long as it is compatible with the ontological commitments of that knowledge base (see figure 11). Making the ontology of an application knowledge base explicit, is a second principle that supports knowledge sharing and reuse. This principle forms one of the cornerstones of the GAMES project [Schreiber *et al.*, 1993a] that aims at the development of reusable medical knowledge bases and tools that provide libraries of partial ontologies.

However, the full ontology of an application knowledge base will often contain task-specific elements. Thus, in order to make at least part of a knowledge base shareable, partitions have to be identified that are to some extent independent of the task. For that purpose we introduce several types of ontologies and corresponding knowledge bases in section 6. First, we will illustrate the importance of explicit ontologies using analysis of DNA sequences as an example domain.

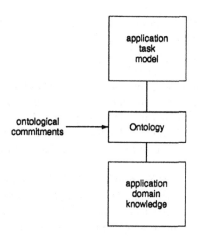

FIGURE 11: Ontology as intermediary between task model and domain knowledge

5 Ontologies in Molecular Biology: a Case Study

The field of Molecular Biology is a particularly good example of a scientific discipline where a large body of information is becoming available in a short period of time. Biologists studying the genome of various organisms make intensive use of large databases such as the GENBANK and EMBL data bases. Many of the problems that we have outlined in the introduction are manifest in this domain.

First, there exist many databases for different purposes. For example, there are the basic sequence databases, such as GENBANK, that contain the data about DNA sequences. For certain organisms, e.g. the plant Arabidopsis thaliana, separate databases are maintained, containing abstracts of selected papers. Data about physical and genetic maps of chromosomes is maintained in yet other databases. Several collections of data exist that provide information about patterns in DNA sequences that indicate particular properties. This is only the top of an iceberg of information sources, and the iceberg is growing fast: while the various "genome" projects are advancing, the need for aggregated information is becoming more pressing. So, new types of databases will continue to emerge. In addition to the multitude of databases there is the problem of proliferation of application software using these databases. These programs are often based on specific assumptions or methods, a fact which is often neglected when interpreting their output.

Most databases in Molecular Biology are represented in flat textual form, and for good reasons. The information in these databases should be interpretable for a large community of users, equiped with a wide variety of hard- and software. A simple text- based database is the most universal representation, but it is very limited in its representational power with respect to querying or reasoning. A simple manifestation of this fact is redundancy: many -universally true- facts are repeated in items of the database. For example, we estimate that the fact that mammalian organisms are a subtype of eukaryote organisms is represented some 50.000 times in the GENBANK database. This may not be a great problem if it only concerned the classification of the organism from which data were taken. But it also concerns other data, such as features detected in a DNA sequence. Many such features have been identified todate and a hierarchical classification would be a very helpful method to reduce complexity of the data. Introducing such hierarchies would enlarge the size of databases enourmously.

The solution to some of these problems could be found in the development and use of proper ontologies for the domain. Although it is unrealistic to assume that all software that will access a knowledge base would be standardised, a shared ontology could be of great help in increasing the effectiveness of using the large amount of knowledge about the genome. Such an ontology could at least serve the following purposes.

1. Standardisation of terminology.

2. Allow translation of one representation format to another.

3. Allow flexible integration of different sources of information.

4. Support more complex queries than are currently possible.

Although the need for a standardised terminology in a domain like Molecular Biology, where many new terms are invented each day (e.g. for newly discovered genes, proteins, motifs etc) is beyond doubt, current technology provides little support for such standardisation. In fact, different databases refer to the same information with different keys, spelling and abbreviation of terms is often not unique, different citation conventions exist, notations vary etc. The agreement of a world-wide standard ontology for domains like Molecular Biology will undoubtedly take a long time to be achieved. In the meantime, the ideas about ontologies developed in knowledge engineering can provide some help in comparing and integrating information from different sources.

GB ontology	TFD ontology	Motif
note="TATA-box" TATA-signal	TATA TATAbox	TATAAA/T
note="G box"	G-box	SGGGTGKGTT
CAAT-signal note="CCAAT-box'	CBP-MSV NF-Y*-tk	CCAAT

TABLE 1: Different terminology in databases

Table 5 shows a few examples of terminological and notational differences between two databases. Even within one database different notations are used. Although translation between terms is straightforward in principle, it requires explication of the respective ontologies and their mappings. A standardised language for defining ontologies such as CommonKADS CML or Ontollingua [Gruber, 1992] would greatly enhance the capabilities for integrating and comparing data.

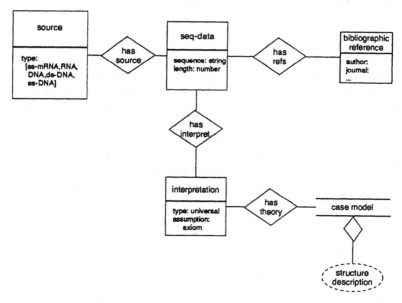

FIGURE 12: Partial meta-model for DNA sequence data

A more serious problem arises when multiple interpretations of the same data exist. New experimental material or integration of data from different sources can cause interpretations to become obsolete or even incorrect. For example, the interpretation of a DNA sequence as a coding sequence is often subject to a number of assumptions. However, such assumptions are not stored in the databases and therefore can not be checked with respect to their consistency when new information becomes available. Representing data, interpretations and their underlying assumptions in a knowledge base would allow more complex queries and consistency checks. Figure 12 shows an example meta-model for a knowledge base storing sequence data together with its interpretations and assumptions. Standard information such as sequence data, source and bibliographic references are represented as concepts with attributes. An interpretation of the data is represented as a theory, i.e. a set of statements about the data such as a description of the putative structure of a gene. A knowledge base structured in this way would allow storage of multiple interpretations and would support complex queries, e.g. for consistency checking. We are currently engaged in the design of a tool that uses explicitly represented ontologies of several data bases and that can import data from these data bases and represent them as knowledge structures. Such a knowledge base, even though it would only contain a small sample of all genomic data, would allow complex analyses, integration and checking, that currently need to be done by hand.

6   Different Types of Ontologies

The separation of the application domain knowledge and the task related knowledge, gives rise to an important question: what are the dependencies between the two parts of the model. Chandrasekaran formulated the *interaction hypothesis* which states that task knowledge and application domain knowledge are highly dependent: one cannot define the application domain knowledge without knowing what the task model is going to be, and vice vera. Domain knowledge and task knowledge must be packaged [Chandrasekaran, 1989]. Early work on KADS [Wielinga & Breuker, 1986], on the other hand, worked under the assumption that application domain knowledge can be formulated independent of the task model.

There is a growing consensus that some interaction between the application domain knowledge and the task model exists, but that different types of such an interaction can be distinguished. Below we will discuss this idea in more detail.

Ontological commitments that are the basis for ontology construction come from different sources and have different flavours, hence we can distinguish different types of ontologies. On the lowest level of complexity, we have the definition of the vocabulary of a knowledge base. In KADS this part of the ontology is called the *application domain terminology*. If in addition we define a set of types and basic relations such is sub/super class relations, we can define a domain ontology: the extensional description of the domain vocabulary, typology and class hierarchy or lattice. Although the second order terms (such as concept, inheritance-relation, property etc) used in defining the domain ontology can be defined in the meta-ontology, these terms are usually a fixed set of types and relations with their standard interpretation. CML in KADS has a number of basic types (see Figure 6) while Ontolingua has a similar set defined in the *Frame Ontology*. Gruber calls such an ontology a *representational ontology*: it makes certain commitments with respect to representational constructs, but makes no commitments about the content of the knowledge [Gruber, 1992].

Although the sharing of domain ontologies is already an important step towards knowledge sharing, it only ensures a commitment to a common vocabulary and typology. It does not imply a consensus on the type of statements that a knowledge base will contain. Such a consensus ontology is what we would call a *domain-model oriented ontology*. This ontology describes general theories within a domain, that are (for all practical purposes) not biased towards particular tasks or methods. For example, in domain concerning devices, there are usually theories about the structure of the device in terms. In that case we can decide to use an ontology based on components with attributes. The goal of reasoning about the structure of a device does imply an ontological commitment, but still leaves the use of the knowledge base large open.

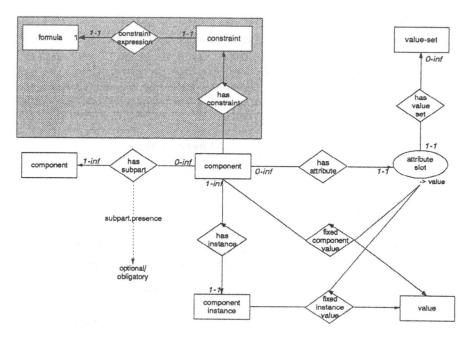

FIGURE 13: Graphical representation of part of the ontology described in [Schreiber *et al.*, 1994]. The main part describes the ontology for modelling a device structure. The upper grey area is an expansion introduced by the task-type (in this case configuration)

The non-grey area of Figure 13 shows an example ontology for components, their properties and component instances. This ontology is derived from the KADS-CML representation of the Ontolingua specification for the VT problem [Schreiber *et al.*, 1994]. This part of the ontology is reusable over all tasks that take a structural view on the device.

If we are, however, interested in a class of tasks such as configuration, we require additional knowledge elements to be able to perform the tasks. For example, configuration tasks generally require knowledge about constraints on components (see the grey area in Figure 13). So, by committing ourselves to a certain class of tasks we introduce additional ontological commitments. The application domain knowledge is extended with a partition that is reusable over a class of tasks, but not usable by any task.

If we take one step further and require the task to be performed through the application of a particular problem solving method, additional requirements on the domain knowledge may come about. For example if we decide to perform the configuration task through the *propose and revise* method, we need knowledge about how to fix violated constraints. Adding this commitment to our ontology makes it not only specific for a class of tasks, but also for the method used.

An example of the use of these types of ontological commitments can be found in the COMMON-KADS realisation [Schreiber *et al.*, 1994] of the VT problem [Yost, 1992]. For this problem, a domain knowledge base specified in Ontolingua was available. Figure 14 shows how the Ontolingua knowledge base for VT was made available in our Prolog environment for executing COMMON-KADS expertise models. This process consisted of the following steps:

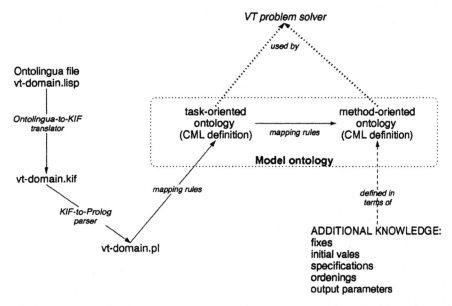

FIGURE 14: Mapping process from the VT domain-knowledge specification in Ontolingua to the COMMON-KADS model ontology

1. As the starting point we used the knowledge base in the KIF form (generated by the Ontolingua-to-KIF translator), because the KIF format is closest to Prolog.
2. The knowledge base *vt-domain.kif* is parsed into a a Prolog-readable knowledge base *vt-domain.pl*. The transformations are syntactical, e.g. handling the different syntactical conventions for symbols/atoms, etc. The parser is *not* a full KIF-to-Prolog parser. It handles only the subset of KIF used in the VT application.
3. The knowledge base *vt-domain.pl* is subsequently interpreted by a set of mapping rules that rewrite the domain expressions into statements of the types defined in the task-type oriented ontology (see Figure 13).
4. The task-type oriented ontology in turn is mapped through a second set of rewrite rules onto method-oriented ontology types, namely those that specify viewpoints on the task ontology.

5. In addition, this method ontology defines a number of conceptualisations that are specific for this method, and thus have no counterpart in the task-oriented ontology. An example in the VT domain is the fix knowledge.
6. The problem solver uses both the method-oriented and the task-oriented ontology to access the knowledge base.

Although in this example only a distinction was made between task-type oriented and method-oriented ontological commitments, it clearly shows how such explicit descriptions can be applied in sharing knowledge bases. The Ontolingua knowledge base, built at another site, on a different platform, using a different representation, etc, could be used in our framework to access the knowledge types defined in the task-type oriented ontology.

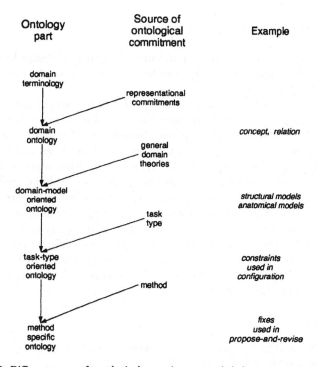

FIGURE 15: Different types of ontological commitments and their corresponding ontologies

Figure 15 summarizes the different sources of ontological commitments and the resulting ontologies:

- Level 1: domain terminology
- Level 2: representational commitments (e.g. class, relation, etc.)

- Level 3: domain-model oriented commitments (e.g. structural models, anatomical models)
- Level 4: task-type oriented commitments (e.g. constraints)
- Level 5: method oriented commitments (e.g. fix knowledge)

We do not consider these levels as fixed borderlines, but instead view them as a hypothesis of useful landmarks in a spectrum of ontological commitments.

The important consequence is that through the use of different ontologies with different generality and by partitioning the application knowledge base accordingly, we can identify different classes of knowledge bases, with different scope, generality and reusability. For example, if one neglects the distinction between task-related and method-related ontologies, this will hamper the reuse of parts of the knowledge base for a similar task but applying a different method.

7 Discussion and Conclusions

In this paper we have discussed the problem of designing knowledge bases that can be shared by many applications, that can be reused or that can be queried by users with a variety of questions.

We have formulated a number of principles that can form the basis for a methodology for building reusable and shareable knowledge bases. The first principle concerns the separation of application domain knowledge and control knowledge. This separation allows the construction of modular knowledge bases and the potential reuse and sharing of knowledge modules. The second principle states that the ontologies -viewed as a meta-model- of the knowledge base should be explicated.

Ontologies have structure: certain parts are based on generally accepted theory, other parts are based on common practice, useful interpretations or on task oriented notions. The third principle for knowledge sharing methodology that we advocate is to distinguish different partial ontologies that are based on different types of ontological commitments. Shareability and Reusability depend critically on the distinctions between the view that underlies the different ontologies: the assumptions and the scope of the ontologies should be made explicit.

References

BENJAMINS, V. R. (1993). *Problem Solving Methods for Diagnosis*. PhD thesis, University of Amsterdam, Amsterdam, The Netherlands.

BREUKER, J. A., WINKELS, R. G. F., & SANDBERG, J. A. C. (1987). A shell for intelligent help systems. In *Proceedings of the 10th IJCAI*, pages 167–173, Milan, Italy.

CHANDRASEKARAN, B. (1989). Task–structures, knowledge acquisition and learning. *Machine Learning*, 4(3/4):337–338.

CLANCEY, W. J. (1983). The epistemology of a rule based system -a framework for explanation. *Artificial Intelligence*, 20:215–251.

GRUBER, T. (1992). Ontolingua: A mechanism to support portable ontologies. version 3.0. Technical report, Knowledge Systems Laboratory, Stanford University, California.

RUMBAUGH, J., BLAHA, M., PREMERLANI, W., EDDY, F., & LORENSEN, W. (1991). *Object-Oriented Modelling and Design*. Englewood Cliffs, New Jersey, Prentice Hall.

SCHREIBER, A. T. (1992). *Pragmatics of the Knowledge Level*. PhD thesis, University of Amsterdam.

SCHREIBER, A. T., TERPSTRA, P., MAGNI, P., & VAN VELZEN, M. (1994). Analysing and implementing VT using COMMON-KADS. In *Proceedings Knowledge Acquisition Workshop KAW'94, Banff, Canada*. Contribution to the Sisyphus-93 experiment. To appear.

SCHREIBER, A. T., VAN HEIJST, G., LANZOLA, G., & STEFANELLI, M. (1993a). Knowledge organisation in medical KBS construction. In Andreassen, S., Engelbrecht, R., & Wyatt, J., editors, *Proceedins of the 4th Conference on Artificial Intelligence in Medicine Europe, 3-6 October 1993, Munich*, volume 10 of *Studies in Health Technology and Informatics*, pages 394–405, Amsterdam. The Netherlands. IOS Press.

SCHREIBER, A. T., WIELINGA, B. J., & BREUKER, J. A., editors (1993b). *KADS: A Principled Approach to Knowledge-Based System Development*, volume 11 of *Knowledge-Based Systems Book Series*. London, Academic Press. ISBN 0-12-629040-7.

STEELS, L. (1990). Components of expertise. *AI Magazine*.

WIELINGA, B. J. & BREUKER, J. A. (1986). Models of expertise. In *Proceedings ECAI-86*, pages 306–318.

WIELINGA, B. J., SCHREIBER, A. T., & BREUKER, J. A. (1992). KADS: A modelling approach to knowledge engineering. *Knowledge Acquisition*, 4(1):5–53. Special issue 'The KADS approach to knowledge engineering'. Reprinted in: Buchanan, B. and Wilkins, D. editors (1992), *Readings in Knowledge Acquisition and Learning*, San Mateo, California, Morgan Kaufmann, pp. 92-116.

WIELINGA, B. J., VAN DE VELDE, W., SCHREIBER, A. T., & AKKERMANS, J. M. (1993). Towards a unification of knowledge modelling approaches. In David, J.-M., Krivine, J.-P., & Simmons, R., editors, *Second Generation Expert Systems*, pages 299–335. Berlin Heidelberg, Germany, Springer-Verlag.

YOST, G. (1992). Configuring elevator systems. Technical report, Digital Equipment Corporation, 111 Locke Drive (LMO2/K11), Marlboro MA 02172.

Tool Integration in Evolving Information Systems Environments*

Matthias Jarke, Hans W. Nissen, Klaus Pohl

Informatik V, RWTH Aachen
Ahornstr. 55, 52056 Aachen, Germany
{jarke, nissen, pohl}@informatik.rwth-aachen.de

Abstract. Evolution is a fact of life in information systems. Not only systems evolve but also their development processes. IS environments must therefore be designed for accommodating and managing change. The management of process meta models in repositories is one important step; we show how process traceability models and process guidance models can be developed and related in a standard repository framework. In addition, the currently available tool integration along the presentation, data, and control perspectives have to be augmented for process integration. In our process-adaptable and interoperable tool concept, tool behavior is directly influenced by the process guidance model and automatically traced according to the traceability model. The approach is demonstrated with a prototype requirements engineering environment developed in ESPRIT project NATURE.

1 Information Systems and the Process Improvement Paradigm

Information systems (IS) are networks of humans and information technology components intended to serve some organizational purpose. It is widely agreed that next-generation IS will have to be better aligned to organizational goals and processes.

Business processes and goals change even more rapidly with a more turbulent and globalized environment. The management of change therefore becomes a critical issue also for information systems. Current reality is studied by reverse analysis, creating a conceptual model. A desired change is defined in terms of this model. This change must be propagated to the level of the real system by a partial re-implementation process, in a careful trade-off between accomplishing the change goal and blending into the existing context. A typical re-engineering step is shown in figure 1.

Today's situation is characterized by the presence of many IS components and accumulated experiences. On the positive side, products, models, and processes gained from these experiences can be reused. On the negative side, this valuable,

---

* This work was supported in part by the Commission of the European Communities under ESPRIT Basic Research Project 6353 (NATURE).

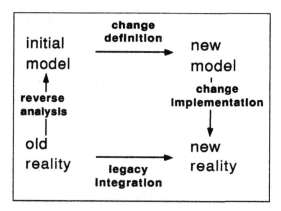

Fig. 1. A change management cycle for information systems

but often dated legacy forces us to integrate multiple generations of systems with vastly heterogeneous intents, technologies, and organizational environments.

Next-generation IS development environments will have to consider evolution of products to be developed (object evolution), of development methods and processes through which they are developed (process evolution), and of the tools used in those processes (tool evolution). In the database and software engineering areas, many people are investigating object evolution; we shall therefore focus on the other two aspects.

Due to the heterogeneous nature of the development environment, and the closer cooperation of systems, consideration of international standards is becoming increasingly important. In section 2, the NIST/ECMA reference model for tool integration is briefly reviewed as a background for our work.

In software engineering, a number of formalisms for process definition have been proposed. A few of them also consider aspects of customization and evolution [4]. To a large degree, this work has been stimulated by the Software Engineering Institute at Carnegie Mellon University (SEI) [9], [5] which associated the maturity of a software development organization with the ability to understand, define, and manage its processes. In previous work [21], we have shown that the SEI maturity levels can be characterized through a *process-oriented IS repository*. Section 3 reviews this work and discusses the relationship between tools and repositories according to a view concept.

The main contribution of this paper, described in section 4, concerns the role that *IS development tools* can play in the change management scenario. The motivation for this work is twofold.

First, capturing process knowledge according to the above-mentioned models (process *traceability*) can be very labor-intensive and costly, and should therefore be automatically done by the tools.

Second, current CASE tools tend to have a fixed functionality whose relationship to the process has to be determined by the development engineer. What we need, are tools that can adapt their behavior to the process even while they are running. In section 4, we develop a concept for process-adaptable interoperability of tools that satisfies these requirements to a large degree.

Our approach is demonstrated in a prototypical requirements engineering environment, developed in ESPRIT Project NATURE[2]. As requirements processes are poorly understood and existing methods tend to be woefully incomplete, process adaptability and traceability as a basis for learning and improvement are particularly relevant. Major lessons learned are summarized in section 5.

2 Background on Tool Integration

The integration of development tools is a long-standing topic in the CASE literature, culminating in the NIST/ECMA reference model shown in figure 2 [3]. This so-called "toaster model" distinguishes four aspects of integration:

- *Data integration* concerns the ability of tools to exchange data with little conversion effort and a high degree of consistency;
- *Control integration*, supported by message services, concerns the sharing of functions among tools, i.e., the ability to control each others behavior;
- *Presentation integration* offers the user of a tool a uniform interface to all tools;
- *Process integration* concerns the cooperation of tools with respect to the steps, events, and constraints of a process definition.

Detailed requirements for each kind of integration have been explicated in [28].

Most progress has been made in the field of data integration. In fully integrated closed environments, deep integration can be achieved through detailed modeling of document structures (e.g., in IPSEN [17]), whereas open environments such as DECs CDD/Repository have to rely on tool envelopes to achieve a more modest data integration.

In control integration, the idea of message servers or software buses to support message exchange among tools has proven quite successful, e.g. in Hewlett-Packards SoftBench system or in the Eureka Software Factory.

For presentation integration, there exist a number of standard platforms with associated style guides, such as X11 and OSF/MOTIF, although further improvements remain desirable.

Most authors agree that little is known about process integration [30]. There exist a number of process modeling facilities, along with process drivers to enact the models, and with monitoring functions to supervise the execution (cf., e.g., [15]). However, little is said about the assumptions such models make about the tools they work with, how process tracing, evaluation, and evolution are supported.

We have found that the goal of process integration has implications for all the other three kinds of tool integration. Therefore, the next sections look in some

---

[2] NATURE stands for Novel Approaches to Theories Underlying Requirements Engineering [13].

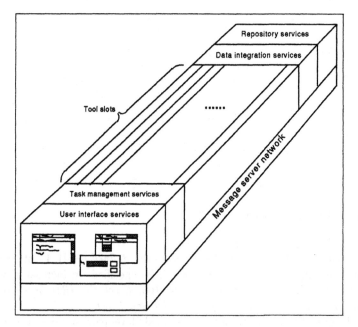

Fig. 2. The NIST/ECMA reference model for tool integration

detail at extensions to data integration (via repositories) and control integration (via communication servers) required for process integration. There are also implications for presentation integration, such as group awareness facilities, but we shall elaborate them here only indirectly, through the discussion of view mechanisms for repositories in section 3.3.

3 Process Repositories: Extending The Data Integration Perspective

In this section, we present the repository concept required to maintain process knowledge, and illustrate it with process meta models used for requirements engineering in the NATURE project.

3.1 The IRDS Standard

Meta information systems, also called data dictionaries, information resource dictionaries, or repositories are information systems about information systems. We shall use the term repositories which was popularized by IBMs AD/Cycle initiative [24]. More precisely, we shall start from the Information Resource Dictionary Standard (IRDS) as recently defined by ISO [10]. Figure 3 sketches this framework.

ISO IRDS is organized along the classification abstraction of semantic data models. In a layered type universe of four levels, level $n+1$ (called the *defining*

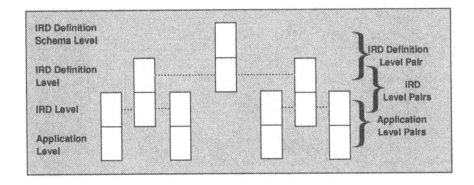

Fig. 3. ISO-IRDS repository framework

level) constitutes a type system for level *n* (the *defined* level). In other words, it defines the language in which level *n* can be specified. In increasing order of abstraction, the four levels are the *Application Level*, the *IRD Level*, the *IRD Definition Level*, and the *IRD Definition Schema Level*.

ISO IRDS additionally promotes a so-called "level pair" architecture in which the relationships among the four levels are defined by a hierarchy of three SQL database specifications on top of each other. *Application Level Pairs* correspond to the actual applications to be integrated. Dictionaries or *IRD Level Pairs* contain as their data the schemata of the application level pairs, and definitions of the underlying data models as their schemata.

A single *IRD Definition Level Pair* manages descriptions of the dictionary schemata under a fixed schema, defined in the standard by a set of SQL tables, together with some basic features of the dictionary level pairs.

3.2 Process Repositories

Due to the level pair concept, application systems as well as dictionary systems can be distributed and heterogeneous. Looking at figure 3 in a different manner, we can see two *application environments*, each coordinated by a dictionary. This is the environment available at system runtime.

Overlapping with the application environments, we also see a *development environment*, consisting of the *IRD Definition Level Pair* and the two dictionaries. This is where the development process is managed. To be consistent with the application systems coordinated by the dictionaries, the development environment must, of course, contain information about the products of IS development – the application data structures, programs, interfaces, and maybe manual operating procedures.

However, the development environment must also contain information about intermediate results, human agents and tools involved, process plans, design decisions, and steps taken to execute them. In short, the product respository must be extended to a process repository.

Ignoring for the moment the distributed nature of the development environment, figure 4 shows what kind of process information is defined at what level of the IRDS hierarchy.

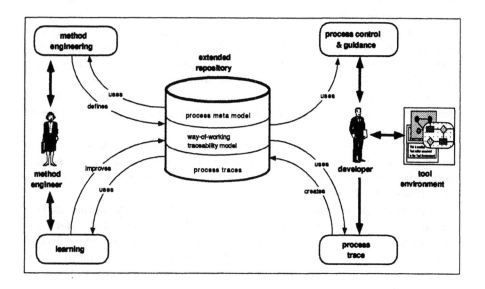

Fig. 4. Process repositories and process-related activities

The *IRD level* (the lowest in figure 4) stores the trace of the actual process; note that part of this trace are descriptions of the product at the schema level (DB schemata and program code, for example).

The *IRD Definition level* defines the actual way-of-working (guidance model), but also the record structure (traceability model) according to which the process trace is to be organized. Note that both structures should not necessarily be the same, as we want to detect discrepancies and use them for process management and improvement. However, the two structures must at least make the actual trace (organized by the traceability model) and the intended trace (defined by the way-of-working) comparable. Traceability model and way-of-working are therefore defined under the same meta process model which is fixed at the *IRD Definition Schema level*, supposedly as a proposed extension to the IRDS standard.

In [21], we have shown how process repositories can be naturally linked to the so-called SEI process maturity model. The Software Engineering Institute at Carnegie Mellon University claims that the maturity of an IS development organization can be characterized through the way the process of gradual system evolution is managed [5]. SEI assesses process maturity by questionnaires followed by in-depth interviews and inspections; we are more interested in the specific repository implications of their model. Briefly, each such level can be associated with the different kinds of actions on the process repository, as shown in figure 4.

At the *initial level*, this process is ad-hoc and no organizational learning takes places from one change cycle to the next. This corresponds to the case where there is no process repository.

At the *repeatable level*, the organization understands sufficiently well what it is doing to have repeatable processes. Technically, this can be supported by capturing process traces according to some record structure and making them accessible for reuse. This is indicated in the lower right of figure 4.

At the *defined level*, process definitions (ways-of-working) can be abstracted from these collected experiences and enforced through process guidance mechanisms (upper right of figure 4).

Once this has been established, the organization can introduce procedures for measuring the actual process execution against the defined process, thus promoting continuous organizational learning of new processes – the *managed level* (lower left of figure 4).

Finally, there may be also an *optimizing level*, in which continuous goal-oriented and measurement-based optimization of process plans takes place. The repository will, in this case, have to be enhanced with corresponding decision support tools. A new group of people, the process engineers, come into play, which changes the process definition (way-of-working), as shown in the upper left of figure 4.

3.3 Requirements Process Models in NATURE

The process meta model and its specializations for defining traceability and guidance are strongly influenced by the domain in which the process operates. In this subsection, we briefly sketch the models we have designed in NATURE for the task of requirements engineering.

Requirements engineering is a poorly understood field, in which no comprehensive process model can be expected. In such unstructured settings, it is known that humans react with situated behavior and cooperative decision making [27]. The NATURE process meta model (cf. figure 5) therefore comprises concepts of:

- *actions* which transform input *objects* to output objects, and can be composed of sub-actions organized, e.g., as nondeterministic finite automata;
- *situations* in which certain actions are applicable, and which can be characterized by views on objects, on the process state, a combination of both, or simply a perception of the application engineer;
- *decisions* taken by *agents* reacting to specific situations according to certain *arguments* that help with the choice among actions applicable to that situation.

Situations and related decisions together form the process *context*.

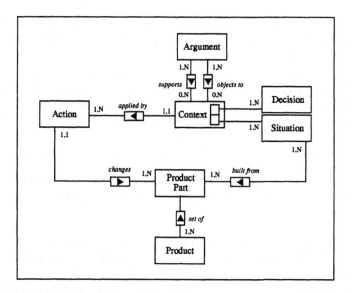

Fig. 5. NATURE process meta model (cf. [25])

Process Guidance Model. The process guidance model (cf. [25]) contains a set of reusable process chunks. Each chunk is described by a situation pattern in which it applies, the possible action patterns known in this situation, and arguments for guiding the choice among them. [3] A chunk can be invoked when its situation pattern is instantiated.

Process guidance can happen at multiple levels of granularity, ranging from long range project planning issues to detailed technical transformations. Firstly, some contexts may be *compound* from more *atomic* ones. Secondly, some contexts are directly applicable by performing product transforming actions while others may be applied in several alternative ways, thus requiring a choice from the developer. Direct action contexts are also called *micro contexts*, contexts with user choices are called *macro contexts*.

As a simple example, consider a requirements engineer working on the refinement of an entity relationship (ER) diagram. The way-of-working for ER contains, for example, a context associating a situation consisting of a pair entity type/relationship type and a decision to "improve" it. As there are several ways to improve entity relationship groupings, this context is a macro context. The process chunk thus relates it to several other contexts that are its alternatives, along with arguments that support the choice between alternatives.

One of these alternatives is the context that "subtypes" the entity type. The "subtypes" context is a compound context as it is built from more atomic

---

[3] In the context of process improvement, these arguments can be seen as abstractions from arguments underlying important design decisions in the traceability model from which a chunk has been gained [12].

ones, including the creation of a sub entity type, of the isA relationship between the sub entity type and the initial entity type, and possibly the addition or re arrangement of attributes.

Although very simple, the example shows how the concepts of our approach can be used to precisely define ways-of-working. This can be done both at a very low level of granularity (as in the example) or at a more macroscopic one, such as defining the organization of project inspections in certain critical project situations.

Process Traceability Model. The traceability model (structure of the design record) is organized by three dimensions along which progress in the requirements process is needed [20]:

- The *specification dimension* records the degree of understanding achieved, compared with a model of the international requirements engineering standards.
- The *representation dimension* records progress from initially completely informal representations to more formal and verified requirements models, according to formalizations of hypertext structures, semi-formal graphics, formal knowledge representations, and their possible process interrelationships ("derived from", "explains", etc.).
- The *agreement dimension* records progress from different individual viewpoints to shared understanding and goals, according to a decision-oriented adaption of the IBIS model similar to the one chosen in REMAP [22].

The actual traceability model relates the three dimensions to the process meta model, to give a structure for the trace. Decisions are views a group of agents takes on an argumentation space within the IBIS model of the agreement dimension. Actions are traced by recording (a) the products obtained, (b) the dependencies from existing products to old ones along any of the three dimensions, (c) the agent or tool actions creating these dependencies, plus some other annotations (e.g., criticality of the dependency). To achieve uniformity, decisions are treated like other objects when it comes to traceability, i.e., they depend on certain input objects and other objects may depend on them.

In a practical sense, the traceability model is supported by specific tool suites for each dimension, and by some generic tools for browsing products and dependencies. For example, a flexible hypertext editor for informal requirements, semi-formal graphical tools for ER and SA, and interfaces for the formal knowledge representation language Telos have been developed for the representation dimension, along with a set of dependency types that characterize the possible relationships between such objects. For the agreement dimension, a tool for recording informal argumentation histories according to the IBIS model has been developed, and a group decision support tool for actually making the choices is under development. Along the specification dimension, tools mainly support reuse of generic domain models or of abstractions of existing instances [13].

3.4   Tool Views

To formally describe and technically implement the relationships between tools and repositories, view concepts are an obvious candidate. But it is far from trivial to decide what is the view and what is the database. Goals to consider when making this choice include consistency of the database, awareness of change across tools within the whole development team, autonomy and coordination of users, and other factors. In our prototype, we have initially followed the usual approach where tools have views on a knowledge base. As the experiences were not uniformly positive, we also briefly discuss alternatives we are currently evaluating.

Our Approach: Tools Have Views on the Repository. Like [14, 23], the NATURE environment uses a central repository in client-server architecture (the ConceptBase system [11]) as the only information store. Tools do not keep any persistent knowledge locally. Typically, a client connected to the database is only concerned with a very small part of this information, possibly structured in a different way – it has a specific view on the global information. Such a view is realized as virtual information which is not explicitly stored in the database but can be computed when needed. An integration of the different views is not necessary because all are derived from the same (global) representation of the world. This enables the application of sophisticated integrity checking techniques [19, 2] for global and local constraints. The tools access the database (i.e., ask and tell) only through their specific view specification which prevents other parts of the database against uncontrolled access.

Views are specified like any other query, but may be parameterized. Updates on explicitly stored information in a database often affect intensional knowledge defined by views. If the view is materialized or in use by a tool, the content of the view must be recomputed in order to capture the consequences of this update. We use incremental view maintenance techniques to propagate updates on base data to updates of a view, i.e. the data used by a tool [8, 29].

The reverse direction, in which updates coming from the tools must be translated to updates on the underlying base data, is much more complicated. In general, there exists no one-to-one mapping. There may be zero, one or many possible translations. An unique translation is only possible for a very restricted number of views. To implement a (partial) translation, the ConceptBase system uses the concept of query classes to specify views in the conceptual modeling language Telos [16] and translates them into event-condition-action rules [26].

Experiences and Alternatives. We have chosen the above approach because of the deductive nature of our repository ConceptBase and the availability of well-understood and efficient algorithms for problems like integrity checking, view maintenance and view update. Our experiences have shown that this approach is very suitable for display tools but has difficulties when updates have to be propagated across tools which do not look at the repository with the same structural organization.

We now briefly describe two alternatives where in the first one the tools have a distributed database on which the repository maintains a view. In the second, the repository is fully distributed across tools (then called viewpoints rather than views) and there is no repository at all.

The Repository Holds Views of the Tools. In [1] the authors describe a way how to manage the coexistence of tools which locally organize their data and a database also representing the data of the tools. They avoid redundant storage and therefore the maintenance problem by using a database not containing the data itself but only a view on the tools. The database extracts the data from the tools (resp. the file) only when needed, e.g., for query evaluation. One can look at the database as an abstract interface to the information stored in the tools while offering standard database facilities. The integration of the different views enables the handling of restricted updates on the database (view updates) and updates on the internal tool data (view maintenance). Then it is also possible to use the database as a medium for tool interoperability in the sense that they can exchange information if their views overlap.

The responsibility of every single tool to keep its own data consistent seems to be a main disadvantage of this approach, because this leads to the implementation of integrity checking techniques in every tool. Only if the views are materialized is it possible to use facilities offered by the connected database for this task. But this contradicts the original approach.

Tools Represent Independent Interrelated Viewpoints. The ViewPoint Oriented Systems Engineering (VOSE [7]) framework proposes the use of largely distributed, locally managed viewpoints as a way of managing the software development process. In contrast to the above approaches, there exists no common database or repository to support the viewpoints. The global perspective on the development process is given by the collection of all involved autonomous viewpoints. They may overlap, complement and contradict each other. Even though absolute consistency can be an unnecessary restriction of the individual development strategy, it is necessary to keep the specifications consistent in some way. This requires constraints satisfied by all viewpoints. The missing common description of all perspectives in, e.g., a repository, makes the check and enforcement of such constraints complicated.

The viewpoint approach has a number of very attractive features for cooperative work in unstructured application domains but is still in its early phases.

4 Process-Adaptable and Interoperable Tools: Extending the Control Integration Perspective

Looking again at figure 4, we have so far discussed models from which the requirements engineering team can obtain guidance for their process, and models into which they can document their activities. This approach is also roughly followed in other recent proposals for process-centered environment, albeit with different process models (e.g., [15]).

The problem is that this solution involves two man machine interfaces: one for guidance, one for tracing. The former creates a reliability problem since it is not clear whether the requirements engineering team will actually see and follow the guidance. The latter creates a workload problem since a detailed trace requires a lot of traceability data which are very inefficient to record manually.

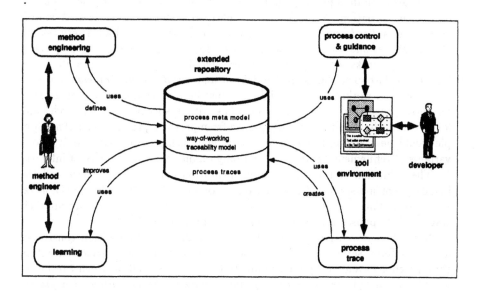

Fig. 6. Integration of tool environment and process repository

We therefore aim at offloading much of this work to the CASE tools available in the environment. CASE tools should be directly put into the right context by the process guidance model (cf. figure 6). They should also trace their own activities in the repository automatically according to the process traceability model. Bringing process guidance and traceability into the CASE tools is particularly demanding, as we cannot expect a fixed process model. Thus, tool behavior must adapt itself to changing process definitions in the process improvement scenario, and traceability should address the relationship of actions not only to the basic traceability model, but also to the guidance situation.

We achieve process adaptability through modeling tools as composite objects, and support process enacting and traceability through a communication server for coordinating short term interoperability of tools. Both are described in the sequel and illustrated with a scenario from the NATURE prototype, extending the entity relationship example from the previous sections.

4.1 Tool Models and Implementation

In our approach, tools have several similarities to objects in languages such as SmallTalk but there are also some important additional aspects to be considered.

It has already been recognized in the Eureka Software Factory project [6] that, as a minimal requirement for adapting tool behavior to processes, tools have to be composed of *individual services* which can be made available and traced independently of each other. At the user interface level, these services are often shown as menu items.

It is also common practice that tools can operate in *different modes* depending on the situation. A mode offers a particular subset of services. A simple example is a *Read only* mode in a text editor in which no change services are offered. Modes and mode combinations can, for example, be supported by selective bitmap masks on the menu services offered. For process adaptability, it is important that such masks can be defined and activated from *outside* the tool.

To set the working context right, it must be further possible to *parameterize* these process adapted tool invocations with a specific product model and focus within that model, typically gained from previous process steps. An example would be a *Refine* mode in an entity-relationship editor which only allows variants of refinement operations, and only on one particular entity of interest.

The definition of the service implementation may include choices and the invocation of sub-services from the same or other tools, without losing the *working context*. Thus, services must be enabled to send messages and maintain their state until responses to these messages have been received.

If all these conditions are satisfied, a specialized tool definition consists of a set of offered services, an appropriate object context, and service execution through choices and compound, multi-tool operations – all of which can be influenced from outside. *This corresponds exactly to the definition of a process chunk in our guidance model!* New tools can therefore be integrated into the repository by simply defining the appropriate process chunks for their available modes.

Conversely, by defining a process chunk composed from the basic services and object types available in the tools and in the repository, we can construct a specialized tool environment for exactly this process chunk. We have thus reached the goal of process-adaptable tool definitions.

4.2 Interoperability and Traceability of Tool Behavior

We now discuss how to make guidance available dynamically to the development environment, and how to execute and trace complex multi-tool process actions. Process-guided and communication-based interoperability is the main pre-requisite, for several reasons.

First, actions are often *nested*. For instance, during the creation of a data store in a data flow diagram, also the corresponding part of the data dictionary must be updated. This causes the need for direct communication between the actions which are provided by a particular tool, not between the whole tools. The "first" action, which leads to the execution of other actions, must be able to control the performance of the others. Figure 7 explains this issue.

Second, actions can be provided by *different tools*. For example, in nested actions, each action which needs another action for assistance, must know by

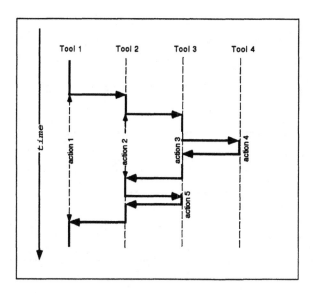

Fig. 7. An example of nested actions across multiple tools

which (set of) tools that action is provided.

Third, actions must know the state of those tools which could potentially offer a required service. The action must know if any tool providing the needed action is currently running and if the "right" objects are loaded. If not, the tool must be started according to the needs, its mode must be reset, new objects may have to be loaded and the user must be focused on the current work task.

Fourth, dependent on the results returned by a sub-service, the further execution of the calling action can be different.

Fifth, for performance reasons, data exchange among tools should not always go through the repository. Especially nonpersistent data should be directly transferred as part of the message. This requires suitable abstraction mechanisms for the product descriptions, such as named aggregates or models reference to which can be made by name.

To encapsulate these properties and to insulate the individual tools from control knowledge about other tools, a communication manager (CM) is needed besides the process repository (see figure 8). Similar to Hewlett-Packards Soft-Bench, the CM controls the communication among currently operational tool instances. That is, it knows (a) which tools are currently running, (b) how they can be accessed, and (c) what situation (mode and objects) they are in (i.e., whether they can provide the required services at present).

This approach has several advantages.

Firstly, the CM hides details of message protocols from the individual tools. Secondly, as all tools are invoked (and tool modes changed) through messages, the CM can easily maintain the status of the process situation at any given point. Last not least, to support process adaptability, the CM also abstracts from the

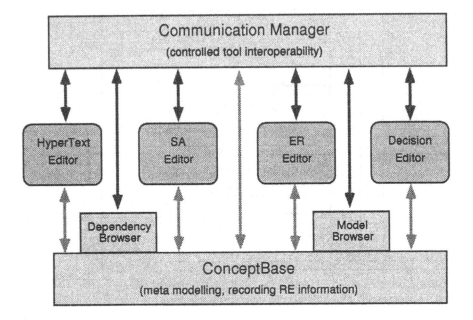

Fig. 8. The NATURE environment

grouping of services into tools. If a tool needs a service performed, it need not know which (combination of) tools offer this service because this information will be brokered by the CM. This is further strengthened by associating default tools for providing a service in particular types of process chunks.

Taken together, we have the following scenario. A service requests a sub-service from the CM. The CM finds the appropriate tool that offers this service, makes it available in the right mode and with the right objects, and restricts its use to the current process state. After the process steps associated to the sub-service have been executed, control is returned to the calling tool. In the current implementation, the calling tool is meanwhile blocked although we are thinking about more parallel ways-of-working.

The trace depends on the results of nested actions. Each sub-action captures the "operational semantics" in the repository by creating dependency links from its output objects to its input objects or to decisions underlying the action. Often, sources and sinks of such dependencies, their types and annotations, depend on sub-actions by other tools. The compound action model of the process guidance must then be used to create a meaningful trace.

4.3 A Session with the NATURE Environment

To illustrate the tool interoperability approach and the use of the guidance and traceability models in it, we shall consider a requirements engineering scenario as supported by the NATURE prototype.

Assume the user has activated an entity-relationship editor to refine a particular entity. The process model for this activity says that he should inspect the reasons behind the current version of a particular entity or relationship, and possibly update them to justify the refinement.

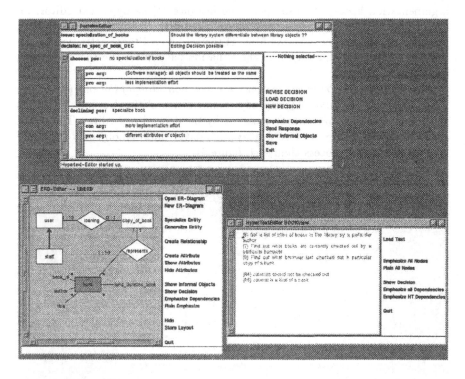

Fig. 9. A screendump demonstrating tool interoperability between entity relationship, decision and hypertext editor

The user first selects the entity to be refined and then the menu option *specialize entity.* Due to the process model, the action *specialize entity* asks the communication manager (CM) for the service of showing the objects the existing entity depends on. The CM knows that this service is provided by the dependency editor, but also, from the kind of message received, that the user is not really interested in the dependencies themselves. It therefore starts the dependency editor in "silence mode" and gives it the task to trace back the dependencies from the entity in question.

Tracing involves retrieving these dependencies from the repository and displaying the target objects. Depending on the kind of objects, the CM is able to start automatically the corresponding tools, which can display the target objects. Since there may be very many such dependencies, the process model allows the user to select the objects to be displayed from the set of retrieved target objects, and thus the tools to be activated.

For the selected entity there are two decisions and a hypertext view consisting of five informal objects retrieved as target objects. The user selects the decision *no specialization of books* and the hypertext view. Depending on the type of object, the CM chooses the tools to be started. It opens an instance of the IBIS browser to show the selected decision in the context of its underlying argumentation history. It also opens one instance of the hypertext editor, for displaying the informal objects. Assume that the decision editor is already open; the CM will then bring it to the front of the screen. All these activities are defined in a process chunk based on the situation pattern for the tool invocation from dependencies.

The user decides to revise the decision *no specialization of the entity book*, due to the retrieved informal objects and argumentation of the decision. He selects the action *revise decision* which is offered by the dependency editor. The action *revise decision* calls the CM to display the related informal objects to the user – as defined in the process chunk (cf. figure 9).

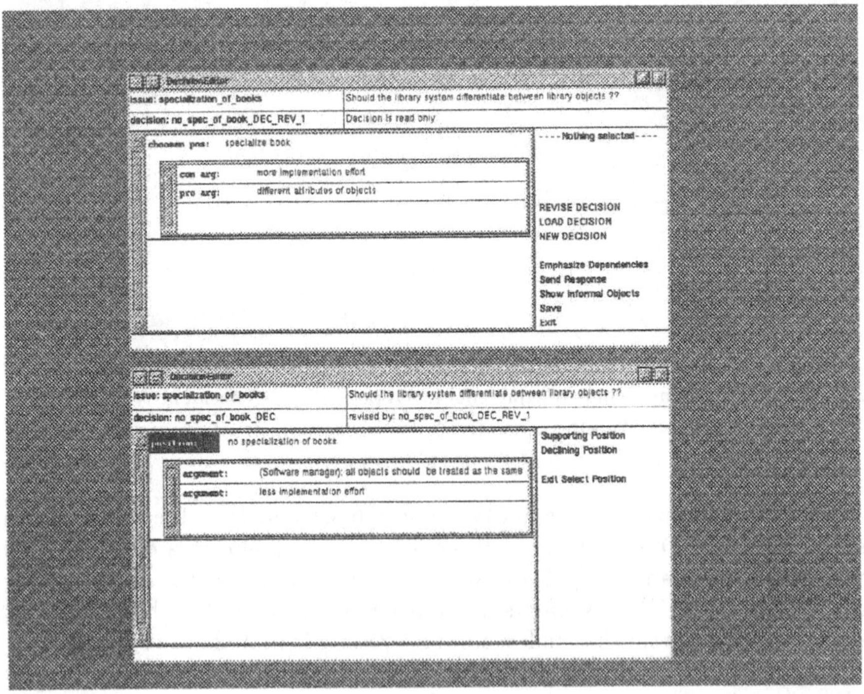

Fig. 10. A screendump demonstrating the revision of a decision

The CM retrieves - again using dependency links - the informal objects and starts automatically the hypertext editor in a predefined mode, the *selection* mode.

The control rests now with the hypertext editor. Within the overall specification, the informal objects, which are related to the decision by dependency links, are automatically highlighted. The user has the possibility to highlight additional parts of the document which he wants to relate to his current action – the revision of the decision *no specialization of books*. After finishing with selection, control returns to the action *revise decision* of the decision editor and the "highlighted" parts of the hypertext are automatically related to the revised decision.

The user now revises the decision (cf. figure 10) by changing the weighting of the positions (arguments) and adding new ones. After finishing with the revision, the control is given back to the ER-Editor – to the action *specialize entity*. Here, the refinement of the entity can now be actually conducted and is automatically related to the revised decision through an additional dependency link derived from the call history of service invocations.

All of the tool interactions and choices are defined by process chunks in the repository, and the actual trace uses the process chunks as well as dependency types coming from the general traceability model to record the process execution.

5 Conclusions

Developing and evolving complex structures do not just pose a challenge to database management, knowledge representation and reasoning. They also require significant extensions to tools and tool integration concepts in IS development environments. The reasonably well established techniques for data integration, control integration, and presentation integration have to be carefully combined and augmented to achieve comprehensive, cost-effective and improvement-oriented process integration.

The NATURE approach presented here attempts to achieve comprehensiveness through a process-oriented extension to the IRDS repository standard, cost-effectiveness through tools that are process-adaptable and offer automated traceability, correctness and group awareness through a view concept that relates tool and repository models. Improvement orientation is achieved through a quality-oriented process meta model, possibly supported by some machine learning techniques, which is presented in a companion paper [12].

Taken together, these techniques should constitute a significant step forward in managing change in complex information systems domains. Application experiments in the requirements engineering and industrial engineering domains are being conducted to substantiate this claim.

Acknowledgments. We are grateful to our NATURE partners for many discussions and contributions, especially to the group of Colette Rolland at Paris-Sorbonne, for their contributions to the process guidance model. Major portions of the NATURE prototype were implemented by our students Michael Gebhardt, Fred Gibbels, Peter Haumer, Ralf Klamma, Christof Lenzen, Ute Loeb, Klaus Weidenhaupt and Claudia Welter.

References

1. S. Abiteboul, S. Cluet, and T. Milo. Querying and updating the file. In *Proc. of the 19th VLDB Conference*, Dublin, Ireland, 1993.

2. F. Bry, H. Decker, and R. Manthey. A uniform approach to constraint satisfaction and constraint satisfiability in deductive databases. In *Proc. Intl. Conf. Extending Database Technology*, Venice, Italy, 1988.

3. M. Chen and R.J. Norman. A framework for integrated CASE. *IEEE Software*, March 1992, 18–22.

4. R. Conradi and M.L.. Jaccheri. Customization and evolution of process models in EPOS. *Proc. IFIP 8.1 Working Conf. Information Systems Development Process*, Como, Italy, 1993, 23–40.

5. B. Curtis. The CASE for processes. *Proc. IFIP 8.2 Working Conf. The Impact of Computer-Supported Techniques on Information Systems Development*, Minneapolis, Mn, 1992, 333–343.

6. C. Fernstroem, K.-H. Naerfelt, and L. Ohlsson. Software factory principles, architectures, experiments. *IEEE Software*, March 1992, 36–44.

7. A. Finkelstein, J. Kramer, B. Nuseibeh, L. Finkelstein, and M. Goedicke. Viewpoints: A framework for integrating multiple perspectives in system development. *Intl. Journal Software Engineering and Knowledge Engineering*, 2(1), March 1992.

8. A. Gupta, I.S. Mumick, and V.S. Subrahmanian. Maintaining views incrementally. In *ACM SIGMOD Conference on Management of Data*, 1993.

9. W. Humphreys. *Managing the Software Development Process*, Addison-Wesley, 1989.

10. ISO/IEC 10027. *Information Technology – Information Resource Dictionary System (IRDS) – Framework*. ISO/IEC International Standard.

11. M. Jarke, (ed.). *ConceptBase V3.1 user manual*. Aachener Informatik Berichte Nr. 92-17, RWTH Aachen, Germany, 1992.

12. M. Jarke, K. Pohl, C. Rolland, J.-R. Schmitt. Experience-based method evaluation and improvement: A process modeling approach. submitted for publication.

13. M. Jarke, K. Pohl, S. Jacobs, J. Bubenko, P. Assenova, P. Holm, B. Wangler, C. Rolland, V. Plihon, J.-R. Schmitt, A. Sutcliffe, S. Jones, N. Maiden, D. Till, Y. Vassiliou, P. Constantopoulos, G. Spanoudakis. Requirements engineering: an integrated view of representation, process, and domain. *Proc. 4th European Software Engineering Conf.*, Garmisch, Germany, 1993.

14. W.L. Johnson, M.S. Feather, and D.R. Harris. Representation and presentation of requirements knowledge. *IEEE Transactions Software Engineering*, 18(10):853–869, October 1992.

15. P. Mi and W. Scacchi. Process integration for CASE environments. *IEEE Software*, March 1992, 45-53.

16. J. Mylopoulos, A. Borgida, M. Jarke, and M. Koubarakis. Telos: representing knowledge about information systems. *ACM Trans. Information Systems*, 10(4):325–362, 1990.

17. M. Nagl. Eng integrierte Software Entwicklungsumgebungen. Ein Erfahrungsbericht ueber das IPSEN Projekt. *Informatik Forschung und Entwicklung*, 8(3),1993.

18. NIST. *Reference Model for Frameworks of Software Engineering Environments*. Draft Version 1.5, Nat'l Inst. Standards and Technology, Gaithersburg, Md., 1991.

19. A. Olive. Integrity constraints checking in deductive databases. In *Proc. 17th VLDB Conf.*, Barcelona, Spain, 1991.

20. K. Pohl. The three dimensions of requirements engineering. Proc. 5th Intl. Conf. Advanced Information Systems Engineering, Paris, France, 1993, 275–292.

21. K. Pohl and M. Jarke. Quality information systems: support for evolving process models. Aachener Informatik Berichte 92-17, RWTH Aachen, Germany, 1992.

22. B. Ramesh and V. Dhar. Supporting systems development by capturing deliberations during requirements engineering. *IEEE Trans. Software Engineering*, 18(6):418–510, 1992.

23. H.B. Reubenstein and R.C. Waters. The Requirements Apprentice: automated assistance for requirements acquisition. *IEEE Transactions on Software Engineering*, 17(3):226–240, March 1991.

24. J.W. Sagawa. Repository manager technology. *IBM Systems Journal*, 29(2),1990, 209–227.

25. J.-R. Schmitt. Product modelling for requirements engineering process modelling. *Proc. IFIP 8.1 Working Conf. on Information Systems Development Process*, Como, Italy, 1993, 231–245.

26. M. Staudt, H.W. Nissen, and M.A. Jeusfeld. Query by class, rule and concept. *Applied Intelligence, Special Issue on Knowledge Base Management*, 1994.

27. L.A. Suchman. *Plans and Situated Actions*, Cambridge University Press, 1987.

28. I. Thomas and B.A. Nejmeh. Definitions of tool integration for environments. *IEEE Software*, March 1992, 29–35.

29. T. Urpi and A. Olive. A method for change computation in deductive databases. In *Proc. of the 18th VLDB Conference*, Vancouver, Canada, 1992.

30. A. Wasserman. IDE: Tool integration in software engineering environments. *Proc. SofTec-NRW Workshop CASE – Stand der industriellen Technik*, RWTH Aachen, October 1992.

Printing and binding: Druckhaus Beltz, Hemsbach

Springer-Verlag
and the Environment

We at Springer-Verlag firmly believe that an international science publisher has a special obligation to the environment, and our corporate policies consistently reflect this conviction.

We also expect our business partners – paper mills, printers, packaging manufacturers, etc. – to commit themselves to using environmentally friendly materials and production processes.

The paper in this book is made from low- or no-chlorine pulp and is acid free, in conformance with international standards for paper permanency.

Lecture Notes in Computer Science

For information about Vols. 1–699
please contact your bookseller or Springer-Verlag

Vol. 736: R. L. Grossman, A. Nerode, A. P. Ravn, H. Rischel (Eds.), Hybrid Systems. VIII, 474 pages. 1993.

Vol. 737: J. Calmet, J. A. Campbell (Eds.), Artificial Intelligence and Symbolic Mathematical Computing. Proceedings, 1992. VIII, 305 pages. 1993.

Vol. 738: M. Weber, M. Simons, Ch. Lafontaine, The Generic Development Language Deva. XI, 246 pages. 1993.

Vol. 739: H. Imai, R. L. Rivest, T. Matsumoto (Eds.), Advances in Cryptology – ASIACRYPT '91. X, 499 pages. 1993.

Vol. 740: E. F. Brickell (Ed.), Advances in Cryptology – CRYPTO '92. Proceedings, 1992. X, 593 pages. 1993.

Vol. 741: B. Preneel, R. Govaerts, J. Vandewalle (Eds.), Computer Security and Industrial Cryptography. Proceedings, 1991. VIII, 275 pages. 1993.

Vol. 742: S. Nishio, A. Yonezawa (Eds.), Object Technologies for Advanced Software. Proceedings, 1993. X, 543 pages. 1993.

Vol. 743: S. Doshita, K. Furukawa, K. P. Jantke, T. Nishida (Eds.), Algorithmic Learning Theory. Proceedings, 1992. X, 260 pages. 1993. (Subseries LNAI)

Vol. 744: K. P. Jantke, T. Yokomori, S. Kobayashi, E. Tomita (Eds.), Algorithmic Learning Theory. Proceedings, 1993. XI, 423 pages. 1993. (Subseries LNAI)

Vol. 745: V. Roberto (Ed.), Intelligent Perceptual Systems. VIII, 378 pages. 1993. (Subseries LNAI)

Vol. 746: A. S. Tanguiane, Artificial Perception and Music Recognition. XV, 210 pages. 1993. (Subseries LNAI).

Vol. 747: M. Clarke, R. Kruse, S. Moral (Eds.), Symbolic and Quantitative Approaches to Reasoning and Uncertainty. Proceedings, 1993. X, 390 pages. 1993.

Vol. 748: R. H. Halstead Jr., T. Ito (Eds.), Parallel Symbolic Computing: Languages, Systems, and Applications. Proceedings, 1992. X, 419 pages. 1993.

Vol. 749: P. A. Fritzson (Ed.), Automated and Algorithmic Debugging. Proceedings, 1993. VIII, 369 pages. 1993.

Vol. 750: J. L. Díaz-Herrera (Ed.), Software Engineering Education. Proceedings, 1994. XII, 601 pages. 1994.

Vol. 751: B. Jähne, Spatio-Temporal Image Processing. XII, 208 pages. 1993.

Vol. 752: T. W. Finin, C. K. Nicholas, Y. Yesha (Eds.), Information and Knowledge Management. Proceedings, 1992. VII, 142 pages. 1993.

Vol. 753: L. J. Bass, J. Gornostaev, C. Unger (Eds.), Human-Computer Interaction. Proceedings, 1993. X, 388 pages. 1993.

Vol. 754: H. D. Pfeiffer, T. E. Nagle (Eds.), Conceptual Structures: Theory and Implementation. Proceedings, 1992. IX, 327 pages. 1993. (Subseries LNAI).

Vol. 755: B. Möller, H. Partsch, S. Schuman (Eds.), Formal Program Development. Proceedings. VII, 371 pages. 1993.

Vol. 756: J. Pieprzyk, B. Sadeghiyan, Design of Hashing Algorithms. XV, 194 pages. 1993.

Vol. 757: U. Banerjee, D. Gelernter, A. Nicolau, D. Padua (Eds.), Languages and Compilers for Parallel Computing. Proceedings, 1992. X, 576 pages. 1993.

Vol. 758: M. Teillaud, Towards Dynamic Randomized Algorithms in Computational Geometry. IX, 157 pages. 1993.

Vol. 759: N. R. Adam, B. K. Bhargava (Eds.), Advanced Database Systems. XV, 451 pages. 1993.

Vol. 760: S. Ceri, K. Tanaka, S. Tsur (Eds.), Deductive and Object-Oriented Databases. Proceedings, 1993. XII, 488 pages. 1993.

Vol. 761: R. K. Shyamasundar (Ed.), Foundations of Software Technology and Theoretical Computer Science. Proceedings, 1993. XIV, 456 pages. 1993.

Vol. 762: K. W. Ng, P. Raghavan, N. V. Balasubramanian, F. Y. L. Chin (Eds.), Algorithms and Computation. Proceedings, 1993. XIII, 542 pages. 1993.

Vol. 763: F. Pichler, R. Moreno Díaz (Eds.), Computer Aided Systems Theory – EUROCAST '93. Proceedings, 1993. IX, 451 pages. 1994.

Vol. 764: G. Wagner, Vivid Logic. XII, 148 pages. 1994. (Subseries LNAI).

Vol. 765: T. Helleseth (Ed.), Advances in Cryptology – EUROCRYPT '93. Proceedings, 1993. X, 467 pages. 1994.

Vol. 766: P. R. Van Loocke, The Dynamics of Concepts. XI, 340 pages. 1994. (Subseries LNAI).

Vol. 767: M. Gogolla, An Extended Entity-Relationship Model. X, 136 pages. 1994.

Vol. 768: U. Banerjee, D. Gelernter, A. Nicolau, D. Padua (Eds.), Languages and Compilers for Parallel Computing. Proceedings, 1993. XI, 655 pages. 1994.

Vol. 769: J. L. Nazareth, The Newton-Cauchy Framework. XII, 101 pages. 1994.

Vol. 770: P. Haddawy (Representing Plans Under Uncertainty. X, 129 pages. 1994. (Subseries LNAI).

Vol. 771: G. Tomas, C. W. Ueberhuber, Visualization of Scientific Parallel Programs. XI, 310 pages. 1994.

Vol. 772: B. C. Warboys (Ed.),Software Process Technology. Proceedings, 1994. IX, 275 pages. 1994.

Vol. 773: D. R. Stinson (Ed.), Advances in Cryptology – CRYPTO '93. Proceedings, 1993. X, 492 pages. 1994.

Vol. 774: M. Banâtre, P. A. Lee (Eds.), Hardware and Software Architectures for Fault Tolerance. XIII, 311 pages. 1994.

Vol. 775: P. Enjalbert, E. W. Mayr, K. W. Wagner (Eds.), STACS 94. Proceedings, 1994. XIV, 782 pages. 1994.

Vol. 776: H. J. Schneider, H. Ehrig (Eds.), Graph Transformations in Computer Science. proceedings, 1993. VIII, 395 pages. 1994.

Vol. 777: K. von Luck, H. Marburger (Eds.), Management and Processing of Complex Data Structures. Proceedings, 1994. VII, 220 pages. 1994.

Vol. 778: M. Bonuccelli, P. Crescenzi, R. Petreschi (Eds.), Algorithms and Complexity. Proceedings, 1994. VIII, 222 pages. 1994.

Vol. 779: M. Jarke, K. Jeffery (Eds.), Advances in Database Technology — EDBT '94. Proceedings, 1994. XII, 406 pages. 1994.